Collins

Maths
Frameworking

3rd edition

Kevin Evans, Keith Gordon,
Trevor Senior, Brian Speed,
Chris Pearce

Contents

How to use this book

Learning objectives

See what you are going to cover and what you should already know at the start of each chapter.

About this chapter

Find out the history of the maths you are going to learn and how it is used in real-life contexts.

Key words

The main terms used are listed at the start of each topic and highlighted in the text the first time they come up, helping you to master the terminology you need to express yourself fluently about maths. Definitions are provided in the glossary at the back of the book.

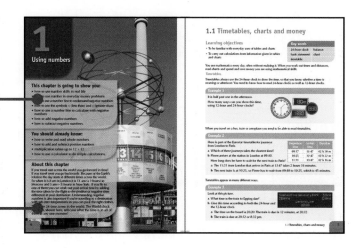

Worked examples

Understand the topic before you start the exercises, by reading the examples in blue boxes. These take you through how to answer a question step by step.

Skills focus

Practise your problem-solving, mathematical reasoning and financial skills.

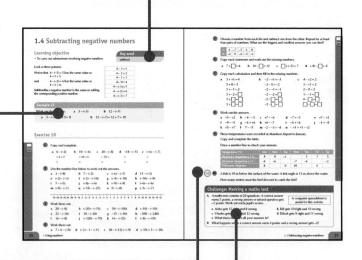

Take it further

Stretch your thinking by working through the **Investigation**, **Problem solving**, **Challenge** and **Activity** sections. By tackling these you are working at a higher level.

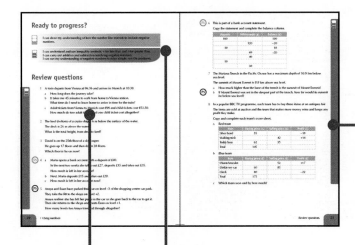

Progress indicators

Track your progress with indicators that show the difficulty level of each question.

Ready to progress?

Check whether you have achieved the expected level of progress in each chapter. The statements show you what you need to know and how you can improve.

Review questions

The review questions bring together what you've learnt in this and earlier chapters, helping you to develop your mathematical fluency.

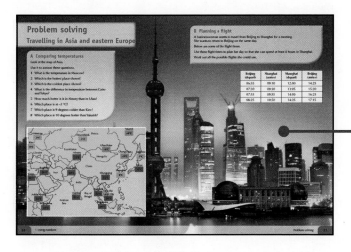

Activity pages

Put maths into context with these colourful pages showing real-world situations involving maths. You are practising your problem-solving, reasoning and financial skills.

Interactive book, digital resources and videos

A digital version of this Pupil Book with interactive classroom and homework activities, assessments, worked examples and tools that have been specially developed to help you improve your maths skills. Also included are engaging video clips that explain essential concepts, and exciting real-life videos and images that bring to life the awe and wonder of maths.

Find out more at www.collins.co.uk/connect

1

Using numbers

This chapter is going to show you:

- how to use number skills in real life
- how to use number in everyday money problems
- how to use a number line to understand negative numbers
- how to use the symbols < (less than) and > (greater than)
- how to use a number line to calculate with negative numbers
- how to add negative numbers
- how to subtract negative numbers.

You should already know:

- how to write and read whole numbers
- how to add and subtract positive numbers
- multiplication tables up to 12 × 12
- how to use a calculator to do simple calculations.

About this chapter

If you travel east across the world you go forward in time! If you travel west you go backwards. Because of the Earth's rotation the day starts at different times across the world. So when it is 8 am in London it is 11 am (+ 3 hours) in Moscow and 3 am (– 5 hours) in New York. If you fly to one of them you can work out your arrival time by adding the time taken by the flight to the positive or negative time difference at your destination. Understanding negative numbers is also important if you're travelling to a destination with sub-zero temperatures so you can pack the right clothes.

There are 24 time zones in the world. The World clock in Berlin, shown here, tells you what the time is in all of them at any one moment!

1.1 Timetables, charts and money

Learning objectives

- To be familiar with everyday uses of tables and charts
- To carry out calculations from information given in tables and charts

Key words

24-hour clock	balance
bank statement	chart
timetable	

You use mathematics every day, often without realising it. When you work out times and distances, read **charts** and spend and save money you are using mathematical skills.

Timetables

Timetables always use the **24-hour clock** to show the time, so that you know whether a time is morning or afternoon. You need to know how to read 24-hour clocks as well as 12-hour clocks.

Example 1

It is half past one in the afternoon.

How many ways can you show this time, using 12-hour and 24-hour clocks?

When you travel on a bus, train or aeroplane you need to be able to read timetables.

Example 2

Here is part of the Eurostar timetable for journeys from London to Paris.

a Which of these journeys takes the shortest time?

b Pierre arrives at the station in London at 09:40.

How long does he have to wait for the next train to Paris?

Departure time	Arrival time	Duration
09:17	11:47	02 h 30 m
10:25	12:47	02 h 22 m
11:31	13:47	02 h 16 m

  a The 11:31 from London that arrives in Paris at 13:47 takes 2 hours 16 minutes.

  b The next train is at 10:25, so Pierre has to wait from 09:40 to 10:25, which is 45 minutes.

Timetables appear in many different ways.

Example 3

Look at this picture.

a What time is the train to Epping due?

b Give this time according to both the 24-hour and the 12-hour clock.

> 1 Hainault via Newbury Park   5 Mins
> 3 Epping   12 Mins
> Central Line
> 20:20

  a The time on the board is 20:20. The train is due in 12 minutes, at 20:32.

  b The train is due at 20:32 or 8:32 pm.

Charts

Maps often have charts attached to them, showing the distances between key places.

Example 4

The table shows the flight distances, in kilometres, between four cities.

a How many kilometres is it from Brussels to Cairo?

b Which two of these places are furthest apart?

Abu Dhabi			
Brussels	5158		
Cairo	2367	3212	
Dublin	5924	776	3977
	Abu Dhabi	Brussels	Cairo	Dublin

  a The distance from Brussels to Cairo is 3212 km.

  b Abu Dhabi and Dublin are furthest apart (5924 km).

Abu Dhabi			
Brussels	5158		
Cairo	2367 →	3212	
Dublin	5924	776	3977
	Abu Dhabi	Brussels	Cairo	Dublin

Planning and making purchases

Information about prices is often given in tables. This makes the information easier to read.

Example 5

A park hires out bicycles. These are the prices.

Hire period	Bicycle	Tandem
2 hours	£7.50 adult	£13.50
	£5.00 child	
All day	£15.00 adult	£25.00
	£10.00 child	

a How much does it cost to hire bicycles for 2 hours for one adult and two children?

b How much more does it cost to hire a tandem for a whole day than for 2 hours?

  a Total cost for 2 hours for one adult and two children is £7.50 + £5.00 + £5.00 = £17.50.

  b It costs £25.00 to hire a tandem for a whole day but £13.50 for 2 hours.

    The difference is £25.00 − £13.50 = £11.50.

Bank statements

A **bank statement** gives detailed information about a bank account. It shows how much money has been paid in or out of the account. The amount of money remaining in the account is called the **balance**.

Example 6

a This is a bank statement. Copy it and complete the balance column.

Statement number: 9				Account number: 13579246
Date	Details	Paid out (£)	Paid in (£)	Balance (£)
31-01-2014	Opening balance			417.80
01-02-2014	Interest		15.40	
03-02-2014	Cash withdrawal	200.00		233.20
05-02-2014	The music shop	9.70		
26-02-2014	Salary		360.00	
28-02-2014	Closing balance			583.50

b How much was paid out from the account in February?

a

Statement No 9				Account No 13579246
Date	Details	Paid out (£)	Paid in (£)	Balance (£)
31-01-2014	Opening balance			417.80
01-02-2014	Interest		15.40	433.20
03-02-2014	Cash withdrawal	200.00		233.20
05-02-2014	The music shop	9.70		223.50
26-02-2014	Salary		360.00	583.50
28-02-2014	Closing balance			583.50

b The amount paid out was £209.70.

Exercise 1A

1 A two-year mobile phone contract costs £27 per month.
How much is the total charge over the two years?

2 A TV programme starts at 18:45 and lasts for 25 minutes.
At what time does it finish?

3 When it is 6:50 pm in Hong Kong it is 3:50 am in Seattle on the same day.
How many hours are there between 3:50 am and 6:50 pm?

I have these coins.

I want to buy milk and cereal.

Milk
£1.10 per litre
or buy
2 litres for £2

Cereal
£1.40 for 750 grams
or £1.90 for 1000 grams

How much milk and cereal can I buy with these coins?

Write down all possible answers.

FS 5   A TV and broadband package costs £24 per month for the first six months and then £48 per month.

Work out the total cost for the first year.

FS 6   Work out the total cost of this mobile phone contract over the length of the plan.

Include the cost of the phone in your total.

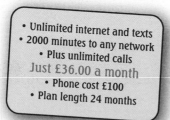

- Unlimited internet and texts
- 2000 minutes to any network
- Plus unlimited calls
Just £36.00 a month
- Phone cost £100
- Plan length 24 months

7   This timetable shows the times of buses from Hedley to Bottomley.

Hedley	07:45	11:20	12:30	13:55	16:20	18:15
Bottomley	08:15	11:55	13:00	14:20	16:55	18:45

a   What time does the bus that gets to Bottomley at 08:15 leave Hedley?

b   How long does the 13:55 bus take to get to Bottomley?

c Moz arrives at the bus stop at Hedley at 12:10.

How long does she have to wait before the bus arrives?

d The bus fare from Hedley to Bottomley is £1.20 for adults and 60p for children.

How much does it cost three adults and two children to travel from Hedley to Bottomley on the bus?

8 The timetable below shows train times from Leeds to Manchester.

Leeds	07:55	08:10	08:25	08:40	08:55
Dewsbury	08:07	...	08:37	...	09:07
Huddersfield	08:15	08:27	08:45	08:58	09:15
Stalybridge	...	08:45	...	...	...
Manchester	08:52	09:05	09:23	09:37	09:50

a How long does the 07:55 take to get from Leeds to Manchester?

b How long does the 08:10 take to get from Leeds to Manchester?

c Jack gets to Huddersfield station at 9:00 am.

How long does he have to wait to catch a train to Manchester?

d Kate wants to travel from Dewsbury to Stalybridge.

　i Explain why she will have to change trains at Huddersfield.

　ii If she catches the 08:07 from Dewsbury, what time will she arrive at Stalybridge?

e Liam lives in Leeds and has to be at a meeting at Manchester University at 10:00 am.

It takes 20 minutes to get from the station to the university.

What train should he catch from Leeds to be sure of getting to the meeting on time?

9 **a** Copy this bank statement and fill in the balance column.

Date	Details	Paid out (£)	Paid in (£)	Balance (£)
31-01-2014	Opening balance			215.70
01-02-2014	Interest		9.30	
05-02-2014	Shirt shop	42.50		
05-02-2014	The hungry café	17.90		
05-02-2104	Birthday shop	21.65		
26-02-2014	Paid in		120.00	
28-02-2014	Closing balance			

b How much was paid out on 5 February?

c What is the difference between the opening and closing balances?

10 Four friends agreed to deposit a fixed amount each month into their bank accounts.

Copy and complete the table.

Who had the most money at the end of 6 months?

	Heather	Iain	Joanna	Ken
Opening bank balance	£215.00	£192.00	£137.00	£96.00
Amount saved per month	£20.00	£25.00	£30.00	£50.00
Amount saved in 6 months				
Closing bank balance				

11 This is part of the timetable for the high-speed train between Rome and Bologna.

Rome (depart)	12:55	13:25	13:55
Florence (arrive)	14:17	14:47	15:17
Florence (depart)	14:25	14:55	15:25
Bologna (arrive)	15:02	15:32	16:02

a How long is the journey time between Rome and Florence?

b How long is the journey time between Florence and Bologna?

 c Why is the total journey time longer than the journey time from Rome to Florence added to the journey time from Florence to Bologna?

12 The chart shows the distances by road, in miles, between six cities in England.

Birmingham					
Leeds	121				
London	120	197			
Manchester	89	44	204		
Oxford	89	171	57	161	
York	134	24	212	71	185
	Birmingham	Leeds	London	Manchester	Oxford	York

a How many miles is it from Leeds to London?

b How many miles is it from Birmingham to Oxford?

c Which two cities are the furthest apart?

d Frances drives from Manchester to Leeds.

She then drives from Leeds to York.

Finally, she returns home from York to Manchester.

How many miles has she driven altogether?

13 Here is a chart showing the distances between four cities.

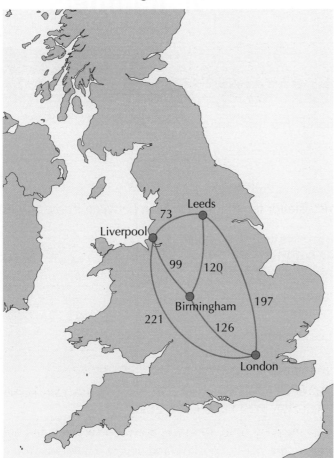

(PS) Copy and complete the mileage chart.

	Leeds	Liverpool	Birmingham	London
Leeds				
Liverpool	73			
Birmingham				
London		221		

Activity: Posting a parcel

Use an internet search to find the cheapest way to send a 7 kg parcel from the United Kingdom to Kuwait. Assume the parcel is 20 cm long, 12 cm wide and 15 cm high.

1.2 Positive and negative numbers

Learning objectives

- To use a number line to order positive and negative numbers
- To understand and use the symbols < (less than) and > (greater than)

Temperature +32 °C

Temperature –13 °C

Look at the two pictures.

How would you describe the two temperatures? What are the differences between the temperatures?

Every number has a sign. Numbers greater than 0 are called **positive numbers**. Although you do not always write it, every positive number has a positive (+) sign in front of it.

Numbers less than 0 are **negative numbers** and must always have the negative (–) sign in front of them.

The positions of positive and negative numbers can be shown on a number line. The value of the numbers increases as you move from left to right. For example, –5 is **greater than** –10, 2 is greater than –5 and 8 is greater than 2.

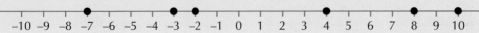

You can use the number line to compare the sizes of positive and negative numbers. You can also use it to solve problems involving addition and subtraction.

Example 7

Which number is greater, –7 or –3?

```
    •           •
-10 -9 -8 -7 -6 -5 -4 -3 -2 -1  0
```

Because –3 is further to the right than –7 is, on the number line, it is the larger number.

Notice that –3 is closer to zero than –7 is.

Example 8

Write these temperatures in order, from lowest to highest.

8 °C, –2 °C, 10 °C, –7 °C, –3 °C, 4 °C

```
        •       •  •                •         •     •
-10 -9 -8 -7 -6 -5 -4 -3 -2 -1  0  1  2  3  4  5  6  7  8  9  10
```

Putting these temperatures on a number line, you can see the correct order.

–7 °C, –3 °C, –2 °C, 4 °C, 8 °C, 10 °C

The symbol > means greater than.
The symbol < means **less than**.

Hint

To remember which symbol is 'less than', notice that < looks similar to the letter L.

For example:

–4 < 7 means 'negative 4 is less than 7'.

–3 > –8 means 'negative 3 is greater than negative 8'.

Example 9

State whether each statement is true or false.

a $6 > 8$ **b** $-7 > -1$ **c** $-3 > -7$

Looking at each of these pairs on the number line shows that:
a is false, **b** is false and **c** is true.

Example 10

Work out the difference between the temperatures in each pair.

a $-4 \,°C$ and $6 \,°C$ **b** $-1 \,°C$ and $-8 \,°C$

Look at each of these pairs on a number line.

a

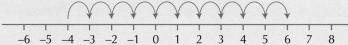

The difference is 10 degrees.

b

The difference is 7 degrees.

Exercise 1B

1. Write down the highest and lowest temperatures in each group.

   a $4 \,°C$, $-2 \,°C$, $0 \,°C$ **b** $-8 \,°C$, $-6 \,°C$, $-10 \,°C$ **c** $-20 \,°C$, $-19 \,°C$, $-5 \,°C$

2. Work out the difference between the temperatures in each pair.

   a $-2 \,°C$ and $5 \,°C$ **b** $-10 \,°C$ and $-22 \,°C$ **c** $4 \,°C$ and $-5 \,°C$

3. On Monday the temperature at noon was $5 \,°C$.

   Over the next few days, these temperature changes were recorded.

Monday to Tuesday	down 3 degrees
Tuesday to Wednesday	up 1 degree
Wednesday to Thursday	down 6 degrees
Thursday to Friday	up 2 degrees

   What was the temperature on Friday?

4 Put these numbers in order, from smallest to largest.

   a   3, −7, 0, −9, 5   **b**   −5, −8, 9, −2, −1   **c**   0, −3, −5, −8, 11

   d   2, −2, 7, −6, −12   **e**   −4, −8, −14, 2, −6   **f**   9, −3, 5, −7, 1

5 State whether each statement is true or false.

   a   7 > 3   **b**   2 < 17   **c**   5 < −6   **d**   −8 > −5   **e**   −2 < − 9

6 Put < or > into each ☐ to make a true statement.

   a   −5 ☐ 4   **b**   −7 ☐ −10   **c**   3 ☐ −3   **d**   −12 ☐ −2

(PS) **7** Find the number that is halfway between the numbers in each pair.

   a ——————— **b** ——————— **c** ———————

       −8   −2   −6   +3   −9   −1

8 Put these temperatures in order, from highest to lowest.

   15 °C, −4 °C, 9 °C, −11 °C, −8 °C

Challenge: Extreme temperatures

Records of extreme temperatures around the world show that a temperature of 56 °C has been recorded in Death Valley, California and a temperature of −88 °C has been recorded at the Vostok Research Station, in Antarctica.

How much higher was the temperature in Death Valley than in Vostok?

1.3 Adding negative numbers

Learning objectives

- To carry out additions involving negative numbers
- To use a number line to calculate with negative numbers

Key words	
add	brackets

You can use a number line to **add** and subtract positive and negative numbers.

Example 11

Use a number line to work out the answers.

a $2 + (-5)$ **b** $(-7) + 4$ **c** $3 + (-2) + (-5)$

  a Starting at zero and 'jumping' along the number line to 2 and then back 5 gives an answer of -3.

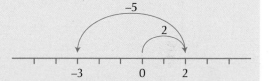

  b Similarly, $(-7) + 4 = -3$.

Notice that you can use **brackets** so that you do not mistake the negative sign for a subtraction sign.

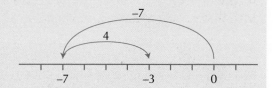

  c Using two steps this time, $3 + (-2) + (-5) = -4$.

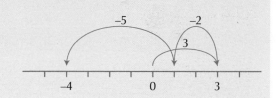

Look at these patterns.

$4 + 2 = 6$	$2 + 4 = 6$
$4 + 1 = 5$	$1 + 4 = 5$
$4 + 0 = 4$	$0 + 4 = 4$
$4 + (-1) = 3$	$(-1) + 4 = 3$
$4 + (-2) = 2$	$(-2) + 4 = 2$

Notice that $4 + (-1) = 3$ and $(-1) + 4 = 3$ have the same value as $4 - 1 = 3$

and $4 + (-2) = 2$ and $(-2) + 4 = 2$ are the same as $4 - 2 = 2$.

Adding a negative number gives the same result as subtracting the corresponding positive number.

Work out the answers.

a 5 + (−2)   **b** 20 + (−3)   **c** (−3) + (−4)

    a 5 + −2 = 5 − 2   **b** 20 + −3 = 20 − 3   **c** (−3) + (−4) = (−3) − 4
            = 3   = 17   = −7

Exercise 1C

1 Work out the answers.

  a 6 − 9   **b** 4 − 3   **c** 2 − 7   **d** 3 + 9
  e 1 − 3   **f** 4 − 4   **g** −6 + 9   **h** −4 − 1
  i −7 − 3   **j** −1 + 8   **k** −2 − 3   **l** −14 + 7
  m −2 − 3 + 4   **n** −1 + 1 − 2   **o** −3 + 4 − 7   **p** −102 + 103 − 5

2 Copy and complete.

  a 6 + (−2)   **b** 8 + (−6)   **c** 20 + (−7)   **d** 16 + (−5)   **e** (−6) + (−7)
    = 6 − 2   = 8 − 6   = 20 − ☐   = ☐☐☐   = ☐☐☐
    = ☐   = ☐   = ☐   = ☐   = ☐

3 Use the number line below to work out the answers.

  a 3 − 5   **b** 8 + (−2)   **c** 4 + (−5)   **d** 3 + (−3)
  e (−2) + (−3)   **f** 2 − 10   **g** (−4) + 10   **h** 0 − 9
  i 10 + (−5)   **j** (−8) + (−6)   **k** 12 + (−10)   **l** 6 + (−6)
  m 9 + (−10)   **n** 15 + (−25)   **o** 0 + (−8)   **p** (−1) + (−7)

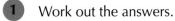

−15 −14 −13 −12 −11 −10 −9 −8 −7 −6 −5 −4 −3 −2 −1 0 1 2 3 4 5 6 7 8 9 10 11 12 13 14 15

4 Work these out.

  a 20 + (−5)   **b** (−5) + (−20)   **c** 60 − 100   **d** (−10) + (−20)
  e 20 + (−16)   **f** (−30) + 30   **g** 15 + (−40)   **h** 120 − 240
  i 13 + (−8)   **j** (−100) + (−20) **k** 16 + (−25)   **l** (−9) + (−19)

5 Work these out.

  a 5 + 6 + (−8)   **b** (−1) − 1 + (−1)   **c** 20 + (−14) + (−6)   **d** (−16) + 3 + (−10)

6 Calculate the total of the numbers in each list.

  a 5, −4, 10, −7, −9, 3   **b** −12, 20, 5, −8, −15, 30

7 In each magic square, all the rows, columns and diagonals add up to the same total. Copy and complete the squares.

a

3		1
	0	
		−3

b

		−8
	−5	−3
−2		

c

0		
−5		
−4		−6

8 Iain has £25 in the bank.

He writes a cheque for £35.

How much has he got in the bank now?

Problem solving: Magic squares

A In this 4 × 4 magic square, all of the rows, columns and diagonals add to −6.

−9			5
2			−4
		6	−1
	1	−5	

Copy and complete the square.

B In this 4 × 4 magic square all of the rows, columns and diagonals add to the same number. Copy and complete the square.

0		−13	−3
	−5		
−7	−9	−10	
−12			−15

1.4 Subtracting negative numbers

Learning objective

• To carry out subtractions involving negative numbers

Key word

subtract

Look at these patterns.

Notice that $4 - (-1) = 5$ has the same value as
$4 + 1 = 5$

and $4 - (-2) = 6$ has the same value as
$4 + 2 = 6$.

Subtracting a negative number is the same as adding the corresponding positive number.

$4 - 3 = 1$
$4 - 2 = 2$
$4 - 1 = 3$
$4 - 0 = 4$
$4 - (-1) = 5$
$4 - (-2) = 6$
$4 - (-3) = 7$

Example 13

Work out the answers.   **a** $3 - (-5)$ **b** $12 - (-7)$

a $3 - (-5) = 3 + 5 = 8$ **b** $12 - (-7) = 12 + 7 = 19$

Exercise 1D

1 Copy and complete.

   a $6 - (-2)$ **b** $10 - (-6)$ **c** $20 - (-8)$ **d** $-14 - (-5)$ **e** $(-6) - (-7)$

      $= 6 + 2$ $= 10 + 6$ $= 20 + $ $=$ $=$

      $=$ $=$ $=$ $=$ $=$

2 Use the number line below to work out the answers.

   a $3 - (-8)$ **b** $7 - (-2)$ **c** $(-6) - (-5)$ **d** $13 - (-2)$

   e $(-2) - (-3)$ **f** $(-2) - (-10)$ **g** $(-4) - (-10)$ **h** $(-10) - (-9)$

   i $7 - (-5)$ **j** $(-8) - (-6)$ **k** $(-9) - (-8)$ **l** $(-6) - (-6)$

   m $(-9) - (-1)$ **n** $(-15) - (-25)$ **o** $0 - (-8)$ **p** $(-3) - (-7)$

```
-15 -14 -13 -12 -11 -10 -9 -8 -7 -6 -5 -4 -3 -2 -1  0  1  2  3  4  5  6  7  8  9 10 11 12 13 14 15
```

3 Work these out.

   a $20 - (-8)$ **b** $(-20) - (-15)$ **c** $30 - (-100)$ **d** $(-10) - (-10)$

   e $22 - (-18)$ **f** $30 - (-30)$ **g** $-15 - (-40)$ **h** $-300 - (-240)$

   i $16 - (-8)$ **j** $(-120) - (-70)$ **k** $16 - (-25)$ **l** $(-8) - (-19)$

4 Work these out.

   a $7 + 6 - (-8)$ **b** $(-2) - 1 - (-1)$ **c** $30 - (-12) + (-9)$ **d** $(-10) + 3 - (-10)$

5 Choose a number from each list and subtract one from the other. Repeat for at least four pairs of numbers. What are the biggest and smallest answers you can find?

A	4	−7	−5	3	8
B	−3	9	−8	−5	−1

6 Copy each statement and work out the missing numbers.

    a $7 + \boxed{} = 6$ **b** $10 - \boxed{} = 12$ **c** $\boxed{} + (-5) = 7$ **d** $(-8) - \boxed{} = 4$

7 Copy each calculation and then fill in the missing numbers.

    a $3 + {+1} = 4$

         $3 + 0 = 3$

         $3 + {-1} = 2$

         $3 + {-2} = \boxed{}$

         $3 + \boxed{} = \boxed{}$

         $3 + \boxed{} = \boxed{}$

    b $-2 - {+1} = -3$

         $-2 - 0 = -2$

         $-2 - {-1} = -1$

         $-2 - {-2} = \boxed{}$

         $-2 - \boxed{} = \boxed{}$

         $-2 - \boxed{} = \boxed{}$

    c $4 - {+2} = 2$

         $3 - {+1} = 2$

         $2 - 0 = 2$

         $1 - {-1} = \boxed{}$

         $0 - \boxed{} = \boxed{}$

         $\boxed{} - \boxed{} = \boxed{}$

8 Work out the answers.

    a $+3 - {+2}$ **b** $-4 - {-3}$ **c** $+7 - {-6}$ **d** $-7 + {-3}$ **e** $+7 - {+3}$

    f $-9 - {-5}$ **g** $-6 + {+6}$ **h** $+6 - {-7}$ **i** $-6 + {-6}$ **j** $-1 + {-8}$

    k $+5 - {+7}$ **l** $7 - {-5}$ **m** $-2 - {-3} + {-4}$ **n** $- {+1} + {+1} - {+2}$

9 These temperatures were recorded at Aberdeen Airport in January.

Copy and complete the table.

Draw a number line to check your answers.

Temperature (°C)	Sun	Mon	Tue	Wed	Thu	Fri	Sat
Maximum temperature (°C)	4	0	−1		2	3	5
Minimum temperature (°C)	−4	−6		−7	−4		−2
Difference (degrees)	8		8	10		6	

10 A fish is 10 m below the surface of the water. A fish eagle is 15 m above the water.

How many metres must the bird descend to catch the fish?

Challenge: Marking a maths test

A A maths test consists of 20 questions. A correct answer earns 3 points, a wrong answer or missed question gets −2 points. Work out each pupil's scores.

> A computer spreadsheet is useful for this activity.

    a Aisha gets 12 right and 8 wrong.   **b** Bill gets 10 right and 10 wrong.

    c Charles gets 8 right and 12 wrong.   **d** Dilash gets 9 right and 11 wrong.

    e What times table are all your answers in?

B What happens when a correct answer earns 4 points and a wrong answer gets −2?

Ready to progress?

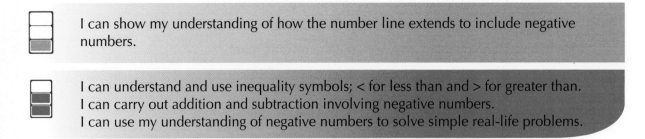

Review questions

1   A train departs from Vienna at 06:36 and arrives in Munich at 10:30.

   a   How long does the journey take?

   b   It takes me 45 minutes to walk from home to Vienna station.
      What time do I need to leave home to arrive in time for the train?

   c   Adult tickets from Vienna to Munich cost €98 and child tickets cost €53.50.
      How much do two adult tickets and one child ticket cost altogether?

2   The keel (bottom) of a cruise ship is 6 m below the surface of the water.

   The deck is 26 m above the water.

   What is the total height, from deck to keel?

3   David is on the 25th floor of a skyscraper.

   He goes up 17 floors and then down 28 floors.

   Which floor is he on now?

(FS) 4   a   Maria opens a bank account with a deposit of £40.

      In the next two weeks she takes out £27, deposits £15 and takes out £35.

      How much is left in her account?

   b   Next, Maria deposits £15 and takes out £20.

   c   How much is left in her account now?

(PS) 5   Anaya and Euan have parked their car on level −3 of the shopping centre car park.

   They take the lift to the shops on level +2.

   Anaya realises she has left her purse in the car so she goes back to the car to get it.
   Then she returns to the shops and meets Euan on level +1.

   How many levels has Anaya travelled through altogether?

6 This is part of a bank account statement.

Copy the statement and complete the balance column.

Deposits	Withdrawals (£)	Balance (£)
100		100
	120	−20
30		10
	60	−50
	40	
10		
	30	

7 The Mariana Trench in the Pacific Ocean has a maximum depth of 10.9 km below sea level.

The summit of Mount Everest is 8.8 km above sea level.

a How much higher than the base of the trench is the summit of Mount Everest?

b If Mount Everest was set in the deepest part of the trench, how far would its summit be below sea level?

8 In a popular BBC TV programme, each team has to buy three items at an antiques fair.

The items are sold at auction and the team that makes more money wins and keeps any profit they make.

Copy and complete each team's score sheet.

a Red team

Item	Buying price (£)	Selling price (£)	Profit (£)
Silver bowl	55		−18
Walking stick		42	+14
Teddy bear	62	55	
Total	145		

b Blue team

Item	Buying price (£)	Selling price (£)	Profit (£)
Charm bracelet		52	+17
Dinkie toy car	60	85	
Clock	80		−22
Total	175		

c Which team won and by how much?

Problem solving
Travelling in Asia and eastern Europe

A Comparing temperatures

Look at the map of Asia.

Use it to answer these questions.

1 What is the temperature in Moscow?

2 Which is the hottest place shown?

3 Which is the coldest place shown?

4 What is the difference in temperature between Cairo and Tokyo?

5 How much hotter is it in Almaty than in Ulan?

6 Which place is at −3 °C?

7 Which place is 9 degrees colder than Kiev?

8 Which place is 10 degrees hotter than Yakutsk?

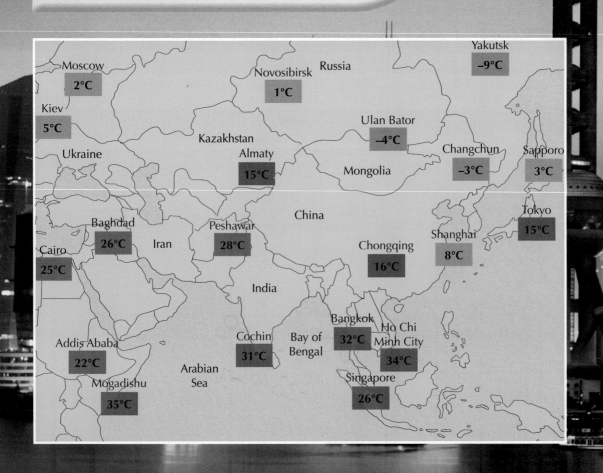

B Planning a flight

A businesswoman wants to travel from Beijing to Shanghai for a meeting.
She wants to return to Beijing on the same day.

Below are some of the flight times.

Use these flight times to plan her day so that she can spend at least 4 hours in Shanghai.

Work out all the possible flights she could use.

Beijing (depart)	Shanghai (arrive)	Shanghai (depart)	Beijing (arrive)
06:55	09:10	12:00	14:25
07:30	09:30	13:05	15:20
07:55	09:55	14:00	16:25
08:25	10:50	14:35	17:15

2

Sequences

This chapter is going to show you:
- how to use function machines to generate input or output values
- how to describe some simple number patterns
- how to create sequences and describe them in words
- how to generate and describe simple whole-number sequences
- how to use the special sequence called the sequence of square numbers
- how to use the special sequence called the sequence of triangular numbers.

You should already know:
- odd and even numbers
- multiplication tables up to 12×12
- how to apply the four rules of arithmetic.

About this chapter
During the Second World War the first computer in the world was invented at Bletchley Park in the UK. At that time, Britain was at war with Germany and needed to break the coded German communications to discover what they were planning to do next. Codes are based on sequences and these were very complex ones, which were changed every day and randomly generated by a machine called Enigma. It was the job of the computer to crack each day's new code sequences from the Enigma machine – and fast. Today, coded sequences are still used in secure communications, for example, encrypting websites used for financial transactions – vital to everyday business.

2.1 Function machines

Learning objectives

- To use function machines to generate inputs and outputs
- To use given inputs and outputs to work out a rule

Function machines can help you to understand how sequences are formed. They use mathematical **rules** to change one number into another. The numbers you start with are called the **input**. The numbers you finish with, after using the rules, are called the **output**.

Example 1

Work out the outputs for this function machine.

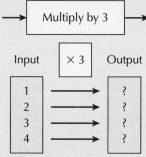

Multiply each input number by 3.
The outputs are:

3
6
9
12

Example 2

Work out the outputs for this function machine.

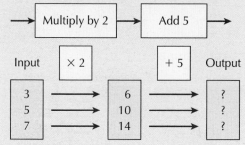

Multiply each input number by 2 and add 5.
The outputs are:

11
15
19

When working backwards from the output to the input, you reverse the operations.

So in Example 2 the reverse of + 5 is – 5 and the reverse of × 2 is ÷ 2.

Example 3

Work out the inputs for this function machine.

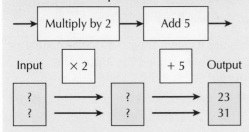

Working backwards from an output of 23 gives 23 – 5 = 18 and then 18 ÷ 2 = 9 so the input is 9.

Similarly, when the output is 31 the input is 13.

Exercise 2A

1 Complete the inputs and outputs for each function machine.

a

Input	+ 3	Output
4	→	?
5	→	?
8	→	?
11	→	?

b

Input	– 2	Output
4	→	?
5	→	?
8	→	?
11	→	?

c

Input	+ 4	Output
3	→	?
?	→	9
8	→	?
?	→	15

2 Complete the inputs and outputs for each function machine.

a

Input	÷ 10	Output
100	→	?
80	→	?
60	→	?
50	→	?

b

Input	× 3	Output
4	→	?
?	→	18
8	→	?
?	→	36

c

Input	× 5	Output
4	→	?
5	→	?
8	→	?
11	→	?

3 Draw a function machine for each set of inputs and outputs.

a

Input	Output
2 →	4
3 →	5
4 →	6
5 →	7

b

Input	Output
3 →	9
4 →	12
5 →	15
6 →	18

c

Input	Output
1 →	6
2 →	12
3 →	18
4 →	24

d

Input	Output
24 →	12
12 →	6
8 →	4
6 →	3

e

Input	Output
2 →	9
3 →	10
4 →	11
5 →	12

f

Input	Output
2 →	16
4 →	32
6 →	48
8 →	64

4 Work out the outputs for each function machine.

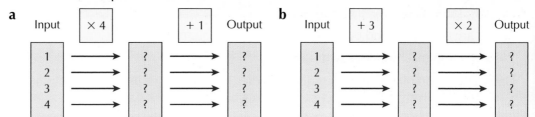

a

Input	× 4		+ 1	Output
1	→	?	→	?
2	→	?	→	?
3	→	?	→	?
4	→	?	→	?

b

Input	+ 3		× 2	Output
1	→	?	→	?
2	→	?	→	?
3	→	?	→	?
4	→	?	→	?

5 Draw diagrams to illustrate these rules. Choose four input numbers and work out the outputs for them.

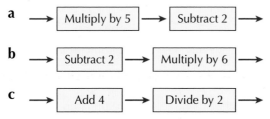

a → | Multiply by 5 | → | Subtract 2 | →

b → | Subtract 2 | → | Multiply by 6 | →

c → | Add 4 | → | Divide by 2 | →

6 Fill in the missing numbers and rules in each function machine.

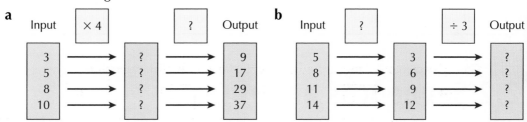

a

Input	× 4		?	Output
3	→	?	→	9
5	→	?	→	17
8	→	?	→	29
10	→	?	→	37

b

Input	?		÷ 3	Output
5	→	3	→	?
8	→	6	→	?
11	→	9	→	?
14	→	12	→	?

7 Work out the number I am thinking of, in each case.

a I think of a number. I multiply it by 4. I then add 8 to my answer.
My final answer is 20.

b I think of a number. I multiply it by 5. I then subtract this from 15.
My final answer is 5.

c I think of a number. I add 4. I then multiply by 6. My final answer is 18.

d I think of a number. I add 3. I then multiply by 2. My final answer is 18.

(MR) 8 Work out the input for each output.

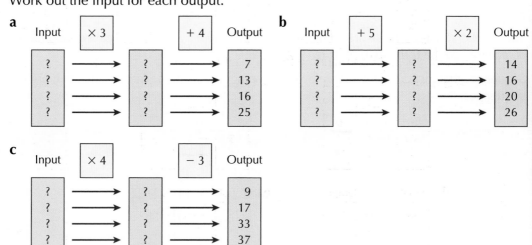

a

Input	× 3		+ 4	Output
?	→	?	→	7
?	→	?	→	13
?	→	?	→	16
?	→	?	→	25

b

Input	+ 5		× 2	Output
?	→	?	→	14
?	→	?	→	16
?	→	?	→	20
?	→	?	→	26

c

Input	× 4		− 3	Output
?	→	?	→	9
?	→	?	→	17
?	→	?	→	33
?	→	?	→	37

Challenge: Rules in sequences

Below are the inputs and outputs from some function machines.

Each function machine uses two rules.

Draw a function machine or describe the rules for each set of inputs and outputs.

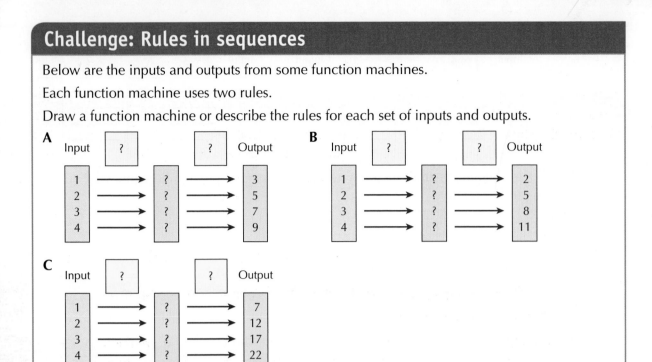

2.2 Sequences and rules

Learning objective

- To recognise, describe and generate sequences that use a simple rule

Key words	
first term	geometric sequence
linear sequence	sequence
term	term-to-term rule

A **sequence** is a list of numbers that follow a pattern or rule.

You can use simple rules to make up many different sequences with whole numbers.

Sequences may also have different starting points.

The numbers in a sequence are called **terms** and the starting number is called the **first term**. The rule is often called the **term-to-term rule**.

Sequences that increase or decrease by a fixed amount, from one term to the next, are called **linear sequences**.

Example 4

Rule: add 3   Starting at 1 gives the sequence 1, 4, 7, 10, 13, …

                   Starting at 2 gives the sequence 2, 5, 8, 11, 14, …

                   Starting at 6 gives the sequence 6, 9, 12, 15, 18, …

Sequences in which you find each term after the first term by multiplying or dividing by a fixed amount are called **geometric sequences**.

Example 5

Rule: multiply by 2   Starting at 1 gives the sequence 1, 2, 4, 8, 16, …

Starting at 3 gives the sequence 3, 6, 12, 24, 48, …

Starting at 5 gives the sequence 5, 10, 20, 40, 80, …

Exercise 2B

1   Use the term-to-term rule to work out the first five terms of each sequence.

Start from a first term of 1.

a	add 3	**b**	multiply by 3	**c**	add 5	**d**	multiply by 10
e	add 9	**f**	multiply by 5	**g**	add 7	**h**	multiply by 2
i	add 11	**j**	multiply by 4	**k**	add 8	**l**	add 105

2   Use the term-to-term rule to work out the first five terms of each sequence.

Start from a first term of 5.

a	add 3	**b**	multiply by 3	**c**	add 5	**d**	multiply by 10
e	add 9	**f**	multiply by 5	**g**	add 7	**h**	multiply by 2
i	add 11	**j**	multiply by 4	**k**	add 8	**l**	add 105

3   Work out the next two terms in each sequence.

Describe the term-to-term rule you have used.

a	2, 4, 6, …, …	**b**	3, 6, 9, …, …	**c**	1, 10, 100, …, …	**d**	1, 2, 4, …, …
e	2, 10, 50, …, …	**f**	0, 7, 14, …, …	**g**	7, 10, 13, …, …	**h**	4, 9, 14, …, …
i	4, 8, 12, …, …	**j**	9, 18, 27, …, …	**k**	12, 24, 36, …, …	**l**	2, 6, 18, …, …

4   Work out the next two terms in each sequence.

Describe the term-to-term rule you have used.

a	50, 45, 40, 35, 30, …, …	**b**	35, 32, 29, 26, 23, …, …
c	64, 32, 16, 8, 4, …, …	**d**	10, 7, 4, 1, −2, …, …
e	9, 5, 1, −3, −7, …, …	**f**	6.5, 1.5, −3.5, −8.5, −13.5, …, …

5   Work out the first four terms of each sequence.

a   Start with a first term of 3. To work out the next term, multiply by 3 and then add 7.

b   Start with a first term of 5. To work out the next term, subtract 2 and then multiply by 4.

c   Start with a first term of 32. To work out the next term, divide by 2 and then subtract 4.

(PS) 6 Work out two terms between each pair of numbers, to form a sequence. Describe the term-to-term rule you have used.

    a 1, ..., ..., 8   **b** 3, ..., ..., 12   **c** 5, ..., ..., 20

    d 4, ..., ..., 10   **e** 80, ..., ..., 10   **f** 2, ..., ..., 54

(PS) 7 Describe each sequence in words, as in question **5**.

    a 7, 15, 31, 63, 127, ...   **b** 6, 4, 3, 2.5, 2.25, ...   **c** 3, 2, 0, −4, −12

(PS) 8 For each pair of numbers, find at least two different sequences and write down the next two terms. Describe the term-to-term rule you have used.

    a 1, 4, ..., ...   **b** 3, 9, ..., ...   **c** 2, 6, ..., ...

    d 3, 6, ..., ...   **e** 4, 8, ..., ...   **f** 5, 15, ..., ...

Investigation: Common terms

Write out the first 20 terms of the sequence that starts 1, 4, 7, 10, 13, ...

Write out the first 20 terms of the sequence that starts 2, 6, 10, 14, 18, ...

10 is a common term in both sequences.

A What are the other common terms?

B Is there a pattern to them?

C Do all linear sequences have common terms?

2.3 Working out missing terms

Learning objective

• To work out missing terms in a sequence

The terms in a sequence are called the first term, second term, third term, fourth term and so on. You need to know how to work out any term in a sequence.

Example 6

Work out the fourth term in the sequence of patterns made with matches, below.

    Look at the number sequence shown by this pattern.

Term number   1   2   3

Number of matchsticks   5   9   13

(Continued)

You can see that four more matches are added each time.

You can draw the pattern for the fourth term and work out that it has 17 matches.

A better way of showing the patterns in the example above is to put the numbers into a table.

Term	Matches
1	5
2	9
3	13
4	17

You could continue this table to find the number of matches for the patterns for all the terms but there is an easier way.

For example, if you want to work out the number of matches in the pattern for the 10th term, you need to add nine more terms to the first term to get to the 10th term. The first term has 5 matches but the rest have 4 matches each so the number of matches you add to the first term is 36 (9×4).

Then add the number of matches in the first term, which is 5.

$$36 + 5 = 41$$

So there are 41 matches in the 10th term.

In Example 6, the tenth term would be:

$$5 + (10 - 1) \times 4 = 5 + 36 = 41 \text{ matches}$$

Example 7

In the sequence 7, 10, 13, 16, ..., what is the fifth term, what is the 25th term and what is the 50th term?

You first need to know what the term-to-term rule is.

You can see that you add 3 from one term to the next.

$$
\begin{array}{ccccc}
 & +3 & +3 & +3 & +3 \\
7 & 10 & 13 & 16 & \dots \\
\text{1st} & \text{2nd} & \text{3rd} & \text{4th} & \text{5th} \dots \text{50th}
\end{array}
$$

To get to the fifth term, you add 3 to the fourth term, which gives 19.

To get to the 25th term, you will have to add on 3 a total of 24 times ($25 - 1$) to the first term, 7.

This will give $7 + 3 \times 24 = 7 + 72 = 79$.

To get to the 50th term, you will have to add on 3 a total of 49 times ($50 - 1$) to the first term, 7.

This will give $7 + 3 \times 49 = 7 + 147 = 154$.

In questions **1** to **4**:

a draw the next pattern of matches

b work out the number of matches in the 10th pattern.

1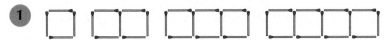

2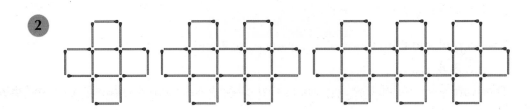

3

4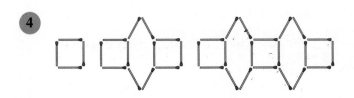

5 Work out the fifth and the 50th term in each sequence.

a	4, 6, 8, 10, …	**b**	1, 6, 11, 16, …
d	5, 8, 11, 14, …	**e**	1, 5, 9, 13, …
g	20, 30, 40, 50, …	**h**	10, 19, 28, 37, …

c 3, 10, 17, 24, …
f 2, 10, 18, 26, …
i 3, 9, 15, 21, …

6 Work out the fifth and the 50th term in each sequence.

a −2, −4, −6, −8, …   **b** −2, −7, −12, −17, …   **c** −4, −11, −18, −25, …
d 8, 5, 2, −1, …   **e** −1, −6, −11, −16, …   **f** −12, −20, −28, −36, …
g 9, 3, −3, −9, …   **h** −37, −28, −19, −10, …   **i** −21, −18, −15, −12, …

(PS) **7** In each sequence, work out the first term, then work out the 25th term.

In each case, you have been given the fourth, fifth and sixth terms.

a …, …, …, 13, 15, 17, …   **b** …, …, …, 18, 23, 28, …
c …, …, …, 19, 23, 27, …   **d** …, …, …, 32, 41, 50, …

8 Work out the 80th term in the sequence with the term-to-term rule 'add 4' and a first term of 9.

PS **9** This is a sequence of patterns made from mauve and white squares.

The diagrams show the patterns for the third and fifth terms.

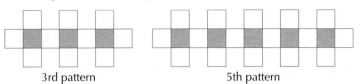

3rd pattern   5th pattern

a How many mauve squares are there in the pattern for the fourth term?

b How many white squares are there in the pattern for the fourth term?

c Draw the pattern for the first term.

PS **10** The second and third terms of a sequence are 2 and 4.

…., 2, 4, …, …

There are several different sequences that could have 2 and 4 as the second and third terms.

a Write down a rule for the way the sequence is building up and work out the first and fourth terms.

b Write down a different rule for the way the sequence is building up and work out the first and fourth terms.

MR **11** In a sequence, the 50th term is 254, the 51st is 259 and the 52nd is 264.

Work out the first term and the 100th term.

Problem solving: Missing terms

In each of the following sequences, work out the missing terms and the 50th term.

Term	1st	2nd	3rd	4th	5th	6th	7th	8th	50th
Sequence A	…	…	…	…	17	19	21	23	…
Sequence B	…	9	…	19	…	29	…	39	…
Sequence C	…	…	16	23	…	37	44	…	…
Sequence D	…	…	25	…	45	…	…	75	…
Sequence E	…	5	…	11	…	…	20	…	…
Sequence F	…	…	12	…	…	18	…	22	…

Challenge: Patterns in squares

In this sequence of patterns, how many squares will there be in:

a the fifth pattern   **b** the 20th pattern?

 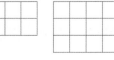

Pattern 1   Pattern 2   Pattern 3   Pattern 4

2.4 Other sequences

Learning objective

- To know and understand the sequences of numbers known as the square numbers and the triangular numbers

Square numbers and triangular numbers

When you multiply a number by itself you are squaring the number. The result is a **square number**. For example:

- 4 is a square number and it is the square of 2 ($2 \times 2 = 4$)
- 9 is a square number and it is the square of 3 ($3 \times 3 = 9$) and so on.

Instead of writing 1×1, 2×2, 3×3 and so on you can write 1^2, 2^2, 3^2. The small 2 is called a **power** and the power of 2 is also called 'square'. You refer to the number it is attached to as 'squared', for example, you say 5^2 as 'five squared'.

This table shows the first 10 square numbers. You can see from the bottom line of the table why they are called square numbers.

1×1	2×2	3×3	4×4	5×5	6×6	7×7	8×8	9×9	10×10
1^2	2^2	3^2	4^2	5^2	6^2	7^2	8^2	9^2	10^2
1	4	9	16	25	36	49	64	81	100

This is the start of the sequence of square numbers. You need to learn the square numbers up to $15^2 = 225$.

Another well-known sequence is 1, 3, 6, 10, 15, 21, ….

This is called the sequence of **triangular numbers**. The sequence builds up like this.

First term: 1

Second term: add 2 to the first term ($1 + 2 = 3$)

Third term: add 3 to the second term ($3 + 3 = 6$)

Fourth term: add 4 to the third term ($6 + 4 = 10$)

Fifth term: add 5 to the fourth term ($10 + 5 = 15$)

This table shows you the first 10 triangular numbers. You can see from the bottom line of the table why they are called triangular numbers.

1	$1 + 2$	$3 + 3$	$6 + 4$	$10 + 5$	$15 + 6$	$21 + 7$	$28 + 8$	$36 + 9$	$45 + 10$
1	3	6	10	15	21	28	36	45	55

The triangular numbers occur in ten-pin bowling and snooker.

Exercise 2D

1 Copy the first three rows of the table of square numbers, opposite, and continue it, up to 15×15.

2 Write each number below as the sum of two square numbers.

The first two have been done for you.

a $5 = 1 + 4$ b $10 = 1 + 9$ c $13 = ... + ...$

d $17 = ... + ...$ e $20 = ... + ...$ f $25 = ... + ...$

g $26 = ... + ...$ h $29 = ... + ...$ i $34 = ... + ...$

j $37 = ... + ...$ k $40 = ... + ...$ l $41 = ... + ...$

m $45 = ... + ...$ n $50 = ... + ...$ o $52 = ... + ...$

3 Copy the first two rows of the table of triangular numbers, opposite, and continue it, to the 15th triangular number.

4 Write each number as the sum of two triangular numbers.

The first two have been done for you.

a $4 = 1 + 3$ b $7 = 1 + 6$ c $9 = ... + ...$

d $11 = ... + ...$ e $13 = ... + ...$ f $16 = ... + ...$

g $18 = ... + ...$ h $21 = ... + ...$ i $22 = ... + ...$

j $24 = ... + ...$ k $25 = ... + ...$ l $27 = ... + ...$

m $29 = ... + ...$ n $31 = ... + ...$ o $34 = ... + ...$

5 Write down two numbers that are both square numbers and also triangular numbers.

6 Look at this pattern of numbers.

$1 \qquad\qquad\quad = 1 = 1^2$

$1 + 3 \qquad\qquad = 4 = 2^2$

$1 + 3 + 5 \qquad\quad = 9 = 3^2$

$1 + 3 + 5 + 7 \quad\ = 16 = 4^2$

$1 + 3 + 5 + 7 + 9 = 25 = 5^2$

a   Write down the next two lines of this number pattern.

b   What is special about the numbers on the left-hand side?

(PS)

c   Without working them out, write down the answers to these calculations.

  i $1 + 3 + 5 + 7 + 9 + 11 + 13 + 15 + 17 + 19 = ...$

  ii $1 + 3 + 5 + 7 + 9 + 11 + 13 + 15 + 17 + 19 + 21 + 23 + 25 + 27 + 29 = ...$

7 Some sums of two square numbers are special because they give an answer that is also a square number. For example:

$3^2 + 4^2 = 9 + 16 = 25 = 5^2$

Which of these pairs of squares give a total that is also a square number?

a $5^2 + 12^2$ b $2^2 + 5^2$ c $6^2 + 8^2$

d $7^2 + 9^2$ e $7^2 + 24^2$ f $10^2 + 24^2$

8 **a** Add up the first 10 pairs of consecutive square numbers, starting with
$1 + 4, 4 + 9, 9 + 16, \ldots$

b Is it possible to get an even number if you add any pair of consecutive square numbers? If not, explain why not.

c Work out the differences between the totals.

d Do they form a sequence? If so, describe the sequence.

9 Look at this pattern of numbers.

$$1 = 1$$
$$1 + 2 = 3$$
$$1 + 2 + 3 = 6$$
$$1 + 2 + 3 + 4 = 10$$
$$1 + 2 + 3 + 4 + 5 = 15$$

a Write down the next two lines of this number pattern.

b What is special about the numbers on the left-hand side?

c What is special about the numbers on the right-hand side?

d Without working them out, write down the answers to these calculations.

    i $1 + 2 + 3 + 4 + 5 + 6 + 7 + 8 + 9 + 10 = \ldots$

    ii $1 + 2 + 3 + 4 + 5 + 6 + 7 + 8 + 9 + 10 + 11 + 12 + 13 + 14 + 15 = \ldots$

10 **a** Add up the first 10 pairs of consecutive triangular numbers, starting with
$1 + 3, 3 + 6, 6 + 10, \ldots$

b What is special about the answers?

11 This number pattern is called Pascal's triangle, after the famous French mathematician, Blaise Pascal.

Row									
1					1				
2				1		1			
3			1		2		1		
4		1		3		3		1	
5	1		4		6		4		1
6	1	5		10		10		5	1

Each row starts and ends with 1.

Each of the other numbers is the sum of the two numbers above it, to the left and right.

For example, in row 5:

    $4 = 1 + 3$ $6 = 3 + 3$ $4 = 3 + 1$

a Write down the next two rows of Pascal's triangle.

b Copy and complete the table to show the numbers and the total for each row.

Row	Sum of numbers in the row	Total
1	1	1
2	1 + 1	2
3	1 + 2 + 1	
4	1 + 3 + 3 + 1	
5		
6		
7		
8		

c Write down the totals as a sequence and then describe the rule for the sequence.

Challenge: Testing the rule

A Here is a rule.

🔲   8 × any triangular number + 1 gives a square number

Test this rule for the first triangular number, 1.

$8 \times 1 + 1 = 8 + 1$

$= 9$

$= 3^2$

Does the rule always work?

Use at least four other triangular numbers to test the rule.

B Now test this rule and say whether it always works.

9 × any triangular number + 1 is also a triangular number

C Now test this rule and say whether it always works.

The sum of the squares of any two consecutive triangular numbers is also a triangular number.

Investigation: Consecutive numbers and Fibonacci numbers

A Take any three consecutive numbers, for example, 7, 8, 9.

Multiply the first and last numbers.

$7 \times 9 = 63$

Square the middle number.

$8^2 = 64$

Subtract the first result from the second.

$64 - 63 = 1$

Try this with at least three different sets of consecutive numbers.

What happens in every case?

B This sequence is called the Fibonacci sequence. It helps to understand some of the patterns in nature.

1   1   2   3   5   8   13   21…

Can you work out what the next term is?

C Now try the process used in part **A** with any three consecutive Fibonacci numbers, for example, 5, 8, 13.

Repeat this with at least three different sets of consecutive Fibonacci numbers subtracting the smaller number from the larger each time.

What happens this time?

Ready to progress?

I can work out the output values for a function machine when I know the input values.
I can work out a sequence, given the first term and a term-to-term rule.
I can work out the term-to-term rule for a sequence.
I can work out the rule for a function machine, when I am given the input and output values.
I know the square numbers up to 15 × 15.

I can work out any term in a sequence, given the first term and the term-to-term rule.
I can recognise and work out the sequence of triangular numbers.
I can investigate the patterns and connections within the square and triangular numbers.
I can work out the inputs to a function machine when given the outputs and the rules.

I can work out the operations in a function machine that uses more than one rule, when I am given the input and output values.
I can investigate a given rule and reach a conclusion about whether it always works.

Review questions

1 a Write down the next two numbers in the sequence below.

72, 66, 60, 54, 48, 42, ... , ...

   b Write down the next two numbers in the sequence below.

1, 3, 6, 10, 15, 21, ... , ...

   c Continue both sequences.
      Which two numbers appear in both sequences?

2 Here is a sequence of shapes made with mauve and white tiles.

Shape number 1 Shape number 2 Shape number 3 Shape number 4

The number of mauve tiles   =   the shape number + 2
The number of white tiles   =   2 × the shape number

   a How many mauve tiles will there be in shape number 7?
   b How many white tiles will there be in shape number 25?
   c How many tiles altogether will there be in shape number 10?
   d Write down the missing numbers from this sentence.
      The total number of tiles = ☐ × the shape number + ☐

3 This is a sequence of huts made from matches.

  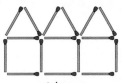

1 hut	2 huts	3 huts
6 matches	11 matches	16 matches

The rule for how many matches you need to make the huts is:

number of matches = 5 × number of huts + 1

a Use the rule to find how many matches you need to make 10 huts.

b I use 76 matches to make some huts. How many huts do I make?

c I have 100 matches. What is the largest number of huts I can make?
How many matches will be left over?

4 a Jeni saves £40 each week for a year.

How much will she have saved after:

i 23 weeks **ii** a year (52 weeks)?

b Lucie saves £1 the first week, £3 the second week, £5 the third week and so on for a year. Copy and complete this table.

Week	1	2	3	4	5	6
Amount saved	£1	£3	£5	£7	£9	£11
Total amount saved	£1	£4				

Work out who will have more money at the end of the year. Show your working.

5 The patterns in this sequence are made from blue and yellow triangles.

Pattern 1	Pattern 2	Pattern 3	Pattern 4

a Copy and complete this table.

Pattern (term) number	Number of blue triangles	Number of yellow triangles	Total number of triangles
1	1	3	4
2	3		
3			
4			

b Describe the sequence formed by the number of blue triangles.

c Describe the sequence formed by the number of yellow triangles.

d Describe the sequence formed by the total number of triangles.

e Work out the total number of triangles in Pattern 10.

Mathematical reasoning
Valencia Planetarium

This is the planetarium in the city of Valencia in Spain. Many of the features of the building are based on a repeating sequence.

This key explains the diagrams on these pages.

Ladders and grids are made from combinations of:

L links   T links   X links   R rods

Each combination can be expressed as an algebraic rule.

Examples

This ladder is a combination of L links, T links and R rods.

The combination can be written as the rule:
$4L + 2T + 7R$

This grid is a combination of L links, T links, X links and R rods.

The combination can be written as the rule:
$4L + 6T + 2X + 17R$

$4L + 2T + 7R$ $4L + 6T + 2X + 17R$

1 Look at the ladders on the right.

  a Use letters to write down a rule for each of them.

  b Copy and complete this table.

Ladder	L links	T links	R rods
1	4	0	4
2	4	2	7
3			
4			
5			

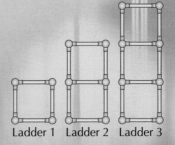

Ladder 1 Ladder 2 Ladder 3

  c Use letters to write down a rule for the links and rods in ladder 10.

2 These rectangles are 2 squares deep.

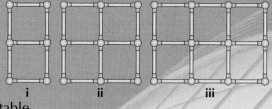

i ii iii

a Use letters to write down a rule for each of them.

b Copy and complete this table.

Rectangle	L links	T links	X links	R rods
2 by 1	4	2	0	7
2 by 2	4	4	1	12
2 by 3				

c Use letters to write down a rule for the links and rods in a 2 by 10 rectangle.

3 These rectangles are 3 squares deep.

a Use letters to write down a rule for each of them.

b Copy and complete this table.

Rectangle	L links	T links	X links	R rods
3 by 1	4	4	0	10
3 by 2	4	6	2	17
3 by 3				
3 by 4				
3 by 5				

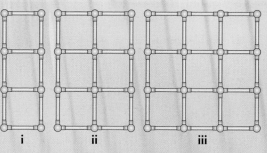

i ii iii

c Use letters to write down a rule for the links and rods in a 3 by 10 rectangle.

3

Perimeter, area and volume

This chapter is going to show you:

- how to work out the perimeters and areas of 2D shapes
- how to work out the volumes of cubes and cuboids
- how to use simple formulae to calculate perimeter, area and volume
- how to work out the capacity of a cube or a cuboid.

You should already know:

- how to measure and draw lines
- that the perimeter of a shape is the distance around its edge
- that area is the space inside a flat shape
- the names of 3D shapes such as the cube and the cuboid.

About this chapter

A five-sided shape is called a pentagon. This is also the name of one of the biggest office buildings in the world, which is the headquarters of the USA Defence Department. The Pentagon has five sides and its perimeter is about 1.4 kilometres long. Its buildings cover an area of 600 000 m^2, with a central plaza of 20 000 m^2. Inside, the lengths of its corridors alone total 28.2 kilometres and over 30 000 people work there.

How does this compare to the area of your house and the perimeter of your bedroom?

3.1 Perimeter and area

Learning objectives

- To work out the perimeters of 2D shapes
- To work out the areas of 2D shapes

Key words	
area	length
metric units	perimeter

The **metric units** of **length** in common use are:

- the millimetre (mm)
- the centimetre (cm)
- the metre (m)
- the kilometre (km).

The metric units of **area** in common use are:

- the square millimetre (mm^2)
- the square centimetre (cm^2)
- the square metre (m^2).

Perimeter

You can calculate or measure the **perimeter** of a shape by adding together the lengths of all its sides.

Example 1

The side of each **square** on the grid represents 1 cm.

Work out the perimeter of the shape.

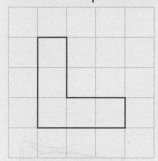

The perimeter of the L-shape = 1 + 2 + 2 + 1 + 3 + 3

                         = 12 cm

Area

One way to calculate the area of a shape is to count the number of square centimetres inside it.

In Example 1 there are five squares inside the shape so the area is 5 cm^2.

You can also estimate the area of an irregular shape in this way.

Example 2

The diagram shows a pond in a garden.

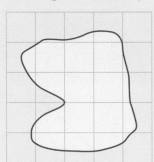

Each square on the grid represents an area of 1 m².

Estimate the area of the pond.

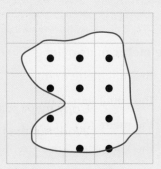

Draw a dot in a square if at least half of it is inside the pond.

There are 11 squares marked with dots. So, an estimate for the area of the pond is 11 m².

Exercise 3A

1   Work out the perimeter of each of these shapes by using your ruler to measure the length of each side.

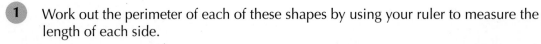

a   **b**   **c**   **d**

2   Copy these shapes onto centimetre-squared paper.

Work out the perimeter of each dark blue square.

a
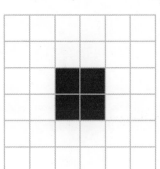

b
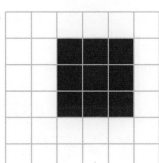

c
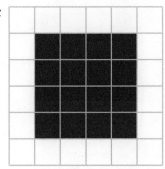

3 Copy these shapes onto centimetre-squared paper.
Work out the area of each dark blue rectangle.

a 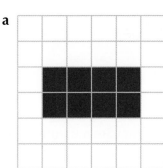   b 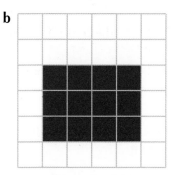   c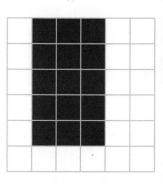

4 Copy these shapes onto centimetre-squared paper.
Work out the perimeter and area of each shape.

a 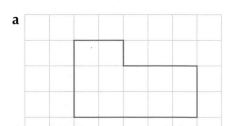   b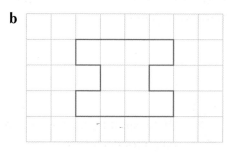

c 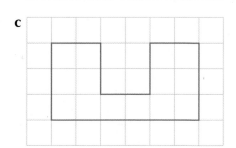   d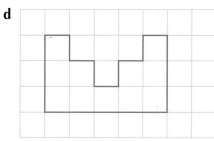

5 Draw each rectangle accurately on centimetre-squared paper.
Work out the perimeter of each rectangle.

a 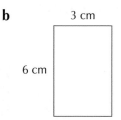   b

6 Draw each rectangle accurately on centimetre-squared paper.
Work out the area of each rectangle.

a 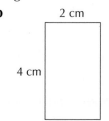   b

7 **a** Draw each square accurately on centimetre-squared paper.

Work out the area of each square.

i

ii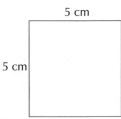

b Explain how you could work out the area of a square measuring 10 cm by 10 cm without drawing it

8 Estimate the area of this oval shape.

Each square on the grid represents one square centimetre.

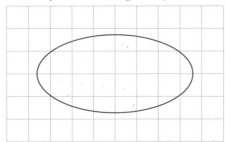

9 Estimate the area of each of these shapes.

Each square on the grid represents one square centimetre.

a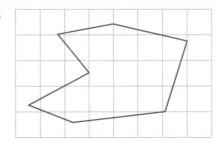

b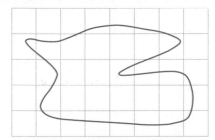

(MR) **10** **a** Work out the area of this rectangle without copying it onto centimetre-squared paper.

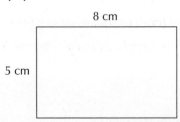

b Explain how you worked out your answer.

Activity: Area of your hand or foot

Work in a group. Draw the outline of each person's hand (or foot) on centimetre-squared paper.

Estimate the area of each hand (or foot).

Make a display of all the hands (and/or feet) for your classroom.

3 Perimeter, area and volume

3.2 Perimeter and area of rectangles

Learning objectives

- To use a simple formula to calculate the perimeter of a rectangle
- To use a simple formula to calculate the area of a rectangle

Key words

formula	rectangle
square	width

A **rectangle** has two long sides and two short sides.

The long sides are equal, and each is referred to as the length of the rectangle.

The short sides are also equal, and each is referred to as the **width**.

length (l)

width (w)

This means that its perimeter equals $2 \times$ length $+ 2 \times$ width.

Perimeter = 2 lengths + 2 widths

You can write this as a **formula**, using the letters P for perimeter, l for length and w for width.

$$P = 2l + 2w$$

The units are millimetres (mm), centimetres (cm) or metres (m).

You can find the area of a rectangle by multiplying its length by its width.

Area = length $\times$ width

This can be shown as a formula, where A = area, l = length and w = width.

$$A = l \times w \text{ or } A = lw$$

The units are square millimetres (mm²), square centimetres (cm²) or square metres (m²).

Using this formula, if you know the area of a shape you can work back to calculate its length or width.

Example 3

Work out the perimeter (P) and area (A) of this wall tile.

$$
\begin{aligned}
P \quad &= 2 \times 6 + 2 \times 4 \\
&= 12 + 8 \\
&= 20 \text{ cm} \\
A \quad &= 6 \times 4 \\
&= 24 \text{ cm}^2
\end{aligned}
$$

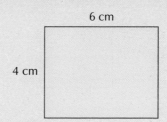

6 cm

4 cm

The length and width of a **square** are the same.

Example 4

Work out the perimeter (P) and area (A) of this square patio.

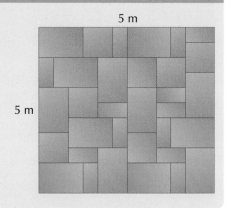

5 m

5 m

$P = 5 + 5 + 5 + 5$

$\quad = 4 \times 5$

$\quad = 20$ m

$A = 5 \times 5 = 5^2$

$\quad = 25$ m^2

Example 5

This fence has an area of 21 m^2.

Work out the height of the fence, shown as h on the diagram.

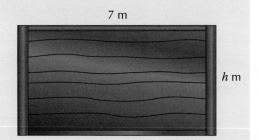

7 m

h m

The fence is a rectangle and its height is its shorter side so take this as its width.

Area = length × width

So $21 = 7 \times w$

To find w, divide both sides of the equation by 7.

$\dfrac{21}{7} = w$

$3 = w$

So the width (or height) of the fence is 3 metres.

You could simply work out $21 \div 7 = 3$.

Exercise 3B

1 Work out the perimeter of each rectangle.

a

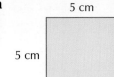

5 cm

5 cm

b

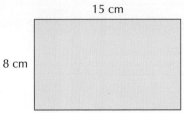

15 cm

8 cm

c

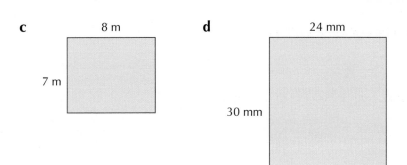

8 m

7 m

d

24 mm

30 mm

2 a Work out the perimeter of this room.

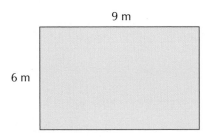

9 m

6 m

b Skirting board is sold in 3 m lengths.
How many lengths are needed to go around the four walls of the room?

3 A paving slab measures 0.8 m by 0.6 m.
Work out the perimeter of the slab.

4 Work out the area of each rectangle.

a

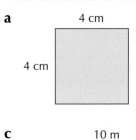

4 cm

4 cm

b

12 cm

7 cm

c

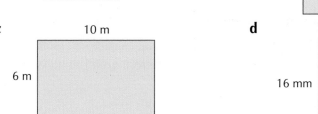

10 m

6 m

d

25 mm

16 mm

e

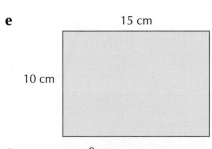

15 cm

10 cm

f

20 cm

8 cm

g

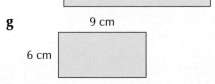

9 cm

6 cm

h

16 cm

8 cm

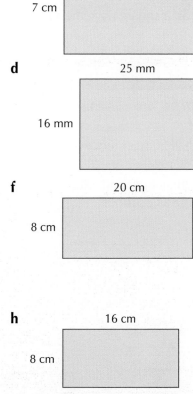

5 Work out the length of each rectangle.

a

Area = 12 cm² | 3 cm

b

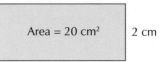

Area = 20 cm² | 2 cm

c

Area = 24 m² | 4 m

d

Area = 48 cm² | 6 cm

6 Work out the perimeter of this square tile.

25 cm²

7 Copy and complete the table for rectangles **a** to **f**.

	Length	Width	Perimeter	Area
a	8 cm	6 cm		
b	20 cm	15 cm		
c	10 cm		30 cm	
d		5 m	22 m	
e	7 m			42 m²
f		10 mm		250 mm²

(PS) **9** Can a square have the same numerical value for its perimeter and its area?

Challenge: How many rectangles?

A How many rectangles can you draw, each having a different area but all with a perimeter of 20 cm?

B A farmer has 60 m of fence to make a rectangular sheep pen against a wall.

Work out the length and width of the pen that will make its area as large as possible.

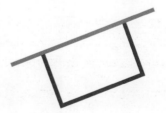

3.3 Perimeter and area of compound shapes

Learning objective

- To work out the perimeter and area of a compound shape

Keyword

compound shape

A **compound shape** is made from more than one shape. You can work out its perimeter and area by dividing it into the shapes that make it up.

Example 6

Work out the perimeter (*P*) and area (*A*) of this compound shape.

10 cm

12 cm

7 cm

4 cm

First split the shape into two rectangles. This split depends on the information you are given. If you split this shape into rectangles A and B, as shown, you will be able to work out all the lengths you need.

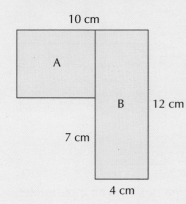

10 cm

A

B   12 cm

7 cm

4 cm

For rectangle A, the length is (10 − 4) = 6 cm and the width is (12 − 7) = 5 cm.

For rectangle B, the length is 12 cm and the width is 4 cm.

$P = 10 + 12 + 4 + 7 + 6 + 5$

$= 44$ cm

Total area = area of A + area of B

$= 6 \times 5 + 12 \times 4$

$= 30 + 48$

$= 78$ cm^2

Example 7

Work out area of the part of this shape that is shaded yellow.

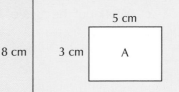

12 m

5 cm

8 cm   3 cm   A

Area of complete rectangle = 12×8

$= 96$ cm^2

Area of rectangle A = 5×3

$= 15$ cm^2

So shaded area = $96 - 15$

$= 81$ cm^2

1 Work out:

i the perimeter   **ii** the area
for each compound shape.

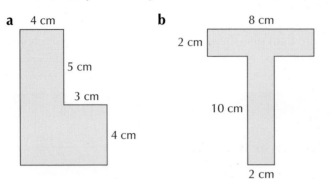

a   4 cm

5 cm

3 cm

4 cm

b   8 cm

2 cm

10 cm

2 cm

c   3 cm   3 cm

4 cm

4 cm

12 cm

4 cm

2 Work out the area of each compound shape.

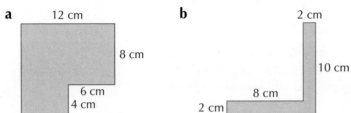
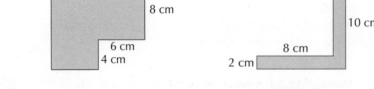

a   12 cm

8 cm

6 cm

4 cm

b   2 cm

10 cm

8 cm

2 cm

3 Zach works out the area of this compound shape.
This is his working.

Area $= 10 \times 4 + 8 \times 5$

$ = 40 + 40$

$ = 80 \text{ cm}^2$

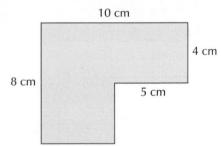

10 cm

4 cm

8 cm

5 cm

MR

a Explain why he is wrong.

b Calculate the correct answer.

4 Nadia uses a rectangular piece of card to
make a picture frame for a photograph of
her favourite band.

a Work out the area of the photograph.

b Work out the area of the card she uses.

c Work out the area of the border.

14 cm   20 cm

24 cm

30 cm

PS **5** A garden is in the shape of a rectangle measuring 16 m by 12 m.

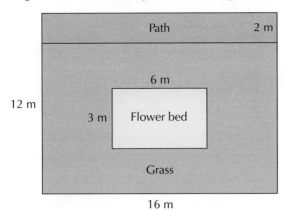

Work out the area of the grass in the garden.

PS **6** Ishmael is painting a wall in his house.

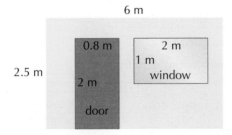

Work out the area of the wall that he needs to paint.

Problem solving: Compound shapes

A This compound shape is made from two identical rectangles.

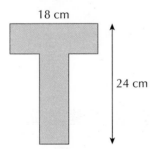

Work out the perimeter of the compound shape.

B The four unmarked sides in this diagram are the same length.

Work out the area of the compound shape.

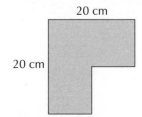

3.4 Volume of cubes and cuboids

Learning objectives

- To use a simple formula to work out the volume of a cube and cuboid
- To work out the capacity of a cube or cuboid

Volume is the amount of space occupied by three-dimensional (3D) shapes like these. They have **height** as well as length and width.

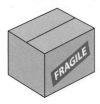 

Shapes that are squares in 3D are called **cubes**. Their width, length and height (edge lengths) are all the same.

Shapes that are rectangles in 3D are called **cuboids**. Their width, length and height can all be different.

This diagram shows a cuboid that measures 4 cm by 3 cm by 2 cm.

It is made up of cubes of edge length 1 cm. The top layer has 12 cubes. There are two layers so the cuboid has 24 cubes altogether.

This number is the same as you would get by multiplying all its edge lengths: $4 \times 3 \times 2 = 24$.

So you can find the volume of a cube or cuboid by multiplying its length by its width by its height.

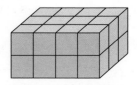

Volume of a cube or cuboid = length × width × height

You can also use letters to write this as a formula:

$V = l \times w \times h = lwh$

where V = volume, l = length, w = width and h = height.

The metric units of volume in common use are:

- the cubic millimetre (mm^3)
- the cubic centimetre (cm^3)
- the cubic metre (m^3)

So, the volume of the cuboid above is 24 cm^3. The cubes that make it up each have a volume of 1 cm^3.

Example 8

Calculate the volume of this cuboid.

The formula for the volume of a cuboid is:

$V = lwh$

$\quad = 5 \times 4 \times 3$

$\quad = 60 \ cm^3$

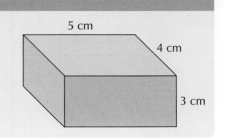

Example 9

Calculate the volume of the shape shown.

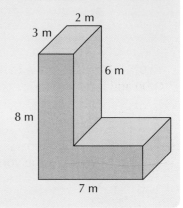

The shape is made up of two cuboids with measurements 7 m by 3 m by 2 m and 2 m by 3 m by 6 m.

So the volume of the shape is given by:

$V = (7 \times 3 \times 2) + (2 \times 3 \times 6)$

$\quad = 42 + 36$

$\quad = 78 \text{ m}^3$

The **capacity** of a 3D shape is the volume of liquid or gas it can hold. The metric unit of capacity is the **litre** (l). One litre equals 1000 cm³.

Example 10

Calculate the volume (*V*) of the tank shown and then work out the capacity of the tank, in litres.

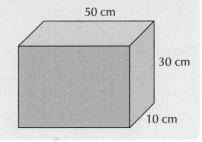

$V = 50 \times 30 \times 10 = 15\,000 \text{ cm}^3$

Since 1000 cm³ = 1 litre, the capacity of the tank is $15\,000 \div 1000 = 15$ litres.

Exercise 3D

1 Work out the volume of each cuboid.

a
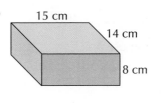

b

c
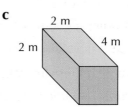

2 Work out the capacity, in litres, of each container.

a
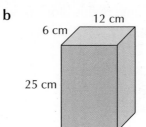

b

c
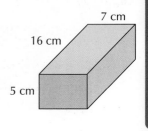

3 Copy and complete the table of cuboids **a** to **e**.

	Length	Width	Height	Volume
a	6 cm	4 cm	1 cm	
b	3.2 m	2.4 m	0.5 m	
c	8 cm	5 cm		120 cm³
d	20 mm	16 mm		960 mm³
e	40 m	5 m		400 m³

4 Work out the volumes of cubes with these edge lengths.

    a 2 cm   **b** 5 cm   **c** 12 cm

5 Work out the volume of a hall that is 30 m long, 20 m wide and 10 m high.

PS **6** How many packets of sweets that each measure 8 cm by 5 cm by 2 cm can be packed into a cardboard box that measures 32 cm by 20 cm by 12 cm?

7 The diagram shows the dimensions of a swimming pool.
Work out the volume of the pool, giving the answer in cubic metres.

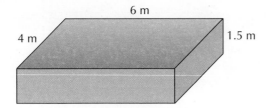

PS **8** The diagram below shows three different packaging boxes.

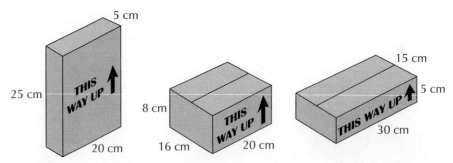

Which box has the greatest volume?

9 Work out the volume of this block of wood, giving your answer in cubic centimetres.

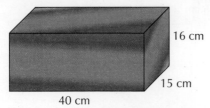

10 Work out the volume of each compound 3D shape.

a

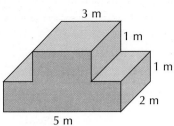

b

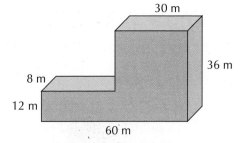

Activity: Volume

Estimate the volume for various cuboid objects in your classroom.

Then copy and complete the table below.

Some examples have already been filled in.

Object	Estimate for volume	Actual volume
Book		
Storage box		
Cupboard		

Challenge: Volume of a cuboid

The diagram shows the areas of the faces of a cuboid.

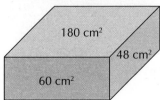

Use this information to calculate the volume of the cuboid.

Ready to progress?

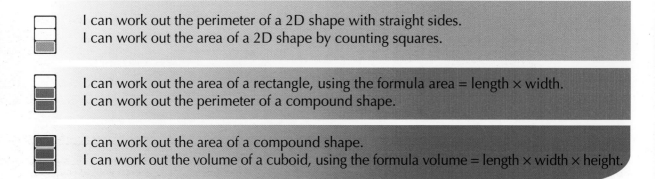

I can work out the perimeter of a 2D shape with straight sides.
I can work out the area of a 2D shape by counting squares.

I can work out the area of a rectangle, using the formula area = length × width.
I can work out the perimeter of a compound shape.

I can work out the area of a compound shape.
I can work out the volume of a cuboid, using the formula volume = length × width × height.

Review questions

1 A circle is drawn on a centimetre-squared grid.

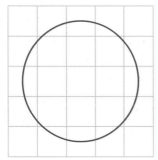

Estimate the area of the circle.

2 Here is a sequence of squares.

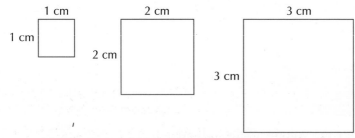

a i Work out the perimeter of the next two squares in the sequence.

ii Describe the pattern for the perimeters of the first five squares.

b i Work out the area of the next two squares in the sequence.

ii What do you notice about the areas of the first five squares?

(PS) 3 A rectangle has an area of 48 cm².

The length is 2 cm longer than the width.

Work out the length of the rectangle.

4   A shop sells square carpet tiles, as shown below.

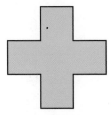

The floor of a rectangular room is 3 m by 1.5 m.

How many tiles are needed to carpet the floor?

 5   This logo is made from five identical squares.

Its total area is 125 cm².

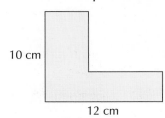

Work out the perimeter of the logo.

 6   Work out the perimeter of this compound shape.

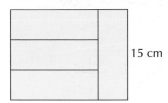

10 cm

12 cm

 7   This shape is made from four identical rectangles.

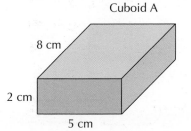

15 cm

Work out the area of the shape.

 8   These two cuboids, A and B, have the same volume.

Cuboid A   Cuboid B

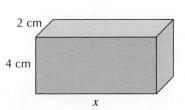

8 cm   2 cm

4 cm

2 cm

5 cm   x

Work out the value of the length marked x on Cuboid B.

Problem solving
Design a bedroom

1 This is a sketch plan for a bedroom.

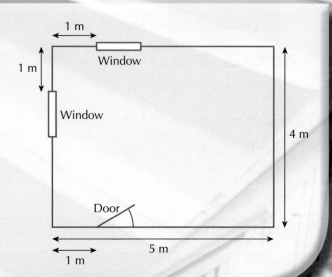

  a What is the perimeter of the bedroom?

  b What is the area of the bedroom?

  c How much does it cost to carpet the bedroom, if 1 m² of carpet costs £30?

2 Posters cost £7.50 each.

  a How many posters can you buy for £50?

  b How much money will you have left over?

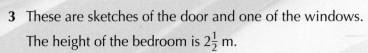

3 These are sketches of the door and one of the windows.

The height of the bedroom is $2\frac{1}{2}$ m.

  a Find the area of each wall that needs to be painted in the bedroom.

  b What is the total area of all four walls?

  c If a one-litre tin of paint covers 12 m², what is the minimum number of tins required to paint the walls?

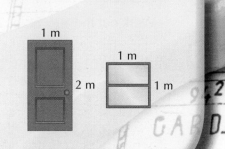

Furniture challenge

4 **a** Copy the plan of the bedroom onto centimetre-squared paper.
Use a scale of 1 cm to $\frac{1}{2}$ m.

Decide where to put this bedroom furniture. Use cut-outs to help.

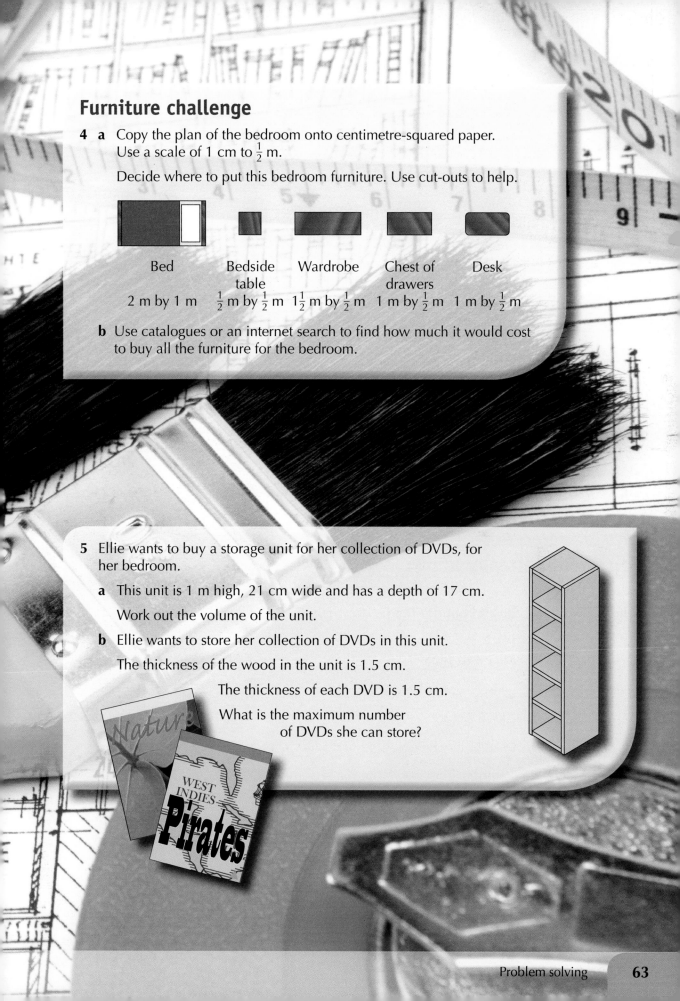

Bed	Bedside table	Wardrobe	Chest of drawers	Desk
2 m by 1 m	$\frac{1}{2}$ m by $\frac{1}{2}$ m	$1\frac{1}{2}$ m by $\frac{1}{2}$ m	1 m by $\frac{1}{2}$ m	1 m by $\frac{1}{2}$ m

b Use catalogues or an internet search to find how much it would cost to buy all the furniture for the bedroom.

5 Ellie wants to buy a storage unit for her collection of DVDs, for her bedroom.

a This unit is 1 m high, 21 cm wide and has a depth of 17 cm.

Work out the volume of the unit.

b Ellie wants to store her collection of DVDs in this unit.

The thickness of the wood in the unit is 1.5 cm.

The thickness of each DVD is 1.5 cm.

What is the maximum number of DVDs she can store?

4

Decimal numbers

This chapter is going to show you:

- how to order decimal numbers by size
- how to multiply and divide decimal numbers by 10, 100 and 1000
- how to use estimation to check your answers
- how to add and subtract decimal numbers
- how to multiply and divide decimals by whole numbers.

You should already know:

- how to write and read whole numbers and decimals
- how to write tenths and hundredths as decimals
- multiplication tables up to 12×12
- how to use a calculator to do simple calculations.

About this chapter

The decimal number system is based on 10. Decimals have been used for so long that no one can say exactly where or when they started. They were the basis of the ancient Chinese, Hindu-Arabic and Roman number systems.

The numbers we use in Europe come from the Hindu-Arabic number system.

Often we refer to decimals when we mean decimal fractions: tenths, hundredths, thousandths and so on.

We express these as 0.1, 0.01, 0.001, etc.

4.1 Multiplying and dividing by 10, 100 and 1000

Learning objective

- To be able to multiply and divide decimal numbers by 10, 100 and 1000

Key words

| decimal | decimal point |

You can already multiply whole numbers by ten, one hundred and one thousand.

You can use the same method to multiply **decimals**.

When you multiply by 10, all the digits move one place to the left.

For example: $4 \times 10 = 40$ $4.15 \times 10 = 41.5$

When you multiply by 100, all the digits move two places to the left.

For example: $4 \times 100 = 400$ $4.15 \times 100 = 415$

When you multiply by 1000, all the digits move three places to the left.

For example: $4 \times 1000 = 4000$ $4.15 \times 1000 = 4150$

Notice that the number of places the digits move left is the same as the number of zeros in the number you are multiplying by. This is true when multiplying decimals as well as whole numbers.

The **decimal point** separates the whole-number part of the number from the tenths, hundredths and thousandths.

Example 1

Work these out.

a 3.5×100 **b** 4.7×10.

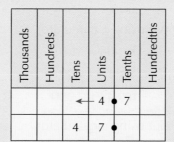

a

	Thousands	Hundreds	Tens	Units	Tenths	Hundredths
		←		3 • 5		
		3	5	0 •		

The digits move two places to the left when you multiply by 100.

$3.5 \times 100 = 350$

b

	Thousands	Hundreds	Tens	Units	Tenths	Hundredths
			←	4 • 7		
			4	7 •		

The digits move one place to the left when you multiply by 10.

$4.7 \times 10 = 47$

You can divide decimals by 10, 100 and 1000 in a similar way as you divide whole numbers.

When you divide by 10, all the digits move one place to the right.

For example: $37 \div 10 = 3.7$ $621.8 \div 10 = 62.18$

When you divide by 100, all the digits move two places to the right.

For example: $37 \div 100 = 0.37$ $621.8 \div 100 = 6.218$

When you divide by 1000, all the digits move three places to the right.

For example: $37 \div 1000 = 0.037$ $621.8 \div 1000 = 0.6218$

Notice that the number of places the digits move right is the same as the number of zeros in the number you are dividing by.

Example 2

Work these out.

a $23 \div 1000$ **b** $13.6 \div 10$

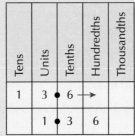

Tens	Units	Tenths	Hundredths	Thousandths
2	3			
	0	0	2	3

The digits move three places to the right when you divide by 1000.

$23 \div 1000 = 0.023$

Tens	Units	Tenths	Hundredths	Thousandths
1	3	6		
	1	3	6	

The digits move one place to the right when you divide by 10.

$13.6 \div 10 = 1.36$

Exercise 4A

1 Work these out without using a calculator.

a	27×10	**b**	63×100	**c**	78×1000
d	$52 \div 10$	**e**	$17 \div 100$	**f**	$38 \div 1000$
g	97×100	**h**	42×1000	**i**	$86 \div 100$

2 Work these out without using a calculator.

a	342×10	**b**	859×100	**c**	197×100
d	134×1000	**e**	$374 \div 10$	**f**	$849 \div 100$
g	$7 \div 100$	**h**	$75 \div 1000$	**i**	$583 \div 1000$
j	714×100	**k**	$374 \div 10$	**l**	189×100

3 Work out the missing number in each case.

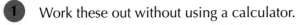

a $3 \times 10 = \boxed{}$ **b** $3 \times \boxed{} = 300$ **c** $3 \div 10 = \boxed{}$ **d** $3 \div \boxed{} = 0.03$

4 Work these out without using a calculator.

a 4.5×10 b 0.6×10 c 5.3×100

d 0.03×100 e 5.8×1000 f 0.7×1000

g $4.5 \div 10$ h $0.6 \div 10$ i $5.3 \div 100$

j $0.03 \div 100$ k $5.8 \div 1000$ l $0.04 \div 10$

m $5.01 \div 10$ n 6.378×100 o $8 \div 1000$

5 Work the missing number in each case.

a $0.3 \times 10 = \square$ b $0.3 \times \square = 300$ c $0.3 \div 10 = \square$

d $0.3 \div \square = 0.003$ e $\square \div 100 = 0.03$ f $\square \div 10 = 30$

g $\square \times 1000 = 30\,000$ h $\square \times 10 = 300$ i $\square \times 100 = 8$

6 Fill in the missing operation in each case.

a $0.37 \; \square \; 37$ b $567 \; \square \; 5.67$ c $0.07 \; \square \; 70$

d $650 \; \square \; 65$ e $0.6 \; \square \; 0.006$ f $345 \; \square \; 0.345$

7 Copy and complete this shopping bill, then work out the total.

1000 sweets at £0.03 each $= \square$

100 packets of mints at £0.45 each $= \square$

10 cans of cola at £0.99 each $= \square$

8 To change metres to centimetres, you multiply by 100.

For example, $4.7 \text{ m} = 4.7 \times 100 \text{ cm} = 470 \text{ cm}$.

Change these lengths to centimetres.

a 3.9 m b 1.75m c 23.5 m

d 0.7 m e 0.25 m f 2.08 m

9 To change grams to kilograms, you divide by 1000.

For example, $250 \text{ g} = 250 \div 1000 \text{ kg} = 0.25 \text{ kg}$.

Change these masses to kilograms.

a 375 g b 75 g c 4550 g

d 5250 g e 615 g f 2008 g

10 How would you explain to someone how to multiply and divide a number by one million?

Activity: Billions and billions

A Find out the difference between an American billion and a UK billion, before and after 1975.

B Explain how to multiply and divide a number by a UK billion, before and after 1975.

4.2 Ordering decimals

Learning objective

- To be able to order decimal numbers according to size

Name	Leroy	Myrtle	Shehab	Baby Jane	Alf	Doris
Height	170 cm	1.58 m	189 cm	0.55 m	150 cm	1.80 m
Mass	75 kg	50.3 kg	68 kg	7.5 kg	75 kg	76 kg 300 g

Look at the people in the picture. How would you put their heights or masses in **order** of size? Before you can compare them you need to rewrite each set of measures in the same units.

For example, the heights are given in metres and in centimetres. There are 100 centimetres in a metre so you can rewrite the heights given in centimetres as heights in metres by dividing them by 100.

Name	Leroy	Myrtle	Shehab	Baby Jane	Alf	Doris
Height	1.70 m	1.58 m	1.89 m	0.55 m	1.5 m	1.80 m

Now you can compare the size of numbers. To do this you have to consider the **place value** of each digit.

Example 3

Put the numbers 2.33, 2.03 and 2.304 in order, from smallest to largest.

It helps to put the numbers in a table like this one.

Use zeros to fill the missing decimal places.

Working across the table from the left, you can see that all of the numbers have the same units digit. Two of them have the same tenths digit, and two have the same hundredths digit. But only one has a digit in the thousandths.

The smallest is 2.03 because it has no tenths, which both of the other numbers have.

Next is 2.304 because it has fewer hundredths than 2.33, even though is has the same number of tenths.

So 2.33 is the largest.

The order is 2.03 , 2.304 , 2.33.

Thousands	Hundreds	Tens	Units	Tenths	Hundredths	Thousandths
			2	3	3	0
			2	0	3	0
			2	3	0	4

Example 4

Put the correct sign, > or <, between each pair of numbers.

a 6.05 and 6.046   **b** 0.06 and 0.065

a Rewrite both numbers with the same number of decimal places.
Use a zero to fill the space.

6.050 ... 6.046

Both numbers have the same units digits and tenths digits, but the hundredths digit is bigger in the first number.
So the answer is 6.05 > 6.046.

b Rewrite both numbers with the same number of decimal places.
Use a zero to fill the space.

0.060 ... 0.065

Both numbers have the same units, tenths and hundredths digits, but the second number has the bigger thousandths digit, as the first number has a zero in the thousandths.
So the answer is 0.06 < 0.065.

Exercise 4B

1 **a** Copy the table in Example 3 (but leave out the numbers).
Write these numbers in the table, placing each digit in the appropriate column.
4.57, 45, 4.057, 4.5, 0.045, 0.5, 4.05

b Use your answer to part **a** to write the numbers in order, from smallest to largest.

2 Write each set of numbers in order, from smallest to largest.

a 0.73, 0.073, 0.8, 0.709, 0.7

b 1.203, 1.03, 1.405, 1.404, 1.4

c 34, 3.4, 0.34, 2.34, 0.034

3 Put these amounts of money in order, from smallest to largest.

a 56p   £1.25   £0.60   130p   £0.07

b $0.04 $1.04 $10 $0.35 $1

4 Put these times in order.
1 hour 10 minutes, 25 minutes, 1.5 hours, half an hour

5 Put the correct sign, > or <, between each pair of numbers.

a 0.315 ... 0.325   **b** 0.42 ... 0.402   **c** 6.78 ... 6.709
d 5.25 km ... 5.225 km   **e** 0.345 kg ... 0.4 kg   **f** £0.05 ... 7p

6 Write each statement in words.

a 3.1 < 3.14 < 3.142   **b** £0.07 < 32p < £0.56

7   One metre is 100 centimetres.

Change all the lengths below to metres and then put them in order, from smallest to largest.

6 m, 269 cm, 32 cm, 27 m, 3400 cm

8   One kilogram is 1000 grams.

Change all the masses below to kilograms and then put them in order, from smallest to largest.

467 g, 1 kg, 56 g, 5 kg, 5500 g

Investigation: Consecutive integers

A Choose a set of five consecutive integers (whole numbers), such as 3, 4, 5, 6, 7.

The reciprocal of a number is the result of dividing 1 by the number.

These are the reciprocals of 3, 4, 5, 6 and 7.

$1 \div 3, 1 \div 4, 1 \div 5, 1 \div 6, 1 \div 7$

B Use a calculator to work out the reciprocal of each of your five numbers.

C Put the reciprocals in order, from smallest to largest.

D Repeat with any five consecutive two-digit whole numbers, such as 12, 13, 14, 15, 16.

E What do you notice?

4.3 Estimates

Learning objective

- To estimate calculations in order to recognise possible errors

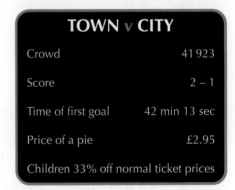

TOWN v CITY	
Crowd	41 923
Score	2 – 1
Time of first goal	42 min 13 sec
Price of a pie	£2.95
Children 33% off normal ticket prices	

Suppose you were telling a friend about the game. Which of the numbers above would you round up to a sensible **approximation**? Which would you round down? Which ones must you give exactly?

You can **round** numbers (up or down) to **estimate** quickly whether the answer to a calculation that you have completed is about right.

There are some other quick checks you can use.

- First, for a multiplication, you can check that the final digit is correct.
- Second, you can round numbers and do a mental calculation to see if an answer is about the right size.
- Third, you use the **inverse operation** (see Example 7).

Example 5

Explain why these calculations must be wrong.

a $23 \times 45 = 1053$ **b** $19 \times 59 = 121$

   a The last digit should be 5, because the product of the last digits (3 and 5) is 15.

      That is, $23 \times 45 = \dots 5$, so the calculation is wrong.

   b The actual answer is roughly $20 \times 60 = 1200$, so the calculation is wrong.

Example 6

Estimate answers to these calculations.

a $\dfrac{21.3 + 48.7}{6.4}$ **b** 31.2×48.5 **c** $359 \div 42$

   a Round the numbers on the top, $20 + 50 = 70$. Round 6.4 to 7. Then $70 \div 7 = 10$.

   b Round to 30×50, which is $3 \times 5 \times 100 = 1500$.

   c Round to $360 \div 40$, which is $36 \div 4 = 9$.

Example 7

Use the inverse operation to check each calculation.

a $450 \div 6 = 75$ **b** $310 - 59 = 249$

   a By the inverse operation, $450 = 6 \times 75$.

      Check mentally.

      $6 \times 70 = 420$, $6 \times 5 = 30$, $420 + 30 = 450$, so is true.

   b By the inverse operation, $310 = 249 + 59$.

      This must end in 8 as $9 + 9 = 18$, so the calculation cannot be correct.

Exercise 4C

1 Explain why each calculation must be wrong.

    a $24 \times 42 = 1080$ **b** $51 \times 73 = 723$ **c** $\dfrac{34.5 + 63.2}{9.7} = 20.07$

    d $360 \div 8 = 35$ **e** $354 - 37 = 323$

 2 A merchant bought 293 kg of grain at \$3.74 per kilogram.

    What is the approximate total cost of this grain?

3 Estimate the answer to each problem.

   a $2768 - 392$ **b** 231×18 **c** $792 \div 38$ **d** $\dfrac{36.7 + 23.2}{14.1}$

   e 423×423 **f** $157.2 \div 38.2$ **g** $\dfrac{135.7 - 68.2}{15.8 - 8.9}$ **h** $\dfrac{38.9 \times 61.2}{39.6 - 18.4}$

4 Amy bought 6 cans of lemonade at 86p per can. The shopkeeper asked her for £6.16. Without working out the correct answer, explain how Amy can tell that this is wrong.

5 A cake costs 47p. I need 8 cakes.

Will £4 be enough to pay for them? Explain your answer clearly.

6 In a shop I bought a chocolate bar for 53p and a model car for £1.47. The total on the till read £54.47. Why?

7 Explain which of these could be the best estimate for $54.6 \div 10.9$.

   a $500 \div 10$ **b** $54 \div 11$ **c** $50 \div 11$ **d** $55 \div 11$

8 Leo wanted to find out approximately how many bricks there were in a large, circular chimney that was being knocked down. He counted 218 bricks on one row, all the way around the chimney. He thought he counted 147 rows of bricks up the chimney.

Approximately how many bricks would Leo expect there to be?

9 Estimate the number each arrow is pointing to, below.

   a ⟨18 ↑ 20⟩   **b** ⟨−2 ↑ 8⟩   **c** ⟨−1.2 ↑ 0.8⟩

10 Delroy had £20. In his shopping basket he had a magazine costing £3.65, some batteries costing £5.92 and a DVD costing £7.99.

   a Without adding up the numbers, how could Delroy be sure he had enough to buy the goods in the basket?

   b Explain a quick way for Delroy to find out if he could afford a 45p bar of chocolate as well.

11 These are the amounts of money a family of four brought home, as wages.

Thomas $280 per week	Dechia $6250 per month
Joseph $490 per week	Sheena $880 per month

To qualify for an educational bursary, they had to be bringing home a total of less than $128 000 per year. Use estimates to decide whether they will qualify.

Challenge: Estimating square roots

The inverse operation of squaring is to find a **square root**.

So, if you square 11 to get 121, the inverse operation is to find the square root of 121 to get 11.

The sign for a square root is $\sqrt{\ }$. So $\sqrt{121} = 11$.

Only the square numbers have square roots that are whole numbers.

The first 15 square numbers are 1, 4, 9, 16, 25, 36, 49, 64, 81, 100, 121, 144, 169, 196 and 225.

(Continued)

You have to find the square roots of other numbers by estimation or by using a calculator. For example, to find the square root of 30, use a diagram like this one to estimate that $\sqrt{30} \approx 5.48$.

A check shows that $5.48^2 = 30.03$ so this a good estimate.

Here is another example.

Find the value of $\sqrt{45}$.

The diagram shows the answer.

$$\sqrt{45} \approx 6.7$$

Using a calculator, a check shows that $6.7^2 = 44.89$ so this is a good estimate.

A Use the above method to estimate $\sqrt{20}$, $\sqrt{55}$, $\sqrt{75}$, $\sqrt{110}$, $\sqrt{140}$, $\sqrt{200}$.

B Use a calculator to check your answers.

4.4 Adding and subtracting decimals

Learning objective

• To be able to add and subtract with decimal numbers

You can add and subtract decimals in the same way as you do whole numbers. As with whole numbers, it is important to get the place values right.

Example 8

Work these out.   **a** $4 + 0.86 + 0.07$ **b** $6 - 1.45$

a Whole numbers have no decimal places, but it can be helpful to write a decimal point after the units digit and show the decimal place values with zeros. Then you can line up the decimal points and place values of all the numbers, like this.

$$
\begin{array}{r}
4.00 \\
0.86 \\
+\ 0.07 \\
\hline
4.93 \\
\scriptstyle 1
\end{array}
$$

b As in part **a**, put a decimal point and zeros after the whole number to show the place values, and line up the decimal points.

$$
\begin{array}{r}
\scriptstyle 5\ 9\ 1 \\
6.00 \\
-\ 1.45 \\
\hline
4.55
\end{array}
$$

Example 9

Nazia has completed 4.3 km of a 20 km bike ride. How far does Nazia still have to go?

The units are the same, so subtract.

$$\begin{array}{r} {\scriptstyle 1\ 9\ 1} \\ 2\cancel{0}.0 \\ -\quad 4.3 \\ \hline 15.7 \end{array}$$

Nazia still has to go 15.7 km.

Example 10

Kilroy has to reduce the mass of his suitcase by 3 kg. So far, he has removed 650 grams. How much more does he need to take out?

The units need to be made the same. So change 650 grams into 0.65 kg. This gives:

$$\begin{array}{r} {\scriptstyle 2\ 9\ 1} \\ \cancel{3}.\cancel{0}0 \\ -\ 0.65 \\ \hline 2.35 \end{array}$$

Kilroy still has to remove 2.35 kg.

Exercise 4D

 1 Work these out without using a calculator.

a 3.5 + 4.7   **b** 6.1 + 2.8   **c** 3.4 + 1.7   **d** 12.41 + 8.69

e 9.3 − 6.1   **f** 3.5 − 2.7   **g** 17.5 − 13.7   **h** 27.65 − 16.47

 2 Work these out without using a calculator.

a 4 − 2.38   **b** 5 − 1.29   **c** 8 − 3.14   **d** 12 − 2.38

e 7 − 1.08   **f** 10 − 2.66   **g** 24 − 12.3   **h** 15 − 6.09

 3 The diagram shows the lengths of the paths in a park.

a How long are the paths altogether?

b Sean wants to visit all the points A, B, C, D, E and F in this order. He wants to start and finish at A and go along each and every path.

Explain why he cannot do this in the distance you worked out for part **a**.

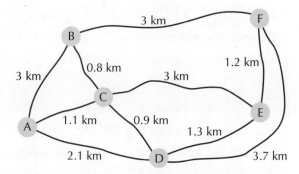

c Work out the shortest distance Sean could walk if he wanted to visit each point, starting and finishing at A.

4 The mass of a Christmas cake is 2 kg. Arthur takes a slice of mass 235 grams.
How much is left?

5 Jack pours 23 cl of water from a jug containing 3 litres. (1 litre = 100 cl)
How much is left?

6 Jasmine cuts 1560 millimetres of ribbon from a piece that is 5 metres long. (1 metre = 1000 mm)
How much ribbon is left?

7 The three legs of a relay are 3 km, 4.8 km and 1800 m.
How long is the race altogether?

8 Three packages have mass 4 kg, 750 grams and 0.08 kg.
How much is their total mass altogether?

9 Talika checks her restaurant bill, She thinks it is wrong.
  a Use estimation to check if the bill is about right.
  b Calculate if the bill is actually correct or not.

2 glasses of wine	£11.60
Soup of the day	£5.95
Madras Curry	£13.95
Cumberland Sausage	£11.85
Rib eye steak	£12.55
Thick cut chips	£3.85
Grilled mushrooms	£3.85
Potato wedges	£3.85
Battered onion rings	£3.85
3 desserts	£18.15
Total	£90.45

10 Estimate which of these has the greatest value, then use a calculator to see if you were right.
  a 14.82 + 7.56
  b 31 − 8.84
  c 106.55 + 135.45

Challenge: Decimals in your head

Ahmed needed to work out 5 − 1.368 without using paper and pencil or a calculator.

He had to do it in his head and tell someone else the answer. This is how he did it.

He first thought of 5 as 5.000, then needed to see what must be added to 1.368 to get 5.000.

He thought: the number must be _ . _ _ 2 as 2 is added to the 8 to get 10

  the number must be _ . _ 32 as 3 is added to the 6 (and the carry 1) to get 10

  the number must be _ . 632 as 6 is added to the 3 (and the carry 1) to get 10

  the number must be 3.632 as 3 is added to the 1 (and the carry 1) to get 10.

Ahmed did all that in his head and could just say that the answer was 3.632.

A Use Ahmed's method to work out each part in your head, then simply write down the answer.
  a 1 − 0.435   **b** 6 − 2.561   **c** 12 − 3.6754

B When you have finished, use a calculator to check your answers and see how accurate you were.

4.5 Multiplying and dividing decimals

Learning objective

• To be able to multiply and divide decimal numbers by any whole number

When you add together 1.2 + 1.2 + 1.2 + 1.2, you get:

$$1.2 + 1.2 + 1.2 + 1.2 = 4.8$$

This sum can be written as:

$$4 \times 1.2 = 4.8$$

It can also be written like this.

$$4.8 \div 4 = 1.2$$

You are now going to look at how to multiply and divide decimals by whole numbers.

These two operations are just like any other type of division and multiplication but you need to be sure where to put the decimal point.

As a general rule, there will be the same number of decimal places in the answer as there were in the original problem.

Example 11

Work these out.   **a** 5×3.7 **b** 8×4.3 **c** 9×1.08 **d** 6×3.5

Each of these can be set out in columns.

$$
\begin{array}{ll}
\textbf{a} & \begin{array}{r} 3.7 \\ \times\,5 \\ \hline 18.5 \\ {\scriptstyle 3} \end{array}
\end{array}
\qquad
\begin{array}{ll}
\textbf{b} & \begin{array}{r} 4.3 \\ \times\,8 \\ \hline 34.4 \\ {\scriptstyle 2} \end{array}
\end{array}
\qquad
\begin{array}{ll}
\textbf{c} & \begin{array}{r} 1.08 \\ \times\,\ 9 \\ \hline 9.72 \\ {\scriptstyle 7} \end{array}
\end{array}
\qquad
\begin{array}{ll}
\textbf{d} & \begin{array}{r} 3.5 \\ \times\,6 \\ \hline 21.0 \\ {\scriptstyle 3} \end{array}
\end{array}
$$

You can see that the decimal point in the answer stays in the same place as it is in the decimal number you are multiplying, with the same number of decimal places after it.

You could also give the answer to part **d** as 21.

Example 12

Work these out.   **a** $22.8 \div 6$ **b** $33.6 \div 7$ **c** $9.59 \div 7$ **d** $26.2 \div 5$

These can be set out as short divisions.

$$
\textbf{a}\ \ 6\overline{)22^4.8}\ \ ^{3\ .8}
\qquad
\textbf{b}\ \ 7\overline{)33^5.6}\ \ ^{4\ .8}
\qquad
\textbf{c}\ \ 7\overline{)9^2.5^4 9}\ \ ^{1\ .3\ 7}
\qquad
\textbf{d}\ \ 5\overline{)26^1.2^2 0}\ \ ^{5\ .2\ 4}
$$

Once again, the decimal point stays in the same place. Notice that you need to add a zero in part **d** in order to complete the division. This means that the answer has one more decimal place than the number being divided.

Exercise 4E

 1 Work these out without using a calculator.

a 3.14×5 b 1.73×8 c 1.41×6 d 2.26×9

e 6×3.35 f 9×5.67 g 5×6.17 h 9×9.12

 2 Work these out without using a calculator.

a $17.04 \div 8$ b $39.2 \div 7$ c $27.2 \div 8$ d $30.6 \div 5$

e $25.88 \div 4$ f $4.44 \div 3$ g $27.72 \div 9$ h $22.4 \div 5$

3 A piece of wood, 2.8 metres long, is cut into five equal pieces.

How long is each piece?

4 Five bars of metal each have mass 2.35 kg.

How much is their total mass altogether?

5 A cake of mass 1.74 kg is cut into six equal pieces.

How much is the mass of one piece?

6 Eight bottles of cola cost £6.24.

What is the price of one bottle?

7 One MP3 player can hold 1.44 Gb of information.

How much information can six MP3 players hold?

8 Ten crayons cost £7.50.

How much would six crayons cost?

 (PS) 9 A can of orange and a chocolate bar cost £1.30 together. Two cans of orange and a chocolate bar cost £2.15 together.

How much would three cans of orange and four chocolate bars cost?

 (MR) 10 A shop was selling a range of DVDs at £7.49 each, or £19.98 for three.

How much would you save if you buy three DVDs together, rather than buying them separately?

(PS) 11 I went into a shop with £20. I wanted to buy three packets of rice at £2.85 each and two bottles of sauce at £3.95 each.

Will I have enough to buy a box of chocolates costing £3.15 as well?

 (PS) 12 Eight packs of cards cost £12.80.

How much would five packs cost?

Reasoning: Decimal multiplication and division

A Use a calculator to work out each of these.

a 46×34 b 4.6×34 c 4.6×3.4 d 0.46×0.34

B You will notice that the digits of all the answers are the same but that the decimal point is in different places. Can you explain a rule for placing the decimal point?

C Use your rule to write down the answers to the problems below, where $152 \times 45 = 6840$.

a 15.2×4.5 b 1.52×45 c 0.152×4.5 d 1520×450

Ready to progress?

I can order decimals by size.

I can add and subtract decimal numbers.
I can multiply and divide decimal numbers by 10, 100 and 1000.
I can estimate answers and check if an answer is about right.
I can multiply and divide decimals by any whole number.

Review questions

1   A meal in a restaurant costs the same for each person.

    For 7 people the cost is £107.45.

    What is the total cost for 4 people?

2   The table shows how much it costs to go to a cinema.

	Before 6 pm	After 6 pm
Adult	£7.20	£9.90
Child (14 or under)	£5.50	£7.50
Senior citizen (60 or over)	£6.45	£7.90

    Mrs Roberts (aged 35), her daughter (aged 8), her son (aged 6) and her mother (aged 64) want to go to the cinema.

    They are not sure whether to go before 6 pm or after 6 pm.

    How much will they save if they go before 6 pm?

    Show your working.

3   Place these masses into order of size, writing the smallest first.

    2 kg   655 g   1.85 kg   3502 g

4 Look at the shapes below. All lengths are in centimetres.

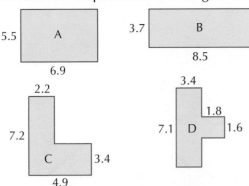

a Which shape has the longest perimeter?

b Use estimation to decide which shape has the smallest area.

5 Write down the next three numbers in each sequence.

    a   1.1, 3.7, 6.3, 8.9, …, …, …

    b   10 , 5.7 , 1.4, …, …, …

    c   1.1, 1.2, 2.3, 3.5, 5.8, …, …, …

6 Write these decimals in ascending order.

   50.9, 12.95, 5.38, 5.7, 50.01, 5.14

(PS) **7** A farmer sells hens for $7.75 and turkeys for $9.50.
One market day he sells twice as many hens as turkeys and takes $10 000.

How many of each did he sell?

(PS) **8** Kath is following a recipe for a chocolate cake and she needs 50 cm³ of milk chocolate.

She has a thick bar of Belgian chocolate, as shown.

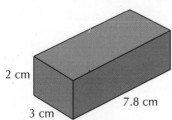

a Show that Kath can estimate that she does not have enough chocolate in this bar.

b Kath decided to use another bar of chocolate. It had the same width and depth but it was 10 cm long.

   What length would Kath need to use from this bar in order to have just over 50 cm³ of chocolate?

Financial skills
Shopping for leisure

Lildi

Table **£48.85** each

Chairs **£37.45** each

Cubed planter **£8.85** each

Outdoor speakers **£39.15** each

Mats **£4.75** each

Fuschia **£1.65** each

Cushions **£6.95** each

Tapestry cube **£15.35** each

Living for less

The Bishop family

All sorts of things are advertised in magazines and newspapers.

The Bishop family saw this advertisement about equipment for relaxing in the garden.

They decided to buy:

- a folding table
- four multi-position chairs
- a cubed planter.

How much will this cost them?

A gift for Pat Visser

Pat Visser had been given a £50 gift voucher.

She thought she would like to buy:

- 2 tapestry cubes
- 3 printed cushions
- a patterned mat.

Estimate if she can buy all these with the gift voucher.

Abbas' outdoor area

Abbas wanted to create an outdoor area with wireless outdoor speakers, a table, some chairs, some mats and some plants all for less than £200.

Select from the advertisement what Abbas needs. Get as close to £200 as you can.

5

Working with numbers

This chapter is going to show you:

- what square roots are
- that you can use a calculator to work out square roots
- how to round whole numbers and decimals
- the order of operations
- how to carry out long multiplication
- how to carry out long division
- how to calculate with measurements.

You should already know:

- how to square a number
- multiplication tables up to 12×12
- place value of digits in a number such as 23.508
- how to use a calculator to do simple calculations
- how to convert units of measurement.

About this chapter

Your school is organising its summer fête, but where should it locate the star attraction: a giant chessboard with an area of 9 m²? The organisers need to work out how long its sides are in order to see where it will fit. As the board is a square, its area is the length of one of its sides squared. This means that the length is the square root of the area. So if the area is 9 m² the sides will be 3 m long. Most square roots are not whole numbers, however. If the chessboard had an area of 10 m², the organisers would need either to approximate the square root or to use a calculator to find it, and then round it up, to be sure of having enough space to fit the board.

5.1 Square numbers and square roots

Learning objectives

• To recognise and use square numbers up to 225 (15×15) and the corresponding square roots

Key words

power	square number
squaring	square root

You learned in Chapter 2 that when you multiply any number by itself, you are **squaring** the number.

You can write it as a number to the **power** of 2, for example, $4 \times 4 = 4^2 = 16$.

When you multiply an integer (whole number) by itself, the result is called a **square number**.

You need to learn all of the first 15 square numbers.

1×1	2×2	3×3	4×4	5×5	6×6	7×7	8×8	9×9	10×10
1^2	2^2	3^2	4^2	5^2	6^2	7^2	8^2	9^2	10^2
1	4	9	16	25	36	49	64	81	100

11×11	12×12	13×13	14×14	15×15
11^2	12^2	13^2	14^2	15^2
121	144	169	196	225

The **square root** of a number is that number which, when squared, gives the starting number. For example:

   2 is the square root of 4

   3 is the square root of 9

and so on.

Finding the square root is the opposite of squaring a number.

A square root is represented by the symbol $\sqrt{}$. For example:

$\sqrt{1} = 1$ $\sqrt{4} = 2$ $\sqrt{9} = 3$ $\sqrt{16} = 4$ $\sqrt{25} = 5$

Only the square root of a square number will give a whole number as the answer.

Example 1

$\sqrt{130}$ lies between two two consecutive whole numbers.
What are they?
   $11 \times 11 = 121$ and $12 \times 12 = 144$, so $\sqrt{130}$ is between 11 and 12.

Note that if you use a calculator to work out $\sqrt{130}$ your answer will be 11.40....

Exercise 5A

  1 Look at this pattern.

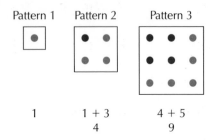

Pattern 1   Pattern 2   Pattern 3

1   1 + 3   4 + 5
              4   9

a Copy the pattern and draw the next two shapes.
b What is special about the total number of dots in each pattern?
c What is special about the number of blue dots in each pattern?
d What is special about the number of red dots in each pattern?
e Write down a connection between square numbers and odd numbers.

2 Copy this table of numbers and their squares.
Fill in the gaps.

Number	Number × number	Number^2	Number squared
3	3 × 3	3^2	9
5	5 × 5	5^2	
	2 × 2	2^2	
			36
7			
	12 × 12		
			121
			1
			81
		4^2	

  3 36 and 64 are two square numbers that add up to another square number (100).
Find two more square numbers that add up to a square number.

  4 36 and 49 are two square numbers that add up to 85.
Find two other square numbers that add up to 85.

  5 Find two square numbers that add up to 130.

  6 Find three square numbers that add up to 300.

7 Write down the value of each square root.
Do not use a calculator.

a $\sqrt{16}$ b $\sqrt{36}$ c $\sqrt{4}$ d $\sqrt{49}$ e $\sqrt{1}$

f $\sqrt{9}$ g $\sqrt{100}$ h $\sqrt{81}$ i $\sqrt{25}$ j $\sqrt{64}$

8 Use a calculator to find the value of each square root.

a $\sqrt{289}$ b $\sqrt{961}$ c $\sqrt{529}$ d $\sqrt{2500}$ e $\sqrt{1296}$

f $\sqrt{729}$ g $\sqrt{3249}$ h $\sqrt{361}$ i $\sqrt{3969}$ j $\sqrt{1764}$

9 Make an estimate of each square root.
Then use your calculator to see how many of your estimates are correct.

a $\sqrt{256}$ b $\sqrt{1089}$ c $\sqrt{625}$ d $\sqrt{2704}$ e $\sqrt{1444}$

f $\sqrt{841}$ g $\sqrt{3481}$ h $\sqrt{441}$ i $\sqrt{4096}$ j $\sqrt{2025}$

(PS) 10 Each square root lies between two consecutive whole numbers.
Work out what they are.

a $\sqrt{30}$ b $\sqrt{85}$ c $\sqrt{50}$ d $\sqrt{160}$ e $\sqrt{200}$

f $\sqrt{75}$ g $\sqrt{600}$ h $\sqrt{1000}$ i $\sqrt{3000}$ j $\sqrt{2014}$

(MR) 11 a Work out these square roots.

  i $\sqrt{25}$ ii $\sqrt{2500}$ iii $\sqrt{250\,000}$

b What do you notice about your answers to part **a**?

c Use your answers to part **a** to write down the value of $\sqrt{25\,000\,000}$.

Problem solving: Squares

A a Choose any two square numbers.
  b Multiply them together.
  c What is the square root of this result?
  d Can you find a connection between this square root and the two starting numbers?
B Try this again with some more square numbers.
C Is the connection the same, no matter what two square numbers you choose?

5.2 Rounding

Learning objectives

• To round numbers to a given degree of accuracy

Key words

decimal places	round
round down	rounding
round up	units digit

To **round** numbers – to the nearest 10, 100 or 1000 – you need to use your knowledge of place value. You always look at the digit to the right of the digit being rounded. For example, if you are **rounding** to the nearest 10, look at the **units digit**, if you are rounding to the nearest 100, look at the tens digit, and so on. If the digit is 4, 3, 2, 1 or 0, **round down**. If the digit is 5, 6, 7, 8 or 9, **round up**.

When you are rounding, you can use the special symbol, ≈, which means is 'approximately equal to'. For example, if you round 34 to the nearest 10, you could write '34 ≈ 30', which means '34 is approximately equal to 30'.

Example 2

Round each number to the nearest: **i** 10   **ii** 100   **iii** 1000.

a 521   **b** 369   **c** 605   **d** 4298

i   Look at the units digit.
If its value is less than 5, round the number down. If its value is 5 or more, round up.

    a 521 ≈ 520   **b** 369 ≈ 370   **c** 605 ≈ 610   **d** 4298 ≈ 4300

ii Look at the tens digit. Round down or up, as before.

    a 521 ≈ 500   **b** 369 ≈ 400   **c** 605 ≈ 600   **d** 4298 ≈ 4300

iii Look at the hundreds digit. Round down or up, as before.

    a 521 ≈ 1000   **b** 369 ≈ 0   **c** 605 ≈ 1000   **d** 4298 ≈ 4000

However, it is not really sensible to round 369 down to 0. When rounding numbers, always check that your answer is sensible.

Look at this picture. Can you see anything wrong?

60 kg ≈ 100 kg   110 kg ≈ 100 kg

It shows that the woman whose mass is 60 kg balances the man whose mass is 110 kg, when both measures are rounded to the nearest 100 kg! This highlights the need to round numbers sensibly, depending on the situation in which they occur.

Example 3

Round each number to the nearest whole number.

a 2.356 **b** 4.75 **c** 6.5 **d** 8.49

Look at the number after the decimal point. Round down or up as before.

a 2.356 ≈ 2 **b** 4.75 ≈ 5 **c** 6.5 ≈ 7 **d** 8.49 ≈ 8

You can also round to one or more **decimal places** if you need an answer that is more accurate than estimating to the nearest whole number.

Example 4

Round each number to one decimal place.

a 9.615 **b** 4.532 **c** 18.857 **d** 12.99

Look at the digit in the second decimal place (hundredths). Round down or up as before.

a 9.615 ≈ 9.6 **b** 4.532 ≈ 4.5 **c** 18.857 ≈ 18.9 **d** 12.99 ≈ 13.0

Exercise 5B

1. The English Academy in Kuwait has 1057 students.
   a How many students is this, to the nearest 100?
   b How many students is this, to the nearest 10?

2. The price of a freezer is £285.
   a What is the price to the nearest £100?
   b What is the price to the nearest £10?

3. A car is advertised for sale at £8965.
   a What is the price to the nearest £100?
   b What is the price to the nearest £1000?
   c What is the price to the nearest £10?

4. These are the attendances at the Champions League quarter-final matches in 2013.
   Copy and complete the table.

Match	Attendance	Attendance (to nearest 100)	Attendance (to nearest 1000)
Paris Saint-Germain v FC Barcelona	45 336	45 300	
FC Barcelona v Paris Saint-Germain	96 022		
Bayern Munich v Juventus	68 047	68 000	68 000
Juventus v Bayern Munich	40 823		
Malaga CF v Borussia Dortmund	28 548		
Borussia Dortmund v Malaga FC	65 829		
Real Madrid v Galatasaray	76 462	76 500	
Galatasaray v Real Madrid	49 975		

5 Round each of these numbers to:

i the nearest 10   **ii** the nearest 100   **iii** the nearest 1000.

a 3731   **b** 807   **c** 2111   **d** 4086

e 265   **f** 3457   **g** 4050   **h** 2999

i 1039   **j** 192   **k** 3192   **l** 964

 6 **a** The table shows the diameters of the planets, in kilometres. Round each diameter to the nearest 1000 km. Then place the planets in order of size, starting with the smallest.

Planet	Earth	Jupiter	Mars	Mercury	Neptune	Pluto	Saturn	Uranus	Venus
Diameter (km)	12 800	142 800	6780	5120	49 500	2284	120 660	51 100	12 100

 b What would happen if you rounded the diameters to the nearest 10 000 km?

7 Round each number to:

i the nearest 10   **ii** the nearest whole number   **iii** one decimal place.

a 15.41   **b** 12.64   **c** 43.75   **d** 72.86

e 57.17   **f** 167.91   **g** 145.86   **h** 799.925

i 84.05   **j** 76.99   **k** 102.445   **l** 143.967

Problem solving: Think of a number

Starla and Morgan are thinking of whole numbers.

When I round my number to the nearest 10 it is 460.

When I round my number to the nearest 100 it is 500.

How many possible answers are there, if Morgan's number is smaller than Starla's number?

5.3 Order of operations

Learning objectives

• To use the conventions of BIDMAS to carry out calculations

Key words	
BIDMAS	operation
order of operations	

Most of the time, the order in which instructions are carried out is important.

These are instructions for making a cup of tea.

If you don't follow them in the right order, the end result might not be drinkable!

| Drink tea | Empty teapot | Fill kettle | Put milk in cup | Put teabag in teapot |
| Switch on kettle | Wait for tea to brew | Rinse teapot with hot water | Pour boiling water in teapot | Pour out tea |

In mathematics, the order in which calculations are carried out is also important. A calculation can be made up of various different **operations**, for example, adding, subtracting, multiplying or squaring.

BIDMAS describes the **order of operations** – the order in which operations should always be carried out.

B	Brackets
I	Indices or powers
D	Division
M	Multiplication
A	Addition
S	Subtraction

This means that you always work out calculations in brackets first, followed by powers, then division and multiplication, and finally addition and subtraction.

For example, in the calculation $2 + 3 \times 4$, you must do the multiplication first.

$$2 + 3 \times 4 = 2 + 12 = 14$$

Example 5

Circle the operation that you do first in each calculation. Then work out each one.

a $2 + 6 \div 2$ **b** $32 - 4 \times 5$ **c** $6 \div 3 - 1$ **d** $6 \div (3 - 1)$

  a Division is done before addition, so you get $2 + (6 \div 2) = 2 + 3 = 5$.

  b Multiplication is done before subtraction, so you get $32 - (4 \times 5) = 32 - 20 = 12$.

  c Division is done before subtraction, so you get $(6 \div 3) - 1 = 2 - 1 = 1$.

  d Brackets are done first, so you get $6 \div ((3 - 1)) = 6 \div 2 = 3$.

Example 6

Work out each of these, showing each step of the calculation.

a $1 + 3^2 \times 4 - 2$ **b** $(1 + 3)^2 \times (4 - 2)$

  a The order will be power, multiplication, addition, subtraction.

    This gives:

$$1 + (3^2) \times 4 - 2 = 1 + (9 \times 4) - 2 = (1 + 36) - 2 = 37 - 2 = 35$$

  b The order will be brackets (both of them), power, multiplication. This gives:

$$(1 + 3)^2 \times (4 - 2) = 4^2 \times 2 = 16 \times 2 = 32$$

Example 7

Put brackets into each equation to make the calculation true.

a $5 + 1 \times 4 = 24$ **b** $1 + 3^2 - 4 = 12$ **c** $24 \div 6 - 2 = 6$

Decide which operation has been done first.

a $(5 + 1) \times 4 = 24$ **b** $(1 + 3)^2 - 4 = 12$ **c** $24 \div (6 - 2) = 6$

If you have two similar operations, complete the calculation in order, from left to right.

Example 8

Calculate: **a** $8 - 3 - 2$ **b** $24 \div 6 \div 2$.

Work from left to right.

a $(8 - 3) - 2 = 5 - 2 = 3$ **b** $(24 \div 6) \div 2 = 4 \div 2 = 2$

Compare the answers you would get, in each case, if you completed the second operation first.

Exercise 5C

1   Write down the operation that you do first in each calculation.

Then complete the calculation.

   a $2 + 3 \times 6$ **b** $12 - 6 \div 3$ **c** $5 \times 5 + 2$ **d** $12 \div 4 - 2$

   e $(2 + 3) \times 6$ **f** $(12 - 3) \div 3$ **g** $5 \times (5 + 2)$ **h** $12 \div (4 - 2)$

2   Work these out, showing each step of the calculations.

   a $2 \times 3 + 4$ **b** $2 \times (3 + 4)$ **c** $2 + 3 \times 4$ **d** $(2 + 3) \times 4$

   e $4 \times 4 - 4$ **f** $5 + 3^2 + 6$ **g** $5 \times (3^2 + 6)$ **h** $3^2 - (5 - 2)$

   i $(2 + 3) \times (4 + 5)$ **j** $(2^2 + 3) \times (4 + 5)$ **k** $4 \div 4 + 4 \div 4$ **l** $44 \div 4 + 4$

   m $(6 + 2)^2$ **n** $6^2 + 2^2$ **o** $3^2 + 4 \times 6$ **p** $54 \div 9 \div 3$

(MR) 3   Put brackets into each equation to make the calculation true.

   a $2 \times 5 + 4 = 18$ **b** $2 + 6 \times 3 = 24$ **c** $2 + 3 \times 1 + 6 = 35$

   d $5 + 2^2 \times 1 = 9$ **e** $3 + 2^2 = 25$ **f** $3 \times 4 + 3 + 7 = 28$

   g $3 + 4 \times 7 + 1 = 35$ **h** $3 + 4 \times 7 + 1 = 50$ **i** $9 - 5 - 2 = 6$

   j $9 - 5 \times 2 = 8$ **k** $4 + 4 + 4 \div 2 = 6$ **l** $1 + 4^2 - 9 - 2 = 18$

(MR) 4   One of the calculations $2 \times 3^2 = 36$ and $2 \times 3^2 = 18$ is wrong.

Which is it? How could you add brackets to make it true?

5   Work out the value of each expression.

   a $(4 + 4) \div (4 + 4)$ **b** $(4 \times 4) \div (4 + 4)$ **c** $(4 + 4 + 4) \div 4$

   d $4 \times (4 - 4) + 4$ **e** $(4 \times 4 + 4) \div 4$ **f** $(4 + 4 + 4) \div 2$

   g $4 + 4 - 4 \div 4$ **h** $(4 + 4) \times (4 \div 4)$ **i** $(4 + 4) + 4 \div 4$

6 Sarah is given three $10 notes and four $20 notes.

Write down the calculation you need to do, to work out how much she is given altogether.

Work out the answer.

 7 Beth orders six garden plants at £1.99 each. Delivery costs £2.50.

Write down the calculation you need to do to work out the total cost.

Work out the answer.

 8 Jack wants to travel on three trams. He has €10.

The fares are €2.70, €4.20 and €2.70.

Does he have enough money?

Write down the calculation you need to do.

Work out the answer.

Problem solving: Fours and fives

In Exercise 5C question **5**, each calculation was made up of four 4s.

A Work out the value of each expression.

   a $44 \div 4 - 4$ **b** $4 \times 4 - 4 \div 4$ **c** $4 \times 4 + 4 - 4$

B Now make up some more calculations, using four 4s, to give answers that you have not yet obtained in Question **5** or in the three calculations above.

Try as many as you can and see whether you can make all the values up to 20.

C Repeat with five 5s. For example:

    $(5 + 5) \div 5 - 5 \div 5 = 1$

    $(5 \times 5 - 5) \div (5 + 5) = 2$

5.4 Long and short multiplication

Learning objectives

- To choose a written method for multiplying two numbers together
- To use written methods to carry out multiplications accurately

Key words

Chinese method

column method

grid or box method

long multiplication

Long multiplication is a method for multiplying large numbers

There are many different methods of multiplying two numbers.

Example 9

Work out 29×5.

Grid or box method (partitioning)	Column method (expanded working)	Column method (compacted working)	Chinese method
$\begin{array}{c|c|c|c} \times & 20 & 9 & \\ \hline 5 & 100 & 45 & 100 + 45 \\ & & & = 145 \end{array}$	$\begin{array}{r} 29 \\ \times\ 5 \\ \hline 45\ \ (5 \times 9) \\ 100\ \ (5 \times 20) \\ \hline 145 \end{array}$	$\begin{array}{r} 29 \\ \times\ 5 \\ \hline 145 \\ {\scriptstyle 4} \end{array}$	(Chinese method lattice diagrams for 2×5 and 9×5)

The answer is 145.

Example 10

Work out 36×43.

Grid or box method (partitioning)	Column method (expanded working)	Column method (compacted working)	Chinese method
$\begin{array}{c|c|c|c} \times & 30 & 6 & \\ \hline 40 & 1200 & 240 & 1440 \\ \hline 3 & 90 & 18 & 108 \\ \hline & & & 1548 \end{array}$	$\begin{array}{r} 36 \\ \times 43 \\ \hline 18\ \ (3 \times 6) \\ 90\ \ (3 \times 30) \\ 240\ \ (40 \times 6) \\ 1200\ \ (40 \times 30) \\ \hline 1548 \end{array}$	$\begin{array}{r} 36 \\ \times 43 \\ \hline 108\ \ (3 \times 36) \\ 1440\ \ (40 \times 36) \\ {\scriptstyle 1\ 2} \\ \hline 1548 \end{array}$	(Chinese lattice method diagram) Note the carried figure, from the addition of 9, 1 and 4.

The answer is 1548.

Exercise 5D

1   Use the grid method or any other method to work these out.

   a 18×6 **b** 25×7 **c** 89×2 **d** 54×3

   e 17×4 **f** 38×2 **g** 265×3 **h** 147×9

2   Use the column method or any other method to work these out.

   a 27×5 **b** 32×7 **c** 46×8 **d** 19×3

   e 39×4 **f** 41×9 **g** 123×4 **h** 263×5

3 Use the Chinese method or any other method to work these out.

    a 35×4 **b** 22×9 **c** 41×7 **d** 18×3

    e 29×5 **f** 55×6 **g** 121×5 **h** 216×6

4 Use any multiplication method to work out each of these.

    a 17×23 **b** 32×42 **c** 19×45 **d** 56×46

    e 12×346 **f** 32×541 **g** 27×147 **h** 39×213

5 Each day 17 Jumbo jets fly from London to San Francisco. Each jet can carry up to 348 passengers. How many people can travel from London to San Francisco each day?

6 A van travels 34 miles for every gallon of petrol. How many miles can it go if the petrol tank holds 18 gallons?

7 The school photocopier can print 82 sheets a minute. If it runs without stopping for 45 minutes, how many sheets will it print?

8 The daily newspaper sells advertising by the square centimetre. On Monday, it sells 232 square centimetres at $15 per square centimetre. How much money does it get from this advertising?

9 Follow these steps.

- Write down a three-digit number.
- Multiply the number by 7.
- Multiply your answer by 11.
- Multiply your answer by 13.
- Write down your final answer.

    a What do you notice?

    b Can you explain why this happens?

10 **a** Work out these multiplications by 11.

    i 34×11 **ii** 71×11 **iii** 26×11 **iv** 45×11

    b What do you notice about the answers?

    c Write down the answer to 16×11.

    d Write down the answer to 85×11.

Activity: Funny face

Another way of multiplying two-digit numbers together is the 'Funny face' method.

This is how to use the method to work out 26×57.

$$26 \times 57 = (20 + 6) \times (50 + 7)$$

1000	(20×50)
140	(20×7)
300	(6×50)
+ 42	(6×7)
1482	

$$(20 + 6) \times (50 + 7)$$

Make a poster showing how to use the 'Funny Face' method for a calculation.

5.5 Long and short division

Learning objectives

- To choose a written method for dividing one number by another
- To use written methods to carry out divisions accurately

Key words

long division

short division

remainder

repeated subtraction

There are many different ways to work out a division calculation.

Example 11

Work out $582 \div 3$.

Long division	Short division	Repeated subtraction
$\begin{array}{r} 194 \\ 3\overline{)582} \\ \underline{3} \\ 28 \\ \underline{27} \\ 12 \\ \underline{12} \\ 0 \end{array}$	$\begin{array}{r} 194 \\ 3\overline{)5^28^12} \end{array}$	$\begin{array}{r} 582 \\ -\ 300 \quad (100 \times 3) \\ \hline 282 \\ 270 \quad (90 \times 3) \\ \hline 12 \\ 12 \quad (4 \times 3) \\ \hline 0 \end{array}$

The answer is 194.

Divisions do not always give exact answers. There is sometimes a number left over. This is called the **remainder**. If you were using a calculator, the answer would have numbers after the decimal point.

Example 12

Work out $171 \div 5$.

Long division	Short division	Repeated subtraction
$\begin{array}{r} 171\,\text{r}\,4 \\ 5\overline{)859} \\ \underline{5} \\ 35 \\ \underline{35} \\ 09 \\ \underline{5} \\ 4 \end{array}$	$\begin{array}{r} 171\,\text{r}\,4 \\ 5\overline{)8^35^49} \end{array}$	$\begin{array}{r} 859 \\ -\ 500 \quad (100 \times 5) \\ \hline 359 \\ 300 \quad (60 \times 5) \\ \hline 59 \\ 55 \quad (11 \times 5) \\ \hline 4 \end{array}$

The answer is 171, remainder 4.

If you use a calculator, your answer will be 171.8 because a remainder of 4 out of 5 is $\frac{4}{5}$ or 0.8.

Exercise 5E

1   Use long division or any other method to work these out.

   a $54 \div 3$ **b** $85 \div 5$ **c** $91 \div 7$ **d** $114 \div 6$
   e $248 \div 4$ **f** $315 \div 9$ **g** $896 \div 4$ **h** $265 \div 5$

2   Use short division or any other method to work these out.

   a $81 \div 3$ **b** $76 \div 4$ **c** $98 \div 7$ **d** $234 \div 9$
   e $144 \div 9$ **f** $156 \div 6$ **g** $924 \div 4$ **h** $875 \div 5$

3   Use repeated subtraction or any other method to work these out.

   a $129 \div 3$ **b** $84 \div 4$ **c** $105 \div 7$ **d** $108 \div 9$
   e $145 \div 5$ **f** $246 \div 6$ **g** $804 \div 4$ **h** $360 \div 5$

4   Use any division method to work these out. Some of the answers will have remainders.

   a $684 \div 4$ **b** $966 \div 6$ **c** $972 \div 9$ **d** $625 \div 5$
   e $930 \div 6$ **f** $624 \div 8$ **g** $950 \div 3$ **h** $800 \div 7$

5   A company has 95 boxes to move by van. The van can carry 8 boxes at a time.

   How many trips must the van make to move all the boxes?

 6   The mathematics department has printed 500 information sheets about long division. They put them into sets of 30 sheets.

   a   How many full sets are there?

   b   How many more sheets should be printed to make another full set?

Decide whether questions **7–10** involve multiplication or division. Then work out the answers.

7   The local library has 10 000 books. Each shelf holds 40 books.

   How many shelves are there?

 8   To raise money, a running club is doing a relay race of 120 kilometres. Each runner except the last one will run 9 km. The last runner will just run the extra distance to the finish.

   a   How many runners are needed to cover the distance?

   b   How far does the last one run?

9   120 packets of screws are packed in a box. There are 35 screws in each packet.

   How many screws are in the box?

(MR) 10   3000 people go on a journey from Paris to Rome. They travel in 52-seater coaches.

   a   How many coaches do they need?

   b   Each coach costs €680.

     What is the total cost of the coaches?

   c   How much is each person's share of the cost?

Activity: Cross-number puzzle

Copy and complete this puzzle.

Across	Down
1 196×12	**2** $1035 \div 3$
4 $225 \div 3$	**3** 339×8
6 $31\ 284 \div 6$	**5** 9×60
9 20×21	**7** $747 \div 3$
10 97×7	**8** $112 \div 2$

5.6 Calculations with measurements

Learning objectives

- To convert between common metric units
- To use measurements in calculations
- To recognise and use appropriate metric units

Key words

cent-	centi-
conversion	convert
metric	milli-

You need to know and use these **metric conversions** for length and capacity.

Length	Capacity
1 kilometre (km) = 1000 metres (m)	
1 metre (m) = 100 centimetres (cm)	1 litre (l) = 100 centilitres (cl)
1 metre (m) = 1000 millimetres (mm)	1 litre (l) = 1000 millilitres (ml)
1 centimetre (cm) = 10 millimetres (mm)	1 centilitre (cl) = 10 millilitres (ml)

Can you see the connections?

Cent- relates to hundreds and **centi-** to hundredths, for example, a century is 100 years.

Mill- relates to thousands and **milli-** to thousandths, for example, a millennium is 1000 years.

There are 100 cents in a dollar.

You also need to know these metric conversions for mass.

Mass
1 kilogram (kg) = 1000 grams (g)
1 tonne (t) = 1000 kilograms (kg)

This table shows the relationships between the most common metric units.

1000	100	10	1	$\frac{1}{10}$	$\frac{1}{100}$	$\frac{1}{1000}$
km			m		cm	mm
kg			g			mg
			l		cl	ml

Example 13

Convert:

a 6 centimetres to millimetres   **b** 1250 grams to kilograms   **c** 5 litres to centilitres.

a 1 cm = 10 mm   So multiply by 10.
   $6 \times 10 = 60$
   So 6 cm = 60 mm
b 1000 g = 1 kg   So divide by 1000.
   $1250 \div 1000 = 1.25$
   So 1250 g = 1.25 kg
c 1 litre = 100 cl   So multiply by 100.
   $5 \times 100 = 500$
   So 5 litres = 500 cl

When adding or subtracting metric amounts that are given in different units, you need to **convert** so that they are in same units first.

Example 14

Add together 1.23 m, 46 cm and 0.034 km.

First convert all the lengths to the same units.

1000	100	10	1	$\frac{1}{10}$	$\frac{1}{100}$	$\frac{1}{1000}$
km			m		cm	mm
			1	2	3	
				4	6	
0	0	3	4			

The answer is 0.035 69 km or 35.69 m or 3569 cm.

The sensible answer is 35.69 m because this is the one that people are most likely to understand or visualise.

Exercise 5F

1 Convert each length to centimetres.

    a 60 mm   **b** 2 m   **c** 743 mm   **d** 0.007 km   **e** 12.35 m

2 Convert each length to kilometres.

    a 456 m   **b** 7645 m   **c** 6532 cm   **d** 21 358 mm   **e** 54 m

3 Convert each length to millimetres.

    a 34 cm   **b** 3 m   **c** 3 km   **d** 35.6 cm   **e** 0.7 cm

4 Convert each mass to kilograms.

    a 3459 g   **b** 215 g   **c** 65 120 g   **d** 21 g   **e** 210 g

5 Convert each mass to grams.

    a 4 kg   **b** 4.32 kg   **c** 0.56 kg   **d** 0.007 kg   **e** 6.784 kg

6 Convert each capacity to litres.

    a 237 cl   **b** 3097 ml   **c** 1862 cl   **d** 48 cl   **e** 96 427 ml

7 Convert each time to hours and minutes.

    a 70 min   **b** 125 min   **c** 87 min   **d** 200 min   **e** 90 min

8 Add together the measurements in each group and give the answer in an appropriate unit.

    a 1.78 m, 39 cm, 0.006 km   **b** 0.234 kg, 60 g, 0.004 kg

    c 2.3 litres, 46 cl, 726 ml   **d** 0.0006 km, 23 mm, 3.5 cm

(MR) 9 Pierre buys 1 kg of sugar, 750 grams of bananas and 1.2 kg of apples.

Is the total mass of the three items more than 3 kilograms?

Show your working.

(PS) 10 Fill in each missing unit.

    a A two-storey house is about 7… high.   **b** Joe's mass is about 47….

    c Ruby lives about 2… from school.   **d** Luka ran a marathon in 3….

11 Read the value from each of these scales.

a

2 kg   3 kg

b

100

200
grams

c

300
200   400
100   500
0   600
grams

d
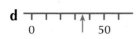

0   50

e

200   100

f

0   20

(PS) 12 Asha has these jugs.

1 litre

800 ml

500 ml

How is it possible to use these jugs to measure 100 ml of water?

Challenge: Area

Area is measured in square millimetres (mm²), square centimetres (cm²), square metres (m²) and square kilometres (km²).

This square shows 1 square centimetre reproduced exactly.

10 mm

10 mm

You can fit 100 square millimetres inside this square because a 1 centimetre square is 10 mm by 10 mm.

A a How many square centimetres are there in 1 square metre?

   b How many square metres are there in 1 square kilometre?

B What unit would you use to measure the area of:

   a a football field   **b** a photograph   **c** a fingernail

   d a national park   **e** the Pacific Ocean   **f** a stamp?

C Convert:

   a 24 cm² to square millimetres (mm²)   **b** 6 km² to square metres (m²)

   c 4000 mm² to square centimetres (cm²)   **d** 3 456 000 m² to square kilometres (km²).

D Look up the areas of some countries on the internet or in an encyclopaedia.

   a Which are the three biggest countries (in terms of area) in the world?

   b Which is the biggest country (in terms of area) in Europe?

Ready to progress?

I can round numbers to make sensible estimates.
I know and can use squares numbers up to 15×15 and corresponding square roots.

I can carry out calculations, knowing the correct order of operations.
I can use written methods to carry out calculations involving multiplications and divisions.
I can convert and calculate with measurements.

Review questions

1   Here is a sequence of square numbers.

      9, 25, 49, 81, ...

  a Write down the next number in the sequence.

  b Write down the rule you used to work out the next number.

2   Work out each of the following.

  a $-2 + 5 \times 3$

  b $(-3 - (-7)) \times (8 - 5)$

  c $5^2 + 4^2 \div 8$

3   Which of these rectangles has the greater area?

You must show your working.

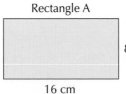

Rectangle A — 8 cm, 16 cm

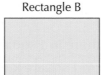

Rectangle B — 9 cm, 13 cm

4   Work out $\dfrac{84 + 27 + 32 + 41 + 75}{5}$.

5   I measured the mass of a melon.

Then I measured the mass of the melon with two bananas.

0 200 400 600 800 1000 200 400 600 800 2000

grams

Complete the sentences below, writing in the missing numbers.

The mass of the melon is ... grams.

The mass of one banana is ... grams.

 6   To work out the amount of water in a person's total body mass, divide the body mass by 3 and then multiply this by 2.

Saanvi measures her mass as 54 kg.

How much of her body is water?

 7   A builder is laying tiles on a patio.

He needs 16 rows with 28 tiles in each row.

The tiles are sold in boxes of 30 tiles.

a   How many boxes does the builder need?

b   How many tiles will he have left?

8   Copy each pair of numbers and write the correct sign, < or >, between them.

a $\sqrt{81}$ ... 2^2 b $\sqrt{144}$ ... 11^2 c $\sqrt{25}$ ... 6^2

d $\sqrt{64}$ ... 7^2 e $\sqrt{169}$ ... 3^2 f $\sqrt{196}$ ... 10^2

9   a $36 = 6^2$ can be called a *D square number* because the sum of its digits is another square number.

$3 + 6 = 9$, which is a square number (3^2).

Find another eight D square numbers.

b   16 can be called a *P square number* because the sum of its digits is a prime number.

$1 + 6 = 7$, which is a prime number.

Find another P square number.

> **Hint** Remember that a prime number is one that can only be divided exactly by itself and 1.

10 2^2 and 3^2 can be called a *prime pair of squares*, because they add up to a prime number.

2^2 and $3^2 = 4 + 9 = 13$

Find another ten prime pairs of squares.

Problem solving

What is your carbon footprint?

Every day we use energy. Scientists can work out our carbon footprint by calculating how much energy we use each year.

Fascinating facts

Our homes take up 30% of the total energy used in the UK.

- The average yearly carbon dioxide emissions in the UK are 9.4 tonnes per person.

- A rule for working out the average yearly carbon dioxide emissions of people in the USA is to double the UK figure and add 1. This gives $2 \times 9.4 + 1 = 19.8$ tonnes per person.

- If we turn down the thermostat by one degree we would save 300 kg of carbon dioxide per household per year.

- A family car with a petrol engine emits about 160 grams of carbon dioxide per kilometre, compared with about 100 grams per kilometre for a small car or 300 grams per kilometre for a large 4 by 4.

Carbon calculator

1 a Work out the carbon dioxide emissions for a journey of 8 kilometres in a small car. Give your answer in grams.

   b Work out the carbon dioxide emissions for a person travelling 8 kilometres in a family car.

   c A large 4 by 4 has 4 passengers and travels 8 kilometres. Work out the carbon dioxide emissions per person.

Carbon dioxide emissions per person

2 a Work out the difference between the average yearly carbon dioxide emissions of people in the UK and the USA.

b A rule for working out the average yearly carbon dioxide emissions of people in China is to add 0.2 to the UK figure and divide by 3.
Use this rule to work out the figure for China.

Save energy

3 If 5000 households turn down their thermostat by one degree for a year, how much carbon dioxide would be saved?

Give your answer in tonnes.

Food miles

4 The food you eat may have travelled a long way across the globe to reach your plate.

For example:

Strawberries from Turkey: 1760 miles
Peas from Egypt: 2181 miles
Tomatoes from Mexico: 5551 miles

• How many miles is this altogether?

Round your answer to the nearest thousand.

6

Statistics

This chapter is going to show you:

- how to calculate the mode, the median, the mean and the range for a set of data
- how to use tally charts and frequency tables to collate data
- how to interpret statistical diagrams and charts
- how to collect and organise data
- how to create data collection forms
- how to create questionnaires
- how to draw simple conclusions from data.

You should already know:

- how to interpret data from tables, graphs and charts
- how to draw line graphs and bar charts
- how to create a tally chart
- how to draw bar charts and pictograms.

About this chapter

How many people are there in the world? Or even in our country? How do they live? What do they eat and drink? How big are their families?

We find out statistics like these by carrying out censuses and surveys. Censuses are huge surveys that find out information about every single man, woman and child in a country.

In the UK a census is carried out every 10 years. When the data is analysed and interpreted it helps the government decide what it needs to do. Charts and graphs give us tools for analysing and representing statistical data – crucial for drawing the right conclusions from it.

6.1 Mode, median and range

Learning objective

- To understand and calculate the mode, median and range of data

Key words

average	median
mode	range

Statistics is all about collecting and organising data, then using diagrams to represent and interpret it.

You often need to find an **average** to help you to interpret data. An average is a single or typical value that represents a whole set of values.

This section explains how to find two types of average: the **mode** and the **median**.

- The mode is the value that occurs most often in a set of data. It is the only average that you can use for non-numerical data, such as favourite colours or football teams. Sometimes there may be no mode because either all the values are different, or no single value occurs more often than any other values.

- The median is the middle value for a set of values when they are put in numerical order.

The **range** of a set of values is the difference between the largest and smallest values.

This is equal to the largest value minus the smallest.

A small range means that the values in the set of data are similar in size, whereas a large range means that the values differ a lot and therefore are more spread out.

Example 1

These are the ages of 11 players in a football squad.

$$23, 19, 24, 26, 27, 27, 24, 23, 20, 23, 26$$

Find: **a** the mode   **b** the median   **c** the range.

First, put the ages in order.

$$19, 20, 23, 23, 23, 24, 24, 26, 26, 27, 27$$

a The mode is the number that occurs most often.

So, the mode is 23.

b The median is the number in the middle of the set.

This will be the sixth of 11 values.

So, the median is 24.

c The largest value is 27, the smallest is 19.

As $27 - 19 = 8$, the range is 8.

Example 2

These are the marks of 10 pupils in a mental arithmetic test.

$$18, 16, 25, 15, 13, 14, 20, 19, 22, 12$$

Find: **a** the mode   **b** the median   **c** the range.

First, put the marks in order.

$$12, 13, 14, 15, 16, 18, 19, 20, 22, 25$$

a There is no mode because no number occurs more often than any others.

(Continued)

12, 13, 14, 15, 16, 18, 19, 20, 22, 25

b In this case there are two numbers in the middle of the set: 16 and 18.

The median is the number that would be between these two numbers.

So, the median is 17.

c The range is the largest number minus the smallest number.

25 − 12 = 13

The range is 13.

Exercise 6A

1 Find the mode of each set of data.

a red, white, blue, red, white, blue, red, blue, white, red

b rain, sun, cloud, fog, rain, sun, snow, cloud, snow, sun, rain, sun

c E, A, I, U, E, O, I, E, A, E, A, O, I, U, E, I, E

d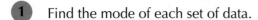

2 Find the mode of each set of data.

a 7, 6, 2, 3, 1, 9, 5, 4, 8, 4, 5, 5

b 36, 34, 45, 28, 37, 40, 24, 27, 33, 31, 41, 34, 40, 34

c 14, 12, 13, 6, 10, 20, 16, 8, 13, 14, 13

d 99, 101, 107, 103, 109, 102, 105, 110, 100, 98, 101, 95, 104

e 12, 13, 13, 15, 18, 18, 18, 19, 19, 19, 19, 20, 20, 20, 21, 21, 21, 21, 21, 21, 21, 21, 21, 23, 29, 36

f 7, 6, 7, 5, 4, 5, 5, 4, 5, 8, 10, 5, 1, 5, 5, 5, 12, 13, 5, 4, 5, 4, 5, 5, 5, 7, 6, 5, 5, 14, 3, 5, 4, 5, 3, 5, 3, 5

3 Find the range of each set of data.

a 23, 37, 18, 23, 28, 19, 21, 25, 36

b 3, 1, 2, 3, 1, 0, 4, 2, 4, 2, 6, 5, 4, 5

c 51, 54, 27, 28, 38, 45, 39, 50

d 95, 101, 104, 92, 106, 100, 97, 101, 99

4 Find the mode and range of each set of data.

a £2.50, £1.80, £3.65, £3.80, £4.20, £3.25, £1.80

b 23 kg, 18 kg, 22 kg, 31 kg, 29 kg, 32 kg

c 132 cm, 145 cm, 151cm, 132 cm, 140 cm, 142 cm

d 32°, 36°, 32°, 30°, 31°, 31°, 34°, 33°, 32°, 35°

5 A group of nine Year 7 pupils had their lunch in the school cafeteria.

These are the amounts that each of them spent.

£2.30, £2.20, £2.00, £2.50, £2.20, £2.90, £3.60, £2.20, £2.80

a Find the mode for the data. **b** Find the range for the data.

6 Find the median of each set of data.

    a 8, 7, 3, 4, 2, 10, 6, 5, 9

    b 30, 28, 39, 22, 31, 34, 18, 21, 27, 25, 35

    c 16, 14, 20, 8, 12, 22, 18, 10

    d 100, 101, 108, 105, 110, 103, 106, 111, 101, 99

7 Find the mode, range and median of each set of data.

    a £3.60, £2.90, £4.75, £4.90, £5.30, £4.35, £2.90

    b 20 kg, 15 kg, 19 kg, 28 kg, 28 kg, 23 kg, 29 kg

    c 121 cm, 134 cm, 140 cm, 121 cm, 129 cm, 131 cm, 121 cm

    d 44°, 48°, 44°, 42°, 43°, 44°, 46°, 45°, 45°, 47°, 46°

    e €2.40, €1.70, €3.55, €4.10, €3.15, €1.70, €3.75

8 **a** Write down a list of seven numbers with a median of 10 and a mode of 12.

    b Write down a list of eight numbers with a median of 10 and a mode of 12.

    c Write down a list of seven numbers with a median of 10, a mode of 12 and a range of 8.

9 These are the names of the 12 people who work for a company.

Abbas	Kathy	Yiiki	Suki
Brian	Kathy	Lucy	Tim
Kathy	James	Ryan	Tim

    a Which name is the mode?

    b One person leaves the company. A different person joins the company.

        Now the name that is the mode is Tim.

        i What is the name of the person who leaves?

        ii What is the name of the person who joins?

10 **a** There are two children in the Bishop family.

        The range of their ages is exactly 5 years.

        What could the ages of the two children be?

        Give an example.

    b In the Patel family, two of the children are twins.

        What is the range of their ages?

Activity: Research

Carry out some research, and find the mode, the median and the range of:

A yesterday's UK temperatures

B yesterday's worldwide temperatures

C the numbers of brothers of the pupils in your class

D the number of sisters of the pupils in your class.

6.2 The mean

Learning objective

• To understand and calculate the mean average of data

Key words	
average	mean
mean average	outlier

The **mean** is the most commonly used average. You may see it called the **mean average** or simply the **average** but, for clarity, it is better to call it the mean. The mean can be used only with numerical data.

The mean of a set of values is the sum of all the values divided by the number of values in the set.

$$\text{Mean} = \frac{\text{sum of all values}}{\text{number of values}}$$

The mean is a useful statistic because it takes all of the values into account, but it can be distorted by an **outlier**. This is a value, in the set of data, that is much larger or much smaller than the rest.

When there is an outlier, the median is often used instead of the mean.

Example 3

Find the mean of 2, 7, 9, 10.

The mean is $\dfrac{2 + 7 + 9 + 10}{4} = \dfrac{28}{4} = 7$

For more complex data, you can use a calculator. When the answer is not exact, the mean is usually given to one decimal place (1 dp).

Example 4

The ages of seven people are 40, 37, 34, 42, 45, 39, 35. Calculate their mean age.

The mean age is $\dfrac{40 + 37 + 34 + 42 + 45 + 39 + 35}{7} = \dfrac{272}{7} = 38.9$ (1 dp)

Exercise 6B

1 Complete each calculation.

a The mean of 3, 5, 10 is $\dfrac{3 + 5 + 10}{3} = \dfrac{\square}{3} = \square$

b The mean of 2, 5, 6, 7 is $\dfrac{2 + 5 + 6 + 7}{4} = \dfrac{\square}{4} = \square$

c The mean of 1, 4, 8, 11 is $\dfrac{1 + 4 + 8 + 11}{4} = \dfrac{\square}{4} = \square$

d The mean of 1, 1, 2, 3, 8 is $\dfrac{1 + 1 + 2 + 3 + 8}{5} = \dfrac{\square}{5} = \square$

2 Complete each calculation.

a The mean of 5, 6, 10 is $\dfrac{5+6+10}{3} = \dfrac{\square}{\square} = \square$

b The mean of 1, 3, 3, 5 is $\dfrac{1+3+3+5}{4} = \dfrac{\square}{\square} = \square$

c The mean of 4, 4, 5, 5, 7 is $\dfrac{4+4+5+5+7}{5} = \dfrac{\square}{\square} = \square$

d The mean of 1, 2, 2, 5, 10 is $\dfrac{1+2+2+5+10}{5} = \dfrac{\square}{\square} = \square$

3 Complete each calculation.

a The mean of 1, 5, 6 is $\dfrac{1+5+6}{\square} = \dfrac{\square}{\square} = \square$

b The mean of 1, 4, 7, 8 is $\dfrac{1+4+7+8}{\square} = \dfrac{\square}{\square} = \square$

c The mean of 2, 2, 3, 6, 7 is $\dfrac{2+2+3+6+7}{\square} = \dfrac{\square}{\square} = \square$

d The mean of 4, 6, 10, 20 is $\dfrac{4+6+10+20}{\square} = \dfrac{\square}{\square} = \square$

4 Complete each calculation.

a The mean of 3, 7, 8 is $\dfrac{\square+\square+\square}{\square} = \dfrac{\square}{\square} = \square$

b The mean of 5, 8, 10, 17 is $\dfrac{\square+\square+\square+\square}{\square} = \dfrac{\square}{\square} = \square$

c The mean of 2, 4, 11, 13, 15 is $\dfrac{\square+\square+\square+\square+\square}{\square} = \dfrac{\square}{\square} = \square$

d The mean of 1, 3, 8, 8 is $\dfrac{\square+\square+\square+\square}{\square} = \dfrac{\square}{\square} = \square$

5 Find the mean of each set of data.

a 8, 7, 6, 10, 4   b 23, 32, 40, 37, 29, 25

c 11, 12, 9, 26, 14, 17, 16   d 2.4, 1.6, 3.2, 1.8, 4.2, 2.5, 4.5, 2.2

6 Calculate the mean of each set of data, giving your answer to 1 dp.

a 6, 7, 6, 4, 2, 3   b 12, 15, 17, 11, 18, 16, 14

c 78, 72, 82, 95, 47, 67, 77, 80   d 9.1, 7.8, 10.3, 8.5, 11.6, 8.9

7 These are the heights, in centimetres, of 10 children.

132, 147, 143, 136, 135, 146, 153, 132, 137, 149

a Calculate the mean height of the children.

b What is the median height of the children?

c What is the modal height of the children?

d Which average do you think is the best one to use? Explain your answer.

8 These are the numbers of children in the families of Marie's class at school.

1, 1, 1, 1, 1, 1, 2, 2, 2, 2, 3, 3, 3, 3, 4

a What is the mode? **b** What is the median? **c** What is the mean?

9 These are the shoe sizes of all the girls in class 7JS.

3, 3, 3, 3, 3, 4, 4, 4, 5, 6, 6

a What is the mode? **b** What is the median? **c** What is the mean?

FS **10** These are the prices of chocolate bars on sale at a school fete.

50p, 70p, 45p, 60p, 90p, 65p, 55p, 60p, 55p, 60p

The mean price of the chocolate bars last year was 60p.

Is the mean price this year higher or lower?

Explain your answer.

Investigation: Find the mean

A Vital statistics

Work in a group. Calculate the mean and the median for your group's ages and heights.

B Average score

a Throw a dice 10 times. Record your results. What is the mean score?

b Repeat the experiment but throw the dice 20 times. What is the mean score now?

c Repeat the experiment but throw the dice 50 times. What is the mean score now?

d Write down anything you notice as you throw the dice more times.

6.3 Statistical diagrams

Learning objective

• To be able to read and interpret different statistical diagrams

Key words	
bar chart	grouped data
icon	line graph
pictogram	pie chart

When you have collected data from a survey, you can display it in various ways, to make it easier to understand and interpret.

The most common ways to display data are **pictograms**, **bar charts**, **pie charts** and **line graphs**.

• In pictograms, you use small diagrams or **icons** to represent the data.

• Bar charts may be drawn in several different ways. The questions in Exercise 5C will show you the different types of bar chart that can be used. Notice that you can show data that has separate or distinct categories in a bar chart with gaps between the bars. For **grouped data**, for example, where data values fall into ranges such as 1–5, 6–7, you will use a bar chart with no gaps between the bars.

• You would generally use line graphs to show trends and patterns in the data. They often show what happens over time.

• A pie chart is a circular diagram divided into sectors to show proportions. A pie chart shows what fraction of the whole sample each category represents.

When you compare pie charts of data from different sources, you must take care. They may not be based on similar numbers. For example, two different classes did a survey of how the pupils travelled to school. These pie charts show their results.

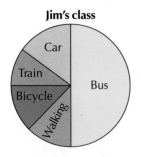

Jim's class

Noriko's class

The pie chart shows that a larger proportion of Jim's class than Noriko's class travelled by bus.

It does not show that a larger number of Jim's class than Noriko's class travel by bus.

In fact, there are 24 people In Jim's class and 12 travel by bus.

There are 36 people in Noriko's class and 14 travel by bus.

Exercise 6C

1 The bar chart shows how the pupils in class 7PB travel to school.

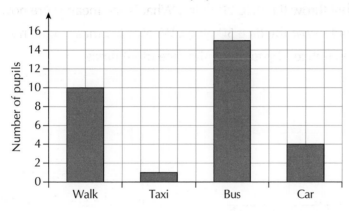

a How many pupils walk to school?

b What is the mode for the way the pupils travel to school?

c How many pupils are there in class 7PB?

2 The pictogram shows the amounts of money collected for charity by different year groups in a school.

a How much money was collected by Year 8?

b How much money was collected by Year 10?

c Which year group collected most money?

d How much money did the school collect altogether?

Year 7	£20	£20	£20	£20	£20
Year 8	£20	£20	£20		
Year 9	£20	£20	£20	£20	£2
Year 10	£20	£20	£20	£2	
Year 11	£20	£20	£20		

Key £20 represents £20

3 The pictogram shows how many DVDs five pupils have in their collections.

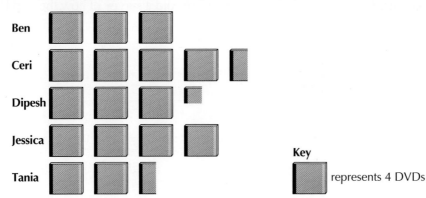

Key

represents 4 DVDs

a Who has the most DVDs?

b How many DVDs does Jessica have?

c How many DVDs does Ceri have?

d How many more DVDs does Dipesh have than Tania?

e How many DVDs do the five pupils have altogether?

4 The dual bar chart shows the daily mean number of hours of sunshine in London and Edinburgh over a year.

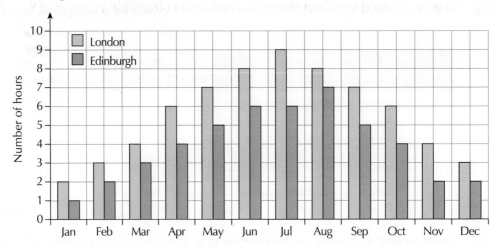

a Which city has the most sunshine?

b Which month is the sunniest for:

  i London

  ii Edinburgh?

c What is the range for the number of hours of sunshine over the year for:

  i London

  ii Edinburgh?

5 The line graph shows the temperature, in Celsius degrees (°C), in Bristol over a 12-hour period.

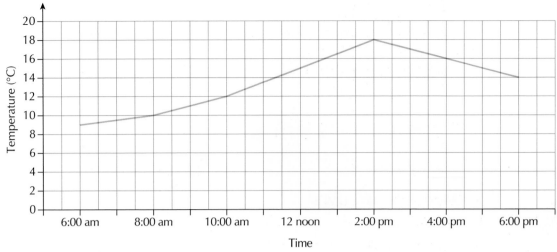

a What was the temperature at midday?

b What was the temperature at 3:00 pm?

c Write down the range for the temperature over the 12-hour period.

d Explain why the line graph is a useful way of showing the data.

6 This compound bar chart shows the favourite colours for a sample of Year 7 pupils.

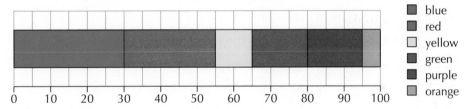

- blue
- red
- yellow
- green
- purple
- orange

a Which colour was chosen by the greatest number of pupils?

b What percentage of the pupils chose yellow?

c Which two colours were equally liked by the pupils?

d Explain why the compound bar chart is a useful way to illustrate the data.

7 The bar chart shows the marks obtained in a mathematics test by the pupils in class 7KG.

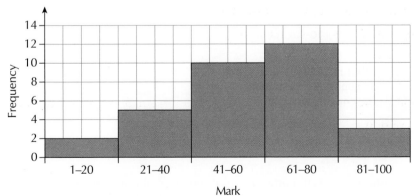

a How many pupils are there in class 7KG?

b How many pupils got a mark over 60?

c Write down the smallest and greatest range of marks possible for the data.

8 In a survey, 60 people were asked which TV channels they watched most often. The pie chart shows the results.

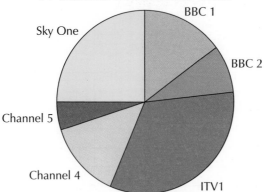

TV channels watched most often

a Which is the most popular channel?

b Which is the least popular channel?

Activity: Statistical diagrams

a Look through newspapers and magazines and find as many statistical diagrams as you can Make a display to show the variety of diagrams used in the press.

b What types of diagram are most common?

c How effective are the diagrams in showing the information?

d Are any of the diagrams misleading? If they are, explain why.

6.4 Collecting and using data

Learning objectives

• To create and use a tally chart

Key words

frequency	modal
sample	tally chart

What method of transport do pupils use to travel to school – and why?

If you ask pupils this question, they will name different methods of transport, such as bus, car, bike, walking, train and they will give various reasons for using them!

A good way to collect this data is to fill in a **tally chart** as each pupil responds to the question.

For example:

Type of transport	Tally	Frequency
Bus	卌 IIII	9
Car	卌	5
Bike	II	2
Walking	卌 卌 IIII	14
Other		
	Total:	30

Each 'stick' represents one pupil. When you get to the fifth, you draw it as a sloping stick across the other four. This can be called a gate – because that's what it looks like – or a bar, as it 'bars the gate'.

Using tallies allows you to collect the data and count it easily, in fives.

The **frequency** is the sum of all the sticks in the tally.

You can see from the tally chart that the most common type of transport is walking. This is the mode of the data and so you can say the **modal** form of transport is walking.

To answer the question 'Why?', the pupils might give answers such as those listed below.

Bus	Because it's quicker.
	Because it's too far to walk.
Car	My mum goes that way to work.
	There's no bus and it's too far.
	It's easier than the bus.
Bike	It's better than walking.
Walking	It's not too far.
	It's better than a crowded bus.

If you look at all the reasons they have given, you will be able to put some together because they are similar. These reasons can be left as a table.

Sometimes collecting every single piece of data would be very time-consuming. How would you find the answer to this question?

Do certain newspapers use more long words than the other newspapers?

The most accurate way would be to count all of the words, in each newspaper, and compare the numbers of letters in the words. Because this would take far too long, instead you would take a **sample**. You would count, say, 100 words from each newspaper and find the length of each of these words.

1 The pupils in a class were asked: 'Where would you like to go for your form trip?'

This is how they voted.

a Draw a chart illustrating the places the pupils wanted to go to.

b Suggest reasons why the pupils might have voted for each place.

c What is the modal place chosen?

Place	Tally
Alton Towers	ⅢⅢ ⅢⅢ
Camelot	ⅢⅢ Ⅰ
Blackpool	ⅢⅢ ⅢⅠ
London	Ⅲ
Bath	ⅢⅠ

2 The students in a class were asked: 'What is your favourite pet?'

This is how they voted.

a Draw a chart illustrating the favourite pets.

b What is the modal pet chosen?

Pet	Tally
Cat	ⅢⅢ ⅢⅠ
Dog	ⅢⅢ ⅢⅠ
Hamster	ⅢⅢ
Rabbit	ⅢⅠ
Other	Ⅲ

3 The pupils in a class were asked: 'What is your favourite sport?'

This is how they voted.

a Draw a chart illustrating the favourite sports.

b What is the modal sport chosen?

Sport	Tally
Athletics	ⅢⅢ Ⅰ
Cricket	ⅢⅢ
Football	ⅢⅢ ⅢⅠ
Tennis	ⅢⅢ ⅢⅠ
Other	Ⅲ

4 The pupils in a class were asked: 'What is your favourite school subject?'

This is how they voted.

a Draw a chart illustrating the favourite subjects.

b Write suitable reasons why the pupils might have voted for each subject.

c What is the modal subject chosen?

Subject	Tally
English	ⅢⅢ
History	ⅢⅠ
Maths	ⅢⅢ ⅢⅢ Ⅰ
PE	ⅢⅢ Ⅰ
Science	Ⅲ
Other	Ⅰ

5 The pupils in a class were asked: 'What is your favourite terrestrial TV channel?'

This is how they voted.

a Draw a chart illustrating the favourite channels.

b What is the modal channel chosen?

Channel	Tally
BBC 1	||||| |||
BBC2	|||
ITV 1	|||||	
Channel 4	||||| ||
Channel 5	|||||
Other	||

6 **a** Use your own class tally sheet to draw a chart illustrating the methods of transport used by pupils in your class to get to school.

b Make a table showing the reasons why.

Activity: How many letters?

Work as a class or a group.

A Select one or two pages from a newspaper.

B Create a data capture form (tally chart) like the one below, adding extra rows as necessary.

Number of letters	Tally	Frequency
1		
2		
3		
4		
5		
6		
7		

C a Select at least two different articles.

b Count the letters in each word and complete the tally.

Note: numbers such as 3, 4, 5 count as 1 letter

numbers such as 15, 58 count as 2 letters

numbers such as 156, 897 count as 3 letters, and so on.

Ignore the hyphen in hyphenated words such as 'vice-versa'.

D Fill in the frequency column.

E Create a bar chart for your results.

F What is the modal number of letters?

G You may find it interesting to compare the differences between the different newspapers before looking at the next section, then again after reading the section.

6.5 Grouped frequency

Learning objective

• To understand and use grouped frequencies

How many times have you walked to school this term?

These are the pupils' replies, when the teacher asked the class this question.

6	3	5	20	15	11	13	28	30	5	2	6
8	18	23	22	17	13	4	2	30	17	19	25
8	3	9	12	15	8						

There are too many different values here to make a sensible bar chart, so you need to organise them into a **grouped frequency table**, as shown below.

The data has been sorted into groups called **classes**. Where possible, you should always keep the classes the same size.

Times walked to school	1–5	6–10	11–15	16–20	21–25	26–30
Frequency	7	6	6	5	3	3

Now you can draw a bar chart, to show the results. Because there is no value between 5 and 6, 10 and 11, and so on, you can draw it like this.

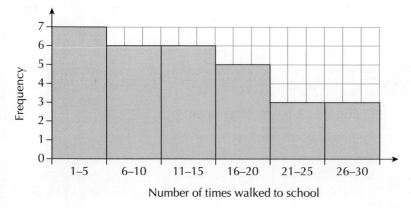

Number of times walked to school

You cannot find a mode for grouped data so, instead, you use the **modal class**. This is the class with the highest frequency.

The modal class of the data above is the class 1–5 times.

Exercise 6E

1 Two classes carried out a survey to find out how many text messages each pupil had sent the day before.

These are the results of this survey.

4	7	2	18	1	16	19	15	13	0	9	17
4	6	10	12	15	8	3	14	2	14	15	18
5	16	3	6	5	18	12	5	9	19	5	17
17	16	5	10	19	7	10	17	16	10	7	19
3	16	16	18	6	5	8	9	3			

a Create a grouped frequency table with a class size of 5, as below.

Number of texts	Tally	Frequency
0–4		
5–9		
10–14		
15–19		
	Total:	

b Use the data above to complete your table.

c Draw a bar chart of the data.

d What is the modal class?

2 A leader of a youth club asked her members: 'How many times this week have you played electronic games?'

These were their responses.

3	6	9	2	23	18	6	8	29	27	2	1
0	5	19	23	13	21	7	4	23	8	7	1
0	25	24	8	13	18	15	16	3	7	11	5
27	23	6	9	18	17	6	6	0	6	21	26
25	12	4	24	11	11	5	25				

a Create a grouped frequency table with a class size of 5, as below.

Number of times	Tally	Frequency
0–4		
5–9		
10–14		
15–19		
20–24		
25–29		
	Total:	

b Use the data above to complete your table.

c Draw a bar chart of the data.

d What is the modal class?

3 At a youth club, the members were asked: 'How many times have you played table tennis this week?'

These are their replies.

5	8	1	15	7	2	0	4	8	10	6	16
3	2	1	1	5	1	6	9	2	3	4	3
2	16	15	0	4	2	11	15	6	7	3	1
2	13	6	5	3	1	2	2	5	6	8	12
1	3	1	1	0	0	15	4	3	5	2	1
12	8	1									

a Create a grouped frequency table:

  i with a class size of 3, i.e. 0–2, 3–5, 6–8, 9–11, 12–14, 15–17

  ii with a class size of 5, i.e. 0–4, 5–9, 10–14, 15–19.

b Draw a bar chart for each frequency table.

c What is the modal class from each chart?

d Which class size seems most appropriate to use? Explain your reason.

 4 In a class sponsorship, the pupils raised these amounts of money.

£12.25	£6.50	£9.75	£23	£1.86	£5.34	£16.75	£11.32
£6.45	£2.50	£5	£18.65	£5.90	£4.34	£2.17	£8.89
£7.86	£19.70	£21.55	£13.87	£23.12	£14.67	£11.98	£13.60
£4.75	£19	£16.41	£1.90	£6.89	£8.33		

a Create a grouped frequency table:

  i with a class size of £4, i.e. £0–£4, £4.01–£8, £8.01–£12,…

  ii with a class size of £6, i.e. £0–£6, £6.01–£12, £12.01–£18,… .

b What is the modal class for each table?

c The teacher was asked to make a display illustrating how well the pupils had done. Select the better class size to illustrate the data.

d Explain why you chose that class size.

Challenge: Boat trips down the Ganges

In Varanasi, India, tourists take boat trips down the river Ganges. One week a boat owner recorded how many people were in his boat on the main days these trips were made.

These are the results.

Saturday:											
18	23	12	17	8	29	13	9	18	21	29	18
14	23	12	14	24	19	17	16	10	9	9	11
23	28	21	22	13	9	24	28	25	12	11	15
9	16	24	16	12	10	26	29	22	17	13	18
21	26	14	9								

(Continued)

Sunday:	17	21	9	13	8	28	11	6	14	16	20	27
	15	10	18	11	12	16	15	12	9	8	6	6
	8	9	20	24	16	21	11	6	20	23	24	10
	8	11	9	15	10	9	6	21	28	20	14	8
	17	19	23	10	9							
Wednesday:	23	29	17	22	14	31	18	24	32	23	20	30
	17	19	20	31	24	23	22	22	17	14	15	18
	28	32	26	28	20	14	20	31	30	18	18	20
	15	23	29	22	19	15	32	33	27	19	20	23
	27	32										

a Complete a grouped frequency tally chart for each day's recorded results. (Decide on your own class size.)

b Draw a bar chart from each frequency chart.

c Comment on your results.

6.6 Data collection

Learning objective

• To develop greater understanding of data collection

Key words

data-collection form

Suppose you wanted to organise a party to celebrate the end of term at school. You need to know what pupils would like. Here are some questions you might ask.

You could ask a sample of the pupils in your school these questions. This means you would not ask everyone, but a few from each group.

You ask each question, then immediately complete your **data-collection form**.

> What shall we charge?
> What time shall we start?
> What time shall we finish?
> What food shall we eat?

An example of a suitable data-collection form is shown below.

Year group	Boy or girl	How much to charge?	Time to start?	Time to finish?	What would you like to eat?
Y7	B	£1	7 pm	11 pm	Crisps, beefburgers, chips
Y7	G	50p	7 pm	9 pm	Chips, crisps, lollies
Y8	G	£2	7:30 pm	10 pm	Crisps, hot dogs
Y9	B	£3	8:30 pm	11:30 pm	Chocolate, pizza
Keep track of the age.	Try to ask equal numbers.	Once you have collected the data, you can sort it into frequency tables.			

The five stages in running this type of data collection are:

• deciding what questions to ask and who to ask

• creating a simple, suitable data-collection form for all the questions

- asking the questions and completing the data-collection form
- after collecting all the data, collating it in frequency tables
- analysing the data to draw conclusions from the data collected.

The size of your sample will depend on many things. It may be simply the first 50 people you meet. Or you may want to target a particular fraction of the available people.

In the above example, a good sample would probably be about four from each class, two boys and two girls.

Exercise 6F

A class completed the data-collection activity described above on a sample of 10 pupils from each of years 7, 8 and 9. This is their data-collection form.

Year group	Boy or girl	How much to charge	Time to start	Time to finish	What would you like to eat?
Y7	B	£1	7 pm	11 pm	Crisps, beefburgers, chips
Y7	G	50p	7 pm	9 pm	Chips, crisps, ice pops
Y8	G	£2	7:30 pm	10 pm	Crisps, hot dogs
Y9	B	£3	8:30 pm	11:30 pm	Chocolate, pizza
Y9	G	£2	8 pm	10 pm	Pizza
Y9	B	£2.50	7:30 pm	9:30 pm	Hot dogs, chocolate
Y8	G	£1	8 pm	10:30 pm	Crisps
Y7	B	75p	7 pm	9 pm	Crisps, beefburgers
Y7	B	£1	7:30 pm	10:30 pm	Crisps, ice pops
Y8	B	£1.50	7 pm	9 pm	Crisps, chips, hot dogs
Y9	G	£2	8 pm	11 pm	Pizza, chocolate
Y9	G	£1.50	8 pm	10:30 pm	Chips, pizza
Y9	G	£2	8 pm	11 pm	Crisps, pizza
Y7	G	£1.50	7 pm	9 pm	Crisps, ice pops, chocolate
Y8	B	£2	7:30 pm	9:30 pm	Crisps, ice pops, chocolate
Y8	B	£1	8 pm	10 pm	Chips, hot dogs
Y9	B	£1.50	8 pm	11 pm	Pizza
Y7	B	50p	7 pm	9:30 pm	Crisps, hot dogs
Y8	G	75p	8 pm	10:30 pm	Crisps, chips
Y9	B	£2	7:30 pm	10:30 pm	Pizza
Y8	G	£1.50	7:30 pm	10 pm	Chips, hot dogs, chocolate
Y8	B	£1.25	7 pm	9:30 pm	Chips, hot dogs, ice pops
Y9	G	£3	7 pm	9:30 pm	Crisps, pizza
Y9	B	£2.50	8 pm	10:30 pm	Crisps, hot dogs
Y7	G	25p	7:30 pm	10 pm	Crisps, beefburgers, ice pops
Y7	G	50p	7 pm	9 pm	Crisps, pizza
Y7	G	£1	7 pm	9:30 pm	Crisps, pizza
Y8	B	£2	8 pm	10 pm	Crisps, chips, chocolate
Y8	G	£1.50	7:30 pm	9:30 pm	Chips, beefburgers
Y7	B	£1	7:30 pm	10 pm	Crisps, ice pops

1 a Copy this chart and complete the tallies for the suggested charges from each year group.

Charges	Tallies					
	Y7	Total	Y8	Total	Y9	Total
25p						
50p						
75p						
£1						
£1.25						
£1.50						
£2						
£2.50						
£3						

b Comment on the differences between the year groups.

2 a Copy this chart and complete the tallies for the suggested starting times from each year group.

Times	Tallies					
	Y7	Total	Y8	Total	Y9	Total
7:00 pm						
7:30 pm						
8:00 pm						
8:30 pm						

b Comment on the differences between the year groups.

3 a Copy this chart and complete the tallies for the suggested finishing times from each year group.

Times	Tallies					
	Y7	Total	Y8	Total	Y9	Total
9:00 pm						
9:30 pm						
10:00 pm						
10:30 pm						
11:00 pm						
11:30 pm						

b Comment on the differences between the year groups.

4 a Create and complete a tally chart, as before, for the food suggestions of each year.

b Comment on the differences between the year groups.

Investigation: Length of the party

Investigate the differences between the views of boys and girls on the suggested length of time for the end-of-term party.

Ready to progress?

I can use a data-collection form to collect data.
I can find the mode and range for a set of data.

I can find the median and the mean for a set of data.
I can compare two simple sets of data.
I can group data, where appropriate, into classes of equal size.

Review questions

1   Twenty 11-year-olds were tweeting about how much it cost them to travel to school on a bus. These are the amounts they paid.

| 20p | £1 | 75p | £1.25 | £1 | 20p | 75p | £1 | £1 | £1.25 |
| 40p | 50p | £1.50 | £1 | 50p | £1 | £1.25 | £1 | 75p | 80p |

What was the modal amount spent on bus fares?

2   These are the temperatures recorded on 1 February in 15 major towns of the UK.

| 1 °C | −4 °C | 0 °C | −1 °C | 1 °C | −2 °C | 0 °C | −1 °C |
| −4 °C | 2 °C | −3 °C | −1 °C | 1 °C | −1 °C | −2 °C | |

What was the median temperature recorded from these temperatures?

(PS) 3   Tom was asked to make a rectangle with a piece of wire, of length 18 cm.

He was told to make the length and width whole numbers of centimetres.

What is the range of areas he could make with that length of wire?

4   Charlie compared the masses of a sample of ten bags of sugar. These are his results.

1.08 kg   1.1 kg   0.95 kg   1.04 kg   0.98 kg   1.09 kg   1.02 kg   0.99 kg   0.97 kg   1.01 kg

What was the mean mass of the ten bags of sugar?

(PS) 5   Kim was asked to draw a rectangle with an area of 24 cm² and with sides that were whole numbers of centimetres.

   a   Show that there are only four different-sized rectangles she can draw.

   b   Calculate the mean of the four different perimeters.

   c   Hence state which rectangle has the closest perimeter to the mean found.

6 Uzma asked children from two different schools: 'How do you travel to school?'
   Here are her results.

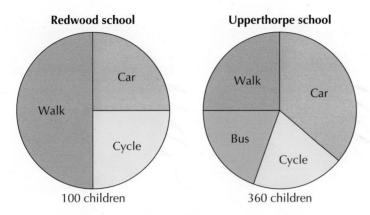

Redwood school — Car, Walk, Cycle — 100 children
Upperthorpe school — Walk, Car, Bus, Cycle — 360 children

a Uzma says: 'The number of children walking to Redwood school is greater than the number walking to Upperthorpe school.'
   Explain why Uzma is incorrect.

b At Upperthorpe school, one-third of the children travel by car.
   The number of children who cycle is the same as the number who go on the bus.

   How many of the children cycle to Upperthorpe school?

7 Efrosyni asked her friends on Facebook to tell her their heights. Her friends sent her the following results.

151 cm	1.53 m	1.44 m	148 cm	1.57 m	138 cm
1473 mm	1535 mm	1.52 m	1.47 m	1432 mm	1.47 m
150 cm	157 cm	1.4 m	1398 mm	1.42 m	139 cm
1.35 m	1458 mm	146 cm	1433 mm	1.49 m	1.32 m
1529 mm	143 cm	136 cm	1.45 m	1503 mm	1.31 m

a Put the heights into a grouped frequency tally chart.
b What is the modal class?

8 Draw a triangle in which the sides have a modal length of 5 cm and a mean length of 6 cm.

Challenge
School sports day

Teams

1 The ages of Ruskin team's seven members are shown in the table.

	Age (years)
Joe	14
Kristen	15
Simon	13
Vikas	15
Helen	14
Sarah	13
Quinn	13

   a Put their ages into order.

   b What is the mode of the ages?

   c What is the range of the ages?

   d What is the median age?

100 m sprint

2 The table shows the times for the girls' 100 m race.

	Time (seconds)
Kate	22
Kerry	25
Maria	21
Oi Yin	25
Sara	23

   a Put these times into order.

   b What is the mode of the times?

   c What is the range of the times?

   d What is the median time?

Long jump

3 Alex had ten practice attempts at the long jump. The bar chart illustrates the range of lengths he jumps.

What is the length of his average jump?

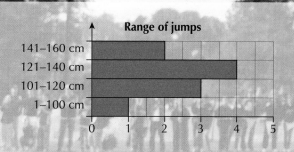

Range of jumps

Range	0	1	2	3	4	5
141–160 cm						
121–140 cm						
101–120 cm						
1–100 cm						

Rounders competition

4 In the rounders game between Huntsman and Chantry, these scorecards were produced as tallies. A tally was put next to a player each time they scored a rounder.

a Which team won the game?

b Which of all the players was the most likely to score a rounder?

Huntsman		Frequency
Afzal	‖	
Claire	‖‖	
Gilbert	‖‖‖ ‖	
John	‖	
Ali	‖	
Izolda	‖‖‖	
Kate	‖‖‖‖ ‖‖‖‖ ‖	
Joy		
Mari	‖	

Chantry		Frequency
Ellen	‖‖‖	
Cynthia	‖	
Runuka	‖‖‖‖ ‖	
Joanne	‖	
Michael	‖	
Emily	‖	
Julie	‖‖‖‖ ‖	
Kay	‖‖‖‖	
Sue	‖‖‖	

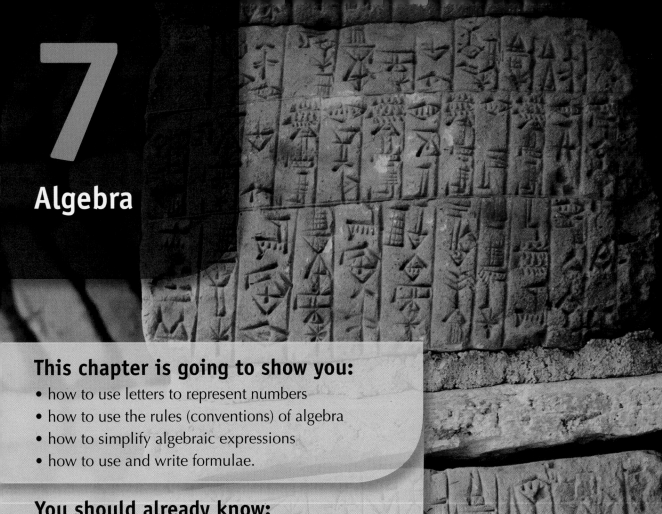

7

Algebra

This chapter is going to show you:

- how to use letters to represent numbers
- how to use the rules (conventions) of algebra
- how to simplify algebraic expressions
- how to use and write formulae.

You should already know:

- how to apply the rules of arithmetic
- the meaning of the words 'term' and 'expression'.

About this chapter

Algebra uses letters instead of numbers to describe and solve problems. It is a universal language and its rules are used all over the world.

Mathematicians have been developing the rules of algebra for over 3000 years. We know that the Babylonians (Babylon was situated in the southern part of today's Iraq) used a form of algebra because they wrote on clay tablets, some of which have survived until today.

Today, we use algebra to help us solve all sorts of problems, from the simplest to the most complex, for example, working out the area of carpet needed for a floor or designing the shape of a racing car to minimise wind resistance.

7.1 Expressions and substitution

Learning objectives

- To use algebra to write simple expressions
- To substitute numbers into expressions to work out their value

Key words

expression	substitute
term	variable

In algebra, you use letters or symbols to represent numbers.

The lengths of the sides of this quadrilateral are 10 cm, a cm, a cm and b cm.

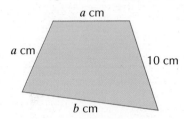

a and b are **variables**. They can take different values.

The two sides labelled a cm are the same length.

An **expression** for the perimeter of the quadrilateral is $2a + b + 10$ cm.

You can write $a + a$ in a short way, as $2a$.

$2a$, b and 10 are the three **terms** in this expression.

You can **substitute** different values for the variables, a and b, and work out the perimeter.

For example, if $a = 7.5$ and $b = 12$, then you can work out the value of the expression $2a + b + 10$.

$$2a + b + 10 = 2 \times 7.5 + 12 + 10$$
$$= 15 + 12 + 10$$
$$= 37$$

The perimeter of the quadrilateral is 37 cm.

Example 1

Write a term or expression to illustrate each sentence.

a 6 more than w **b** 8 less than x **c** y multiplied by 4   **d** z multiplied by z

  a 6 more than w is written as $w + 6$.

  b 8 less than x is written as $x - 8$.

  c y multiplied by 4 is written as $4y$.

  d $z \times z$ is written as z^2.

For example, $3^2 = 3 \times 3 = 9$ or $8^2 = 64$.

Example 2

Work out the value of these expressions when $x = 8$ and $y = 4$.

a $5x$ **b** $x + 3y$ **c** $x^2 - 2y$ **d** $\frac{x}{4}$ **e** $5(x + y)$

a $5x$ means $5 \times x = 5 \times 8 = 40$.

b $x + 3y$ means $8 + 3 \times 4 = 8 + 12 = 20$.

c $x^2 - 2y$ means $8^2 - 2 \times 4 = 64 - 8 = 56$.

d $\frac{x}{4}$ means $x \div 4 = 8 \div 4 = 2$.

e Work out the value of the expression in brackets first.

$5(x + y)$ means $5 \times (8 + 4) = 5 \times 12 = 60$.

Exercise 7A

1 Write terms, or expressions, to illustrate these sentences.

    a   4 more than m

    b t multiplied by 8

    c y less that 9

    d m multiplied by itself

    e n divided by 5

    f t subtracted from seven.

    g   Multiply n by 3, then add 5.

    h   Multiply 6 by t.

    i   Multiply m by 5, then subtract 5.

    j   Multiply x by x.

2 **a**   Show that the perimeter of this shape is $a + 22$ cm.

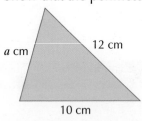

    b   Work out the value of $a + 22$, if $a = 8.5$.

3 **a**   Write down an expression for the perimeter of this triangle.

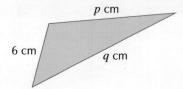

    b   Work out the value of your expression, if $p = 10.5$ and $q = 12.5$.

4 a Show that the perimeter of this parallelogram is $2(d + 14)$ cm.

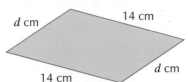

b Work out the value of $2(d + 14)$, if $d = 6$.

5 All the sides of this pentagon are s cm long.

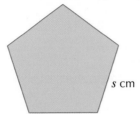

a Write down an expression for the perimeter of the pentagon.

b Work out the value of your expression, if $s = 25$.

6 The length of side AB of this triangle is x cm.

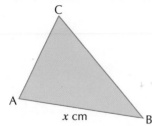

a Side BC is 2 cm longer than side AB.

Write down an expression for the length of BC.

b Side AC is 1.5 cm shorter than side AB.

Write down an expression for the length of AC.

c Write an expression for the perimeter of the triangle.

d Work out the value of your expression, if $x = 20$.

7 Write down the values of each term for the three values of n.

a $4n$ where: **i** $n = 2$ **ii** $n = 5$ **iii** $n = 11$.

b $\dfrac{n}{2}$ where: **i** $n = 6$ **ii** $n = 14$ **iii** $n = 8$.

c n^2 where: **i** $n = 3$ **ii** $n = 6$ **iii** $n = 7$.

d $3n$ where: **i** $n = 7$ **ii** $n = 5$ **iii** $n = 9$.

e $\dfrac{n}{5}$ where: **i** $n = 10$ **ii** $n = 5$ **iii** $n = 20$.

f $3(n + 2)$ where: **i** $n = 2$ **ii** $n = 4$ **iii** $n = 8$.

g $\dfrac{n}{10}$ where: **i** $n = 20$ **ii** $n = 50$ **iii** $n = 100$.

8 Write down the values of each expression for the three values of n.

   a $n + 7$ where: **i** $n = 3$ **ii** $n = 4$ **iii** $n = -6$.

   b $n - 5$ where: **i** $n = 8$ **ii** $n = 14$ **iii** $n = 2$.

   c $10 - n$ where: **i** $n = 4$ **ii** $n = 7$ **iii** $n = -3$.

   d $2n + 3$ where: **i** $n = 2$ **ii** $n = 5$ **iii** $n = 0$.

   e $5(n - 1)$ where: **i** $n = 3$ **ii** $n = 11$ **iii** $n = 1$.

   f $2(n + 8)$ where: **i** $n = 1$ **ii** $n = 5$ **iii** $n = 12$.

   g $4n + 5$ where: **i** $n = 4$ **ii** $n = 3$ **iii** $n = 20$.

9 Write down the values of each expression for the three values of n.

   a $n^2 - 1$ where: **i** $n = 2$ **ii** $n = 3$ **iii** $n = 1$.

   b $n^2 + 1$ where: **i** $n = 5$ **ii** $n = 6$ **iii** $n = 10$.

   c $5 + n^2$ where: **i** $n = 8$ **ii** $n = 9$ **iii** $n = 0$.

10   **a**   Write down an expression for the perimeter, in centimetres, of each rectangle.

   i 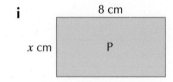   **ii** 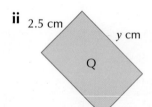   **iii**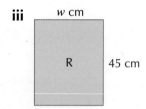

   b   Write down an expression for the area, in square centimetres, of each rectangle.

(PS) **11** The diagram shows an L-shape divided into two rectangles.

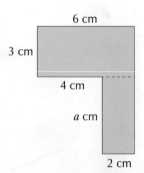

   a   Show that the area of one of the rectangles is 18 cm².

   b   Write down an expression for the area of the other rectangle.

   c   Write down an expression for the area of the whole shape.

   d   Show that the length of the missing side is $a + 3$ cm.

   e   Work out an expression for the perimeter of the whole shape.

PS **12** The areas of these two shapes are A cm² and B cm².

A cm² B cm²

Work out an expression for the area of each of these shapes.

The first one has been done for you.

a
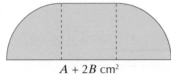
$A + 2B$ cm²

b

c

d

e
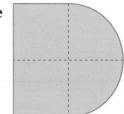

f
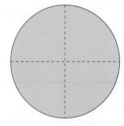

g
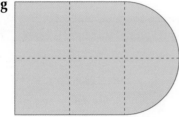

h

i

j
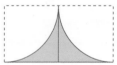

PS **13** Here are the two shapes from Question **12**, again.
Draw shapes that have these areas.

A cm² B cm²

a $3A$ cm²   **b** $3B$ cm²

c $3A + B$ cm²   **d** $2A + 4B$ cm²

Investigation: Making shapes

The areas of these two shapes are C cm² and D cm².

C cm² D cm²

A Draw different compound shapes made up from copies of these two basic shapes.

B Write an expression for the area of each one.

7.2 Simplifying expressions

Learning objective

• To learn how to simplify expressions

Keywords

coefficient	like terms
simplify	

The lengths of the sides of this trapezium are $2a$ cm, b cm, $3a$ cm and b cm.

The perimeter is $2a + b + 3a + b$ cm.

You can **simplify** this by adding the a terms and adding the b terms separately.

$$2a + 3a = 5a$$
$$b + b = 2b$$

The perimeter is $5a + 2b$.

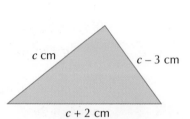

Simplifying an expression in this way is called collecting **like terms**.

The lengths of the sides of this triangle are c cm, $c - 3$ cm and $c + 2$ cm.

The perimeter of the triangle is $c + c - 3 + c + 2$ cm.

This simplifies to $3c - 1$ cm. $c + c + c = 3c$ and $-3 + 2 = -1$.

It cannot be simplified any further. It is <u>not</u> the same as $2c$.

Example 3

Simplify each expression.

a $a + a + a$ **b** $3x + 7x$ **c** $9w - 4w$ **d** $2xy + 5xy - 3xy$

a $a + a + a$ simplifies to $3a$.

b $3x + 7x$ simplifies to $10x$.   Because $3 + 7 = 10$.

c $9w - 4w$ simplifies to $5w$.   Because $9 - 4 = 5$.

d $2xy + 5xy - 3xy$ simplifies to $4xy$.   Because $2 + 5 - 3 = 4$.

Example 4

Simplify each expression.

a $3a + 5b + 6a - 2b$ **b** $x^2 + 4x + 7 - 7x + 3x^2 + 2$

a $3a + 5b + 6a - 2b$

$= 3a + 6a + 5b - 2b$ Putting like terms together.

$= 9a + 3b$ Simplifying.

You cannot make this any simpler because $9a$ and $3b$ contain different variables.

b $x^2 + 4x + 7 - 7x + 3x^2 + 2$ simplifies to $4x^2 - 3x + 9$.

Note: In the term $-3x$, the **coefficient** of x is -3.

Example 5

Work out the missing numbers.

a $2x + y + \square x + 6y = 8x + \square y$ **b** $5x + 7y - 4x - 9y = \square x - \square y$

a $2x + y + 6x + 6y = 8x + 7y$

Check: Coefficients of x give $2 + 6 = 8$, coefficients of y give $1 + 6 = 7$.

b $5x + 7y - 4x - 9y = x - 2y$

Check: Coefficients of x give $5 - 4 = 1$, coefficients of y give $7 - 9 = -2$.

Exercise 7B

1 Simplify each expression.

a $a + a$ **b** $b + 3b$ **c** $9c - c$ **d** $d + d + 3d$

e $x + 2x - x$ **f** $8y - y$ **g** $z + z - z$ **h** $p + 6p - p$

i $4q + q - q$ **j** $2x + x - x$ **k** $4y + y - 5y$ **l** $5z - z - z$

2 Simplify each expression.

a $4c + 2c$ **b** $6d + 4d$ **c** $7p - 5p$ **d** $2x + 6x + 3x$

e $4t + 2t - t$ **f** $7m - 3m$ **g** $q + 5q - 2q$ **h** $a + 6a - 3a$

i $4p + p - 2p$ **j** $2w + 3w - w$ **k** $4t + 3t - 5t$ **l** $5g - g - 2g$

3 Simplify each expression.

a $2x + 2y + 3x + 6y$ **b** $4w + 6t - 2w - 2t$ **c** $4m + 7n + 3m - n$

d $4x + 8y - 2y - 3x$ **e** $8 + 4x - 3 + 2x$ **f** $8p + 9 - 3p - 4$

g $2y + 4x - 3 + x - y$ **h** $5d + 8c - 4c + 7$ **i** $4f + 2 + 3d - 1 - 3f$

j $8c + 7 - 7c - 4$ **k** $2p + q + 3p - q$ **l** $3t + 9 - t$

4 Simplify each expression.

a $5x + 3y + 2x - 6y$ **b** $9x + 5y - 4x - 9y$ **c** $7a + 7b - 8a - b$

d $5x - 8y - 7x - 5y$ **e** $10 + 5w - 13 + 7w$ **f** $11x + 4 - 12x - 8$

g $4x + 6y + x - 9y$ **h** $6a + 9b - 4a - 11b$ **i** $5x + 5 + 3x - 9$

j $10x + 9 - 17x - 14$ **k** $12x - y + 4x - 8y$ **l** $7t - 8 - 6t - 6$

MR **5** Work out the missing coefficients.

a $2x + 8y + \square x + 6y = 6x + \square y$ **b** $5w - 5t - \square w - \square t = w - 9t$

c $4m + \square n + \square m - 4n = 10m + 2n$ **d** $\square x + \square y - 2y - 3x = 7x + 5y$

e $8p + \square x - \square p + 2x = p + 7x$ **f** $8p + 9q - \square p - \square q = 5p - q$

6 This is a number wall.

Add the two numbers in the bricks below, to get the number in the brick above.

4 + 2 = 6 and 2 + 3 = 5

The missing top number is 11.

Work out the top number or expression in each of these number walls. Write any expressions as simply as possible.

a
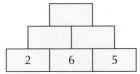

b
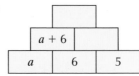

c
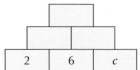

d
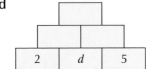

e
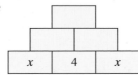

f

g
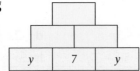

h
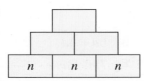

7 In each of these number walls, there is more than one variable.

Work out the top expression. Write it as simply as possible.

a
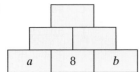

b
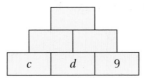

c
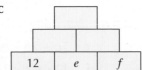

d
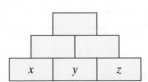

Investigation: Making addition expressions

Here are 10 expression cards.

Cards can be added together, like this.

$(x + 1) + (x + 2) = (2x + 3)$

Use all of the cards to find as many addition expressions as you can.

You cannot use any card more than once in any addition.

x + 1	x − 1	2x + 1	2x + 3	2x
x + 2	x − 2	3x + 4	3x − 1	2x − 1

7.3 Using formulae

Learning objective

• To use formulae

You have already used simple **formulae** in Chapter 3.

Remember that a **formula** can be written in words or using letters.

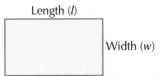

Length (*l*)

Width (*w*)

Hint Formulae is the plural of formula.

The perimeter of the rectangle is equal to 2 lengths + 2 widths.

$$P = 2l + 2w \text{ or } 2(l + w)$$

The area of the rectangle is equal to length × width.

$$A = l \times w \text{ or } A = lw$$

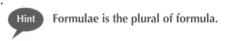

Height (*h*)

Width (*w*)

Length (*l*)

The volume of a cube or cuboid is equal to length × width × height.

$$V = l \times w \times h \text{ or } V = lwh$$

Example 6

A rule for calculating the cost of hiring a hall for a wedding is £200 plus £6 per person.
Write this as a formula.

Taking c = cost in pounds (£) and n = number of people:

$c = 200 + 6n$

Example 7

Use the formula $c = 200 + 6n$ to calculate the cost of hiring a hall for a wedding attended by 70 people.

$c = 200 + 6 \times 70$

$\quad = 200 + 420$

$\quad = £620$

The cost is £620.

The formula could also be written as $c = 6n + 200$

Then the calculation is:

$c = 6 \times 70 + 200$

$\quad = 420 + 200$

$\quad = 620$

The result is the same as before.

Exercise 7C

1. A cleaner uses the formula:

   $$c = 5 + 8h$$

   where c is the cost (in £) and h is the number of hours worked.

   Calculate what the cleaner charges to work for:

   a 5 hours   **b** 3 hours   **c** 8 hours.

2. A mechanic uses the formula:

   $$c = 25t + 20$$

   where c is the cost (in £) and t is the time, in hours, to complete the work.

   Calculate what the mechanic charges to complete the work in:

   a 1 hour   **b** 3 hours   **c** 7 hours.

3. A singer uses the formula:

   $$c = 8 + 5s$$

   where c is the cost (in £) and s is the number of songs sung.

   Calculate what the singer charges to sing:

   a 2 songs   **b** 4 songs   **c** 8 songs.

4. The formula for the average speed of a car is:

   $$A = D \div T$$

   where A is the average speed (in miles per hour)

   D is the distance travelled (in miles)

   T is the time taken (in hours).

   Use the formula to calculate the average speed for each journey.

   a 300 miles in 6 hours   **b** 200 miles in 5 hours

   c 120 miles in 3 hours   **d** 350 miles in 5 hours

5. The formula for the cost of a newspaper advert is:

   $$C = 5W + 10A$$

   where C is the charge (in £)

   W is the number of words used

   A is the area of the advert (in cm^2).

   Use the formula to calculate the charge for the following adverts.

   a 10 words with an area of 20 cm^2 **b** 8 words with an area of 6 cm^2

   c 12 words with an area of 15 cm^2 **d** 17 words with an area of 15 cm^2

6 The formula for the perimeter, P cm, of a rectangle is:

$$P = 2(l + w)$$

where l is the length (in centimetres)

w is the width (in centimetres).

a Work out the perimeter of a rectangle measuring 5 cm by 9 cm.

b Work out the perimeter of a rectangle measuring 14 cm by 12 cm.

7 The diagram shows a regular five-sided polygon and a regular six-sided polygon.

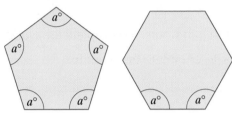

All the angles of a regular polygon are the same size.

If a regular polygon has n sides, the size of the angle marked $a°$ is given by the formula:

$$a = 180 - \frac{360}{n}$$

In this formula, $\frac{360}{n}$ means $360 \div n$.

a Show that the angle of a regular polygon with 5 sides is 108°.

b Work out the angle of a regular polygon with 6 sides.

c Work out the angle of a regular polygon with 8 sides.

d Work out the angle of a regular polygon with 10 sides.

Challenge: Calculating the cost

Ivor Flex, the electrician, charges £A for a call-out charge and then £B per hour when he does a job.

He uses the formula: $C = A + B \times \text{hours}$

He does jobs for Mrs Smith and Mr Khan.

A How much extra did the fourth hour cost Mr Khan?

B Work out the values of A and B.

Ivor did a job that took 4 hours and he charged me £150.

Ivor did a job that took 3 hours and he charged me £118.

7.4 Writing formulae

Learning objective

• To write formulae

Sometimes you will need to create your own formula to represent a statement or to solve a problem.

Example 8

A mechanic charges £15 per hour plus a call-out fee of £30.

A job lasts h hours.

The cost is £c.

Write down a formula for c in terms of h.

    The cost is: number of hours $\times$ 15 + call-out fee of 30.

    So you can write the formula as: $c = 15h + 30$

Example 9

Write down a formula for the sum, S, of three consecutive whole numbers, starting from n.

    Consecutive whole numbers go up in ones, so they can be represented by n, $n + 1$ and $n + 2$.

    So the formula is:

    $S = n + n + 1 + n + 2$

    $S = 3n + 3$

Exercise 7D

1   In each case below, there are two variables. Write a formula to connect them.
The first one has been done for you.

  a It costs £6 per hour to hire a rowing boat.

      Pete rents a boat for h hours.

      The cost is £c.

      A formula for c in terms of h is $c = 6h$.

  b Derek is 40 years older than Joy.

      Derek is d years old.

      Joy is j years old.

      A formula for d in terms of j is $d = \ldots$

  c Petrol costs £1.40 per litre.

      Sally buys b litres and the cost is £a.

      Write a formula for a in terms of b.

d Jason has j sweets.

Cassie has 10 fewer sweets than Jason.

Cassie has c sweets.

Write a formula for c in terms of j.

e There are 7 days in a week.

Building a house takes w weeks or d days.

Write a formula for w in terms of d.

f It takes 5 minutes to answer each question in an examination.

Jack answers q questions.

It takes him m minutes.

Write a formula for m in terms of q.

g Apples cost 20p each and oranges cost 30p each.

Alice buys x apples and y oranges.

She pays t pence altogether.

Write a formula for t in terms of x and y.

h The cost of hiring a room is £20 plus £8 per person.

The room is hired for n people.

The total cost is £t.

Write a formula for t in terms of n.

i The time to cook a chicken is 30 minutes plus 20 minutes per kilogram.

The mass of a chicken is x kg.

It takes m minutes to cook.

Write a formula for m in terms of x.

j Chickens have 2 legs and sheep have 4 legs.

There are f chickens and s sheep in a field.

The chickens and sheep have a total of n legs.

Write a formula for n in terms of f and s.

2 Use the letters given, write down a simple formula for:

a the product, P, of two numbers a and b

b the sum, S, of two numbers x and y

c the number of weeks, W, in Y years

d the number of minutes, m, in h hours

e the difference, d, between the ages of Bert, who is b years old and his little brother Ernie, who is e years old

f the total mark, M, scored in an examination with two papers, when you score X marks on paper 1 and Y marks on paper 2.

3 **a** Work out the lengths of the sides of this rectangle, if $n = 3$.

b Work out the perimeter of the rectangle, if $n = 13$.

c Work out a formula for the perimeter, p cm, of the rectangle.

d Work out the value of p, if $n = 30$.

$n + 5$ cm

n cm

MR **4** A boy is b years old. His mother is m years old.

   a Write down an expression for the difference, d, between their ages.

   b Write down a formula for the sum, s, of their ages.

   c Work out the value of s if $b = 9$ and $m = 41$.

   d Write down an expression for the boy's age in six years' time.

   e Write down an expression for his mother's age in six years' time.

   f Work out a formula for the sum, t, of their ages in 6 years' time.

PS **5** I start with the number 4. I multiply it by x and then add y.

The result is r.

   a Write down a formula for r.

   b Work out the value of r, if $x = 8$ and $y = 5$.

   c Work out the value of r, if $x = 6$ and $y = 13$.

   d Work out the value of r, if $x = 13$ and $y = 6$.

6 This is a quadrilateral.

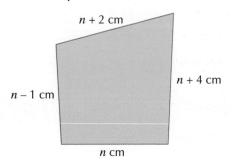

   a Work out the lengths of the four sides of the quadrilateral, if $n = 13.5$.

   b Work out a formula for the perimeter, p cm, of the quadrilateral. Write your formula as simply as possible.

   c Work out the value of p, if $n = 50$.

7 Look at this number wall.

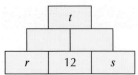

   a Work out a formula for the top number, t, in terms of r and s.

   b Work out the value of t, if r is 15 and s is 25.

   c Work out the value of t, if r and s are both 50.

   d Work out the value of t, if r and s add up to 30.

8 Look at this number wall.

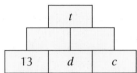

  a Work out a formula for the top number, *t*, in terms of *c* and *d*.
  b Work out the value of *t*, if *c* is 10 and *d* is 15.
  c Work out the value of *t*, if *c* is 15 and *d* is 10.

9 This number wall has four layers.

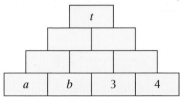

  a Work out a formula for the top number, *t*, in terms of *a* and *b*.
  b Work out the value of *t*, if *a* is 8 and *b* is 2.
  c Work out the value of *t*, if *a* is 2 and *b* is 8.
  d Work out the value of *t*, if *a* and *b* are both 5.

Investigation: Dots and squares

You will need centimetre-square dotted paper for this investigation.

Here are three shapes.

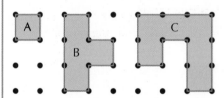

A Copy this table and complete the first three lines.

Shape	Number of dots on the perimeter (*n*)	Area (*a* cm²)
A		
B		
C		

B Draw some more shapes on centimetre-square dotted paper. Follow these rules.

The shapes are made from vertical and horizontal lines joining dots.

Diagonal lines are not allowed.

There must not be any dots inside the shape.

C Add your shapes to the table.

D Work out a formula for *a* in terms of *n*.

Ready to progress?

I can write simple algebraic expressions.
I can substitute numbers into algebraic expressions, such as $2n + 3$.
I can simplify algebraic expressions, such as $2a + 5a$, by collecting like terms

I can substitute values into simple formulae.
I can write simple formulae.
I can simplify algebraic expressions such as $2a + 5b + 5a + 7b$ by collecting like terms.

Review questions

1   The area of this square is Q cm² and the area of the semicircle is S cm².

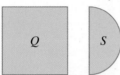

This shape has an area of $Q + 2S$ cm².

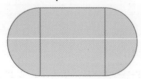

a   Write the area of these shapes, in terms of Q and S.

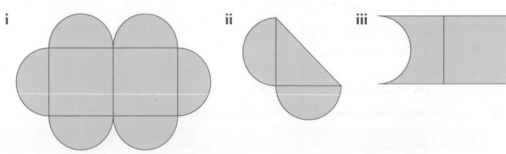

i   ii   iii

b   Draw diagrams to show shapes with these areas.
   i $Q + 4S$ cm²   ii $3Q - 2S$ cm²

PS   2   Given that $r = 5$ and $t = 20$, work out the value of:

a $10 + 4r$ b $1.5t - 12$ c $6r + 3t - 35$ d $6(12 - r)$

e $3r + t$ f $3(r + t)$ g $\dfrac{t}{r}$ h $r^2 - t$.

3 Given that $k = -6$ and $m = -8$, work out the value of:

   a $k + m$ **b** $k - m$ **c** $m - k$ **d** $3k$.

4 **a**   Show that the perimeter of this shape is $2x + 2y + 18$ cm.

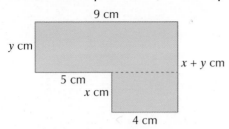

   b   Work out the perimeter, if $x = 3.4$ and $y = 2.8$.

   c   The shape is divided into two rectangles. Work out an expression for the area of each rectangle.

   d   Write down a formula for the area, a cm², of the whole shape.

   e   Find the value of a, if $x = 3.4$ and $y = 2.8$.

5 The width of this rectangle is w cm and the length is $w + 1$ cm.

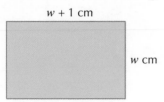

   a   Work out the perimeter, if $w = 10$.

   b   Write down, as simply as possible, a formula for the perimeter, p cm, of the rectangle.

   c   Work out the value of p, if $w = 30$.

   d   Work out the area, if $w = 10$.

   e   Write down a formula for the area, a cm², of the rectangle.

6 Copy and complete these number walls.

Simplify each expression as much as possible.

a 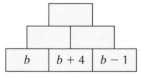   **b** 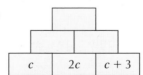   **c**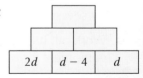

7 Here are three cards, each with an algebraic expression on it.

   a   Find the sum of the first two expressions.

   b   Find the sum of the second and third expressions.

   c   Show that the sum of the three expressions is $6(x + 2)$.

Problem solving
Winter sports

You can hire equipment for skiing and snowboarding.

The cost depends on the number of days for which you want to hire the equipment.

A hire company uses these formulae to work out the cost.

	Skiing	Snowboarding
Adults	$C = 8 + 17D$	$C = 9 + 23D$
Children	$C = 4 + 9D$	$C = 6 + 12D$

C is the cost in pounds.
D is the number of days of hire.

1 Work out the cost of snowboarding for one adult, for five days.

2 Work out the cost of skiing for one child, for four days.

3 Work out the difference between the costs of skiing and of snowboarding for one adult, for seven days.

4 Work out the total cost for a family of two adults and two children to hire skiing equipment for eight days.

5 a Copy and complete this table.

Number of days	6	7	8	9	10
Skiing hire for one adult (£)					

b What is the extra cost for one extra day's hire?

6 A group of 15 children are hiring equipment for three days.
Five of them are skiing and the rest are snowboarding.
Work out the total cost for this group.

7 a Draw axes like this on graph paper.

b Plot crosses to show the cost of ski hire for one adult for from one to ten days. One cross has been plotted for you. You will find some of the costs you need in your table from Q5.

c Draw a dashed line through your ten points. It should be a straight line.

d On the same graph, plot and join crosses to show the cost of ski hire for one child.

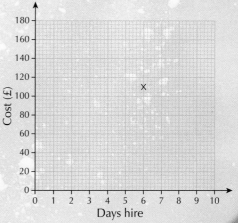

8 Fractions

This chapter is going to show you:

- how to find equivalent fractions
- how to write a fraction in its simplest form
- how to add and subtract fractions with the same and different denominators
- how to convert a simple improper fraction to a mixed number
- how to convert a mixed number into an improper fraction
- how to add and subtract mixed numbers with the same and different denominators.

You should already know:

- a common multiple of two numbers is a number that they both divide into, without leaving a remainder
- how to recognise and use simple fractions
- how to compare and order fractions with the same denominator.

About this chapter

For thousands of years the fraction system used in Europe was based on the ancient Egyptian one. Egyptian fractions were all unitary fractions, that means they only had 1 as a numerator, for example, $\frac{1}{2}$, $\frac{1}{4}$, $\frac{1}{6}$. Big fractions were written as unitary fractions added together, for example, $\frac{3}{4}$ would be $\frac{1}{2} + \frac{1}{4}$.

The fractions $\frac{1}{2}$, $\frac{1}{4}$, $\frac{1}{8}$, $\frac{1}{16}$ and $\frac{1}{64}$ were sacred. They were linked to the Eye of the Horus, an Egyptian god, and were all used as measures for grain. You will have a chance to try Egyptian fractions in this chapter!

8.1 Equivalent fractions

Learning objectives

- To find simple equivalent fractions
- To write fractions in their simplest form

In the fraction $\frac{3}{8}$, the number on the top, 3, is the **numerator** and the number on the bottom, 8, is the **denominator**.

The term **equivalent** means 'of equal value'. You can find **equivalent fractions** by multiplying the numerator and the denominator by the same number.

For example: $\frac{1}{2} = \frac{2}{4} = \frac{3}{6}$ multiplying top and bottom by 2, 3, ...

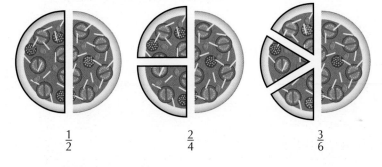

$$\frac{1}{2} \qquad \frac{2}{4} \qquad \frac{3}{6}$$

You can also find equivalent fractions if you can divide the numerator and denominator by the same number.

For example: $\frac{4}{8} = \frac{1}{2}$ dividing top and bottom by 4.

$$\frac{4}{8}$$

Example 1

Fill in the missing number in each of these pairs of equivalent fractions.

a $\frac{1}{3} = \frac{\square}{15}$ **b** $\frac{5}{8} = \frac{\square}{32}$ **c** $\frac{5}{9} = \frac{15}{\square}$

a Multiply top and bottom by 5: $\frac{1 \times 5}{3 \times 5} = \frac{5}{15}$

b Multiply top and bottom by 4: $\frac{5 \times 4}{8 \times 4} = \frac{20}{32}$

c Multiply top and bottom by 3: $\frac{5 \times 3}{9 \times 3} = \frac{15}{27}$

A fraction is in its **simplest form** if you cannot divide both numerator and denominator by any whole number, other than 1. If you are asked to **simplify** a fraction it means finding its simplest form.

Example 2

Write each of these fractions in its simplest form.

a $\frac{6}{8}$ **b** $\frac{9}{15}$ **c** $\frac{40}{60}$

a Divide top and bottom by 2: $\frac{6 \div 2}{8 \div 2} = \frac{3}{4}$

b Divide top and bottom by 3: $\frac{9 \div 3}{15 \div 3} = \frac{3}{5}$

c Divide top and bottom by 20: $\frac{40 \div 20}{60 \div 20} = \frac{2}{3}$

Or divide by 10 and then divide by 2: $\frac{40 \div 10}{60 \div 10} = \frac{4}{6}$ and $\frac{4 \div 2}{6 \div 2} = \frac{2}{3}$

Exercise 8A

1 Copy and complete each series of equivalent fractions.

a $\frac{1}{2} = \frac{2}{\square} = \frac{\square}{6} = \frac{8}{\square} = \frac{\square}{20} = \frac{\square}{150}$

b $\frac{3}{4} = \frac{6}{\square} = \frac{\square}{12} = \frac{12}{\square} = \frac{\square}{40} = \frac{\square}{160}$

 2 Here is part of a multiplication table.

4	8	12	16	20	24
5	10	15	20	25	30
6	12	18	24	30	36

Use the rows in the table to write fractions that are equivalent to each of these fractions.

a $\frac{4}{5}$ **b** $\frac{5}{6}$

(MR) 3 Look again at the fractions in question **1a**.

What is the connection between the numerator and the denominator in each one?

4 Look at the fractions listed here.

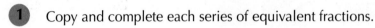

$\frac{3}{9}$ $\frac{14}{42}$ $\frac{2}{10}$ $\frac{25}{75}$ $\frac{45}{90}$ $\frac{24}{48}$ $\frac{4}{8}$ $\frac{16}{32}$ $\frac{3}{12}$ $\frac{22}{88}$ $\frac{50}{100}$ $\frac{1}{4}$

$\frac{60}{300}$ $\frac{1}{5}$ $\frac{10}{20}$ $\frac{3}{15}$ $\frac{60}{240}$ $\frac{30}{90}$ $\frac{15}{45}$ $\frac{4}{16}$ $\frac{20}{100}$ $\frac{7}{20}$ $\frac{4}{20}$ $\frac{27}{54}$

$\frac{22}{44}$ $\frac{5}{15}$ $\frac{12}{48}$ $\frac{1}{3}$ $\frac{8}{24}$ $\frac{12}{60}$ $\frac{2}{8}$ $\frac{16}{80}$ $\frac{1}{2}$ $\frac{35}{70}$ $\frac{15}{60}$ $\frac{100}{400}$

Write down all the fractions that are equivalent each of these fractions.

a $\frac{1}{2}$ **b** $\frac{1}{3}$ **c** $\frac{1}{4}$ **d** $\frac{1}{5}$

5 Fill in the missing number in each set of equivalent fractions.

a $\dfrac{2}{3} = \dfrac{\square}{9}$

b $\dfrac{3}{8} = \dfrac{\square}{16}$

c $\dfrac{5}{9} = \dfrac{\square}{27}$

d $\dfrac{2}{5} = \dfrac{\square}{15}$

e $\dfrac{3}{7} = \dfrac{\square}{28}$

f $\dfrac{4}{9} = \dfrac{\square}{36}$

g $\dfrac{1}{5} = \dfrac{\square}{25}$

h $\dfrac{2}{11} = \dfrac{14}{\square}$

i $\dfrac{4}{9} = \dfrac{20}{\square}$

6 Write each fraction in its simplest form.

a $\dfrac{4}{12}$ **b** $\dfrac{6}{9}$ **c** $\dfrac{14}{21}$ **d** $\dfrac{15}{20}$ **e** $\dfrac{18}{20}$ **f** $\dfrac{20}{50}$

g $\dfrac{8}{24}$ **h** $\dfrac{6}{12}$ **i** $\dfrac{4}{24}$ **j** $\dfrac{12}{20}$ **k** $\dfrac{16}{24}$ **l** $\dfrac{25}{35}$

m $\dfrac{6}{14}$ **n** $\dfrac{12}{9}$ **o** $\dfrac{18}{27}$ **p** $\dfrac{45}{20}$ **q** $\dfrac{28}{20}$ **r** $\dfrac{120}{40}$

(PS) 7 There are 20 fractions in the sequence: $\dfrac{1}{20}, \dfrac{2}{20}, \dfrac{3}{20}, \dfrac{4}{20}, \ldots, \dfrac{20}{20}$.

How many of them cannot be cancelled to a simpler form?

(PS) 8 This compass rose has eight divisions around its face.
What fraction of a turn takes you from:

a NW to SW clockwise

b E to S anticlockwise

c NE to S clockwise

d S to NE anticlockwise

e W to SE clockwise

f N to NW clockwise?

Write your fractions in their simplest form.

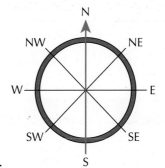

Problem solving: Shaded fraction

What fraction of this shape is shaded?
Give your fraction in its simplest form.

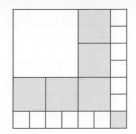

8.2 Comparing fractions

Learning objective

• To compare and order two fractions

You can compare fractions to each other, in terms of size. For example, $\frac{6}{8}$ is equivalent to $\frac{3}{4}$ but $\frac{1}{2}$ is bigger than $\frac{1}{4}$.

You can use a **fraction wall** to compare and order fractions.

$\frac{1}{8}$	$\frac{1}{8}$	$\frac{1}{8}$	$\frac{1}{8}$	$\frac{1}{8}$	$\frac{1}{8}$	$\frac{1}{8}$	$\frac{1}{8}$
$\frac{1}{7}$	$\frac{1}{7}$	$\frac{1}{7}$	$\frac{1}{7}$	$\frac{1}{7}$	$\frac{1}{7}$	$\frac{1}{7}$	
$\frac{1}{6}$	$\frac{1}{6}$	$\frac{1}{6}$	$\frac{1}{6}$	$\frac{1}{6}$	$\frac{1}{6}$		
$\frac{1}{5}$	$\frac{1}{5}$	$\frac{1}{5}$	$\frac{1}{5}$	$\frac{1}{5}$			
$\frac{1}{4}$	$\frac{1}{4}$	$\frac{1}{4}$	$\frac{1}{4}$				
$\frac{1}{3}$	$\frac{1}{3}$	$\frac{1}{3}$					
$\frac{1}{2}$	$\frac{1}{2}$						
1							

Example 3

Which is bigger, $\frac{2}{5}$ or $\frac{3}{8}$?

Look at the fraction wall.

Compare the eighths and the fifths.

$\frac{1}{8}$	$\frac{1}{8}$	$\frac{1}{8}$	$\frac{1}{8}$	$\frac{1}{8}$	$\frac{1}{8}$	$\frac{1}{8}$	$\frac{1}{8}$
$\frac{1}{5}$	$\frac{1}{5}$	$\frac{1}{5}$	$\frac{1}{5}$	$\frac{1}{5}$			

You should see that the region for two-fifths is slightly larger than the region for three-eighths.

This means that $\frac{2}{5}$ is larger than $\frac{3}{8}$.

Exercise 8B

1 Use the fraction wall to write down fractions that are equivalent to:

  a $\frac{1}{2}$ **b** $\frac{1}{4}$ **c** $\frac{2}{3}$ **d** $\frac{3}{4}$

2 Refer to the fraction wall opposite.

  Write the correct sign (<, = or >) between the fractions in each pair.

  a $\frac{2}{7} > \frac{1}{5}$ **b** $\frac{3}{8} \cdots \frac{1}{3}$ **c** $\frac{3}{4} \cdots \frac{6}{8}$ **d** $\frac{1}{2} \cdots \frac{4}{7}$

  e $\frac{2}{8} \cdots \frac{1}{4}$ **f** $\frac{3}{7} \cdots \frac{1}{3}$ **g** $\frac{3}{5} \cdots \frac{2}{3}$ **h** $\frac{1}{2} \cdots \frac{5}{8}$

  i $\frac{5}{8} \cdots \frac{3}{5}$ **j** $\frac{3}{6} \cdots \frac{1}{2}$ **k** $\frac{5}{7} \cdots \frac{3}{4}$ **l** $\frac{2}{3} \cdots \frac{4}{6}$

3 Refer to the fraction wall opposite.

  Work out a fraction that lies between the fractions in each pair.

  a $\frac{1}{4}$ and $\frac{1}{6}$ **b** $\frac{1}{3}$ and $\frac{1}{5}$ **c** $\frac{2}{8}$ and $\frac{2}{6}$

  d $\frac{2}{5}$ and $\frac{1}{2}$ **e** $\frac{4}{6}$ and $\frac{6}{8}$ **f** $\frac{5}{7}$ and $\frac{4}{5}$

4 Rewrite each pair of fractions as fractions with the same denominator.

  Then circle the smaller fraction.

  a $\frac{1}{3}$ and $\frac{4}{6}$ **b** $\frac{4}{6}$ and $\frac{7}{12}$ **c** $\frac{3}{4}$ and $\frac{5}{8}$

  d $\frac{1}{2}$ and $\frac{3}{5}$ **e** $\frac{2}{6}$ and $\frac{3}{8}$ **f** $\frac{5}{6}$ and $\frac{3}{4}$

(PS) 5 Refer to the fraction wall opposite.

  Work out the missing fractions to complete these statements.

  a $\square$ is twice $\frac{1}{8}$ **b** $\frac{1}{6}$ is half of $\square$ **c** $\frac{3}{4}$ is twice $\square$

  d $\frac{1}{2}$ is four times $\square$ **e** $\frac{1}{6}$ is one-third of $\square$ **f** $\square$ is half of $\frac{2}{7}$

(MR) 6 Decide which of the fractions in each pair is larger.

  Use the fraction wall opposite to help you, if you need to.

  a $\frac{1}{6}$ and $\frac{1}{3}$ **b** $\frac{1}{4}$ and $\frac{3}{8}$ **c** $\frac{3}{5}$ and $\frac{3}{8}$

  d $\frac{3}{4}$ and $\frac{5}{6}$ **e** $\frac{3}{7}$ and $\frac{5}{8}$ **f** $\frac{4}{7}$ and $\frac{1}{2}$

7 Rewrite each pair of fractions as fractions with the same denominator, then decide which is bigger.

    a $\frac{1}{2}$ and $\frac{2}{5}$ **b** $\frac{1}{4}$ and $\frac{5}{8}$ **c** $\frac{2}{3}$ and $\frac{7}{9}$

    d $\frac{7}{12}$ and $\frac{3}{4}$ **e** $\frac{8}{15}$ and $\frac{3}{5}$ **f** $\frac{3}{16}$ and $\frac{1}{4}$

Problem solving: Choose two numbers

A Choose two of the numbers on these six cards to make a fraction that is equivalent to $\frac{1}{4}$.

B Now choose two of the numbers to make a fraction that is less than 1 but greater than $\frac{3}{4}$.

8.3 Adding and subtracting fractions

Learning objectives

- To add and subtract fractions with the same denominator
- To add and subtract fractions with different denominators

<table>
<tr><td>Key words</td></tr>
<tr><td>addition</td></tr>
<tr><td>subtraction</td></tr>
</table>

Fractions with the same denominator

Look at this fraction **addition**.

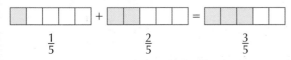

This addition is simple because both shapes are cut into pieces that are the same size, so the fractions have the same denominator. You just add together the numerators.

Example 4

Work these out.   **a** $\frac{1}{7} + \frac{3}{7}$ **b** $\frac{3}{8} + \frac{1}{8}$ **c** $\frac{1}{3} + \frac{1}{3} + \frac{1}{3}$

In each addition, the denominators are the same, so add the numerators.

a $\frac{1}{7} + \frac{3}{7} = \frac{4}{7}$

b $\frac{3}{8} + \frac{1}{8} = \frac{4}{8} = \frac{1}{2}$ The answer has been simplified.

c $\frac{1}{3} + \frac{1}{3} + \frac{1}{3} = \frac{3}{3} = 1$ The answer is a whole number.

Subtraction of fractions with the same denominator works the same way.

Example 5

Work these out.   **a** $\frac{5}{9} - \frac{1}{9}$ **b** $\frac{3}{8} - \frac{1}{8}$

In each subtraction, the denominators are the same, so subtract the numerators.

a $\frac{5}{9} - \frac{1}{9} = \frac{4}{9}$

b $\frac{3}{8} - \frac{1}{8} = \frac{2}{8} = \frac{1}{4}$ The answer has been simplified.

Exercise 8C

1 Add each pair of fractions. Simplify where necessary.

    a $\frac{1}{3} + \frac{1}{3}$ **b** $\frac{2}{5} + \frac{1}{5}$ **c** $\frac{1}{7} + \frac{2}{7}$ **d** $\frac{1}{4} + \frac{1}{4}$

    e $\frac{1}{5} + \frac{3}{5}$ **f** $\frac{3}{8} + \frac{3}{8}$ **g** $\frac{5}{6} + \frac{1}{6}$ **h** $\frac{2}{9} + \frac{1}{9}$

2 Complete these subtractions of fractions. Simplify where necessary.

    a $\frac{2}{3} - \frac{1}{3}$ **b** $\frac{2}{5} - \frac{1}{5}$ **c** $\frac{2}{7} - \frac{1}{7}$ **d** $\frac{3}{4} - \frac{1}{4}$

    e $\frac{3}{5} - \frac{1}{5}$ **f** $\frac{5}{8} - \frac{1}{8}$ **g** $\frac{5}{6} - \frac{1}{6}$ **h** $\frac{5}{9} - \frac{2}{9}$

3 Work these out.

    a $\frac{3}{7} + \frac{2}{7}$ **b** $\frac{3}{11} + \frac{4}{11}$ **c** $\frac{3}{5} + \frac{1}{5}$ **d** $\frac{7}{13} + \frac{3}{13}$

    e $\frac{7}{11} - \frac{2}{11}$ **f** $\frac{4}{9} - \frac{2}{9}$ **g** $\frac{3}{7} - \frac{2}{7}$ **h** $\frac{3}{5} - \frac{1}{5}$

4 Work out each of these. Simplify your answers to the lowest terms.

    a $\frac{3}{8} + \frac{1}{8}$ **b** $\frac{1}{12} + \frac{5}{12}$ **c** $\frac{3}{10} + \frac{1}{10}$ **d** $\frac{7}{15} + \frac{2}{15}$

    e $\frac{4}{9} - \frac{1}{9}$ **f** $\frac{3}{10} - \frac{1}{10}$ **g** $\frac{5}{6} - \frac{1}{6}$ **h** $\frac{7}{12} - \frac{5}{12}$

5 Add the fractions. Simplify to the lowest terms.

    a $\frac{1}{3} + \frac{1}{3}$ **b** $\frac{3}{10} + \frac{3}{10}$ **c** $\frac{1}{9} + \frac{2}{9}$ **d** $\frac{5}{12} + \frac{1}{12}$

(MR) **6** Matt, Dave and Richard cut a cake into eighths. Matt ate one piece, while Dave and Richard ate three pieces each. What fraction of the cake was left?

7 Laura lives $\frac{1}{6}$ km from the shops. How far is it to walk from her house to the shops and back? Simplify your answer.

8 A bread recipe needs $\frac{1}{5}$ kg of wholemeal flour and $\frac{3}{5}$ kg of white flour. How much flour is needed altogether?

Fractions with different denominators

Look at this fraction addition.

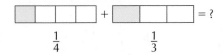

This addition is more difficult because, although the whole shapes are the same size, they have been cut into different-sized pieces. This means that the fractions have different denominators. Before you can add or subtract fractions, you need to find a common multiple of the denominators.

Remember that a common multiple of two numbers is a number that is in the list of multiples of each number.

It is a good idea to use the smallest of these common multiples, to keep the numbers low.

When you have found a common multiple, you then need to change each fraction to its equivalent fraction, with this common multiple as its denominator. You do this by multiplying their numerators by the same number as the denominators.

Example 6

Work these out.

a $\frac{1}{4} + \frac{1}{3}$ **b** $\frac{7}{9} - \frac{2}{5}$

a $\frac{1}{4} + \frac{1}{3}$

$= \frac{3}{12} + \frac{4}{12}$ Convert to equivalent fractions, 12 is a common multiple of 3 and 4.

$= \frac{7}{12}$ Add the fractions.

b $\frac{7}{9} - \frac{2}{5}$

$= \frac{35}{45} - \frac{18}{45}$ Convert to equivalent fractions, a common multiple of 9 and 5 is 45.

$= \frac{17}{45}$ Subtract the fractions.

Exercise 8D

1 Find a common multiple of each pair of numbers.

   a 3 and 4   **b** 5 and 6   **c** 3 and 5   **d** 2 and 3

   e 4 and 5   **f** 2 and 4   **g** 6 and 9   **h** 4 and 6

2 Add these fractions. Use your answers from Question **1** to help.

   a $\frac{2}{3} + \frac{1}{4}$ **b** $\frac{2}{5} + \frac{1}{6}$ **c** $\frac{1}{3} + \frac{2}{5}$ **d** $\frac{1}{3} + \frac{1}{2}$

   e $\frac{1}{5} + \frac{1}{4}$ **f** $\frac{1}{2} + \frac{1}{4}$ **g** $\frac{5}{6} + \frac{1}{9}$ **h** $\frac{1}{6} + \frac{1}{4}$

(3) Subtract these fractions.

a $\dfrac{1}{3} - \dfrac{1}{4}$ **b** $\dfrac{2}{5} - \dfrac{1}{6}$ **c** $\dfrac{2}{5} - \dfrac{1}{3}$ **d** $\dfrac{1}{2} - \dfrac{1}{3}$

e $\dfrac{2}{5} - \dfrac{1}{4}$ **f** $\dfrac{1}{2} - \dfrac{1}{4}$ **g** $\dfrac{5}{6} - \dfrac{1}{9}$ **h** $\dfrac{5}{6} - \dfrac{3}{4}$

(4) Convert each set of fractions to equivalent fractions with a common denominator. Then work out the answer, simplifying if appropriate.

a $\dfrac{1}{3} + \dfrac{1}{4}$ **b** $\dfrac{1}{6} + \dfrac{1}{3}$ **c** $\dfrac{3}{10} + \dfrac{1}{4}$ **d** $\dfrac{1}{8} + \dfrac{5}{6}$

e $\dfrac{4}{15} + \dfrac{3}{10}$ **f** $\dfrac{7}{8} + \dfrac{5}{6}$ **g** $\dfrac{7}{12} + \dfrac{1}{4}$ **h** $\dfrac{3}{4} + \dfrac{1}{3} + \dfrac{1}{2}$

i $\dfrac{2}{3} - \dfrac{1}{8}$ **j** $\dfrac{5}{6} - \dfrac{1}{3}$ **k** $\dfrac{3}{10} - \dfrac{1}{4}$ **l** $\dfrac{8}{9} - \dfrac{1}{6}$

m $\dfrac{4}{15} - \dfrac{1}{10}$ **n** $\dfrac{7}{8} - \dfrac{5}{6}$ **o** $\dfrac{7}{12} - \dfrac{1}{4}$ **p** $\dfrac{3}{4} + \dfrac{1}{3} - \dfrac{1}{2}$

(5) Convert each set of fractions to equivalent fractions with a common denominator. Then work out the answer. Simplify if appropriate.

a $\dfrac{1}{8} + \dfrac{3}{5}$ **b** $\dfrac{5}{7} + \dfrac{1}{4}$ **c** $\dfrac{3}{14} + \dfrac{3}{8}$ **d** $\dfrac{1}{9} + \dfrac{5}{6}$

e $\dfrac{5}{12} + \dfrac{3}{10}$ **f** $\dfrac{3}{8} + \dfrac{1}{6}$ **g** $\dfrac{7}{12} + \dfrac{1}{8}$ **h** $\dfrac{1}{3} + \dfrac{5}{12}$

i $\dfrac{3}{5} - \dfrac{1}{8}$ **j** $\dfrac{5}{7} - \dfrac{1}{4}$ **k** $\dfrac{1}{4} - \dfrac{3}{16}$ **l** $\dfrac{5}{9} - \dfrac{1}{6}$

m $\dfrac{5}{12} - \dfrac{1}{10}$ **n** $\dfrac{7}{8} - \dfrac{5}{16}$ **o** $\dfrac{7}{12} - \dfrac{1}{8}$ **p** $\dfrac{3}{4} + \dfrac{3}{16} - \dfrac{3}{8}$

(6) A magazine reserves $\frac{1}{3}$ of its pages for advertising, it uses $\frac{1}{12}$ for letters and the rest for articles.

What fraction of the pages is for articles?

(7) A survey of pupils showed that $\frac{1}{5}$ of them walked to school, $\frac{2}{3}$ came by bus and the rest came by car.

What fraction came by car?

 (8) A farmer plants $\frac{2}{7}$ of his land with wheat and $\frac{3}{8}$ with maize. The rest is used for cattle.

a What fraction of the land is used to grow crops?

b What fraction is used for cattle?

 (9) John gives $\frac{1}{2}$ his pocket money to Sarah and $\frac{1}{3}$ of it to Dave.

a What fraction of his pocket money has he given away?

b What fraction does he have left?

 (10) In the fridge there is a carton of milk containing $\frac{2}{5}$ of a litre. There is also another carton of milk containing $\frac{3}{4}$ of a litre. Harry drinks $\frac{1}{3}$ of a litre of milk from one of the cartons.

How much milk is left in the fridge altogether?

8.4 Mixed numbers and improper fractions

Learning objectives

- To convert mixed numbers to improper fractions
- To convert improper fractions to mixed numbers

Key words

convert
improper fraction
mixed number

Here are five pizza halves.

Altogether they make $2\frac{1}{2}$ pizzas. This is 5 halves or $\frac{5}{2} = 2\frac{1}{2}$.

This diagram shows the **mixed number** $3\frac{2}{5}$.

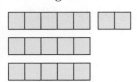

Each whole shape is divided into fifths. Altogether there are 17 fifths.

This is written as $\frac{17}{5}$. So $3\frac{2}{5}$ is the same as $\frac{17}{5}$.

Fractions such as $\frac{17}{5}$ are called **improper fractions** because the numerator is bigger than the denominator.

You can **convert** (change) improper fractions to mixed numbers and mixed numbers to improper fractions.

Example 7

Change $3\frac{1}{4}$ to an improper fraction.

The mixed number has $\frac{1}{4}$ in it so change to quarters.

3 whole ones = 3 × 4 = 12 quarters

So $3\frac{1}{4}$ = 12 + 1 quarters = 13 quarters

$3\frac{1}{4} = \frac{13}{4}$

Example 8

Convert these mixed numbers to improper fractions.

a $2\frac{1}{3}$ **b** $5\frac{3}{8}$

a There are 3 thirds in 1 whole so there are 2 × 3 = 6 thirds in 2 wholes.

This gives a total of 6 + 1 = 7 thirds in $2\frac{1}{3}$.

Therefore, $2\frac{1}{3} = \frac{7}{3}$.

b There are 8 eighths in 1 whole.

Therefore there are 5 × 8 = 40 eighths in 5 wholes.

This gives a total of 40 + 3 = 43 eighths in $5\frac{3}{8}$.

Therefore, $5\frac{3}{8} = \frac{43}{8}$.

Exercise 8E

1   **a**   How many sixths are there in 1?   **b**   How many sixths are there in 3?

     c   How many eighths are there in 1?   **d**   How many eighths are there in 4?

2   **a**   How many sixths are there in $3\frac{5}{6}$?   **b**   How many eighths are there in $4\frac{1}{2}$?

     c   How many tenths are there in $2\frac{3}{10}$?   **d**   How many ninths are there in $5\frac{7}{9}$?

3   Convert each mixed number to an improper fraction.

     a $1\frac{1}{4}$ **b** $2\frac{1}{2}$ **c** $3\frac{1}{6}$ **d** $4\frac{2}{7}$ **e** $5\frac{1}{8}$ **f** $2\frac{3}{5}$

     g $1\frac{7}{9}$ **h** $3\frac{3}{4}$ **i** $4\frac{2}{5}$ **j** $2\frac{3}{11}$ **k** $4\frac{5}{8}$ **l** $3\frac{2}{9}$

     m $1\frac{3}{4}$ **n** $1\frac{4}{5}$ **o** $2\frac{2}{3}$ **p** $2\frac{3}{4}$ **q** $3\frac{1}{6}$ **r** $3\frac{2}{3}$

MR **4**   Match the improper fractions to mixed numbers.

$\frac{5}{2}$ $\frac{7}{4}$ $\frac{7}{5}$ $\frac{11}{5}$

$2\frac{1}{2}$ $1\frac{2}{5}$ $1\frac{3}{4}$ $2\frac{1}{5}$

5 Write each improper fraction as a mixed number.

    a $\dfrac{5}{4}$ **b** $\dfrac{7}{2}$ **c** $\dfrac{11}{6}$ **d** $\dfrac{9}{2}$

    e $\dfrac{11}{8}$ **f** $\dfrac{10}{7}$ **g** $\dfrac{5}{3}$ **h** $\dfrac{16}{5}$

6 Convert each improper fraction to a mixed number.

    a $\dfrac{9}{4}$ **b** $\dfrac{7}{3}$ **c** $\dfrac{11}{7}$ **d** $\dfrac{8}{3}$ **e** $\dfrac{8}{7}$ **f** $\dfrac{13}{8}$

    g $\dfrac{10}{3}$ **h** $\dfrac{14}{3}$ **i** $\dfrac{14}{5}$ **j** $\dfrac{17}{6}$ **k** $\dfrac{17}{5}$ **l** $\dfrac{21}{5}$

7 Write each of these as a mixed number in its simplest form.

    a seven-thirds   **b** sixteen-sevenths   **c** twelve-fifths   **d** nine-halves

    e $\dfrac{20}{7}$ **f** $\dfrac{24}{5}$ **g** $\dfrac{13}{3}$ **h** $\dfrac{19}{8}$

    i $\dfrac{146}{12}$ **j** $\dfrac{78}{10}$ **k** $\dfrac{52}{12}$ **l** $\dfrac{102}{9}$

8 Write each improper fraction as a mixed number in its simplest form.

    a $\dfrac{14}{12}$ **b** $\dfrac{15}{9}$ **c** $\dfrac{24}{21}$ **d** $\dfrac{35}{20}$ **e** $\dfrac{28}{20}$ **f** $\dfrac{70}{50}$

    g $\dfrac{28}{24}$ **h** $\dfrac{26}{12}$ **i** $\dfrac{44}{24}$ **j** $\dfrac{32}{10}$ **k** $\dfrac{36}{24}$ **l** $\dfrac{75}{35}$

(PS) **9** Sort the numbers on these cards into order, from smallest to largest.

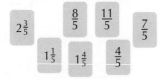

Challenge: Sharing fractions

Change each mixed number to an improper fraction to answer these questions.

A Share $3\frac{3}{5}$ kg of sand equally between three bags.

B Jack has $7\frac{1}{2}$ chocolate bars.

   If he shares the chocolate equally among five people, how much will each person get?

C A plank of wood is $5\frac{1}{4}$ metres long. It is cut three into equal pieces.

   How long is each piece?

8.5 Adding and subtracting mixed numbers

Learning objectives

- To add two mixed numbers
- To subtract one mixed number from another

Adding mixed numbers

When you add two mixed numbers you can add the whole-number parts and the fraction parts separately. Then you can combine the two parts, to find your final answer.

Example 9

Add these mixed numbers. **a** $3\frac{1}{2} + 1\frac{1}{4}$ **b** $2\frac{3}{4} + 2\frac{5}{8}$

a $3\frac{1}{2} + 1\frac{1}{4} = 3 + \frac{1}{2} + 1 + \frac{1}{4}$ Think of $3\frac{1}{2}$ as $3 + \frac{1}{2}$ and $1\frac{1}{4}$ as $1 + \frac{1}{4}$.

      $= 3 + 1 + \frac{1}{2} + \frac{1}{4}$ Add the whole numbers and the fractions separately.

      $= 4\frac{3}{4}$ $\frac{1}{2} + \frac{1}{4} = \frac{2}{4} + \frac{1}{4} = \frac{3}{4}$

b $2\frac{3}{4} + 2\frac{5}{8} = 2 + \frac{3}{4} + 2 + \frac{5}{8}$

      $= 4 + \frac{3}{4} + \frac{5}{8}$

Now $\frac{3}{4} + \frac{5}{8} = \frac{6}{8} + \frac{5}{8}$

          $= \frac{11}{8}$

          $= 1\frac{3}{8}$ This is what to do if the fractions add to more than 1.

So $2\frac{3}{4} + 2\frac{5}{8} = 4 + 1\frac{3}{8}$

          $= 5\frac{3}{8}$

Exercise 8F

Write your answers in their simplest form.

1   Add the mixed numbers.

    a $1\frac{1}{3} + 2\frac{2}{3}$ **b** $2\frac{1}{6} + \frac{5}{6}$ **c** $4\frac{3}{10} + 2\frac{1}{10}$ **d** $3\frac{1}{9} + 5\frac{2}{9}$

    e $3\frac{4}{15} + 2\frac{7}{15}$ **f** $2\frac{7}{9} + 3\frac{1}{9}$ **g** $4\frac{5}{12} + 1\frac{1}{12}$ **h** $3\frac{3}{7} + 3\frac{2}{7}$

2 Add the mixed numbers.

    a $\frac{1}{2} + 1\frac{1}{2}$ **b** $1\frac{1}{8} + \frac{3}{8}$ **c** $2\frac{2}{8} + 1\frac{5}{8}$ **d** $1\frac{1}{2} + \frac{3}{8}$

    e $1\frac{5}{8} + 1\frac{1}{4}$ **f** $2\frac{1}{8} + 1\frac{1}{4}$ **g** $1\frac{3}{8} + 2\frac{3}{8}$ **h** $4\frac{3}{8} + 3\frac{1}{2}$

3 Add these mixed numbers.

    a $2\frac{3}{4} + \frac{1}{2}$ **b** $1\frac{1}{4} + 1\frac{7}{8}$ **c** $1\frac{5}{8} + 2\frac{1}{2}$ **d** $2\frac{3}{4} + 2\frac{3}{4}$

    e $4\frac{3}{4} + 3\frac{5}{8}$ **f** $1\frac{5}{6} + 3\frac{1}{3}$ **g** $1\frac{7}{10} + 2\frac{3}{5}$ **h** $1\frac{2}{3} + 3\frac{1}{2}$

    i $2\frac{1}{2} + 2\frac{7}{10}$ **j** $2\frac{5}{8} + 2\frac{5}{8}$ **k** $5\frac{1}{2} + \frac{2}{3}$ **l** $8\frac{3}{8} + 12\frac{3}{4}$

4 Sam watches two films. One lasts $1\frac{3}{4}$ hours and the other lasts $2\frac{1}{2}$ hours. How long do the two last altogether?

Subtracting mixed numbers

You can subtract mixed numbers in a similar way.

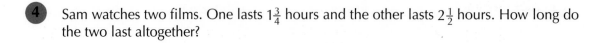

Example 10

Subtract these mixed numbers.   **a** $3\frac{1}{2} - 1\frac{1}{4}$ **b** $4\frac{1}{4} - 2\frac{5}{8}$

a $3\frac{1}{2} - 1\frac{1}{4} = 3 + \frac{1}{2} - 1 - \frac{1}{4}$ Compare this with Example 9a above.

       $= 3 - 1 + \frac{1}{2} - \frac{1}{4}$ Subtract the whole numbers and the fractions separately.

       $= 2\frac{1}{4}$ $3 - 1 = 2$ and $\frac{1}{2} - \frac{1}{4} = \frac{2}{4} - \frac{1}{4} = \frac{1}{4}$.

b $4\frac{1}{4} - 2\frac{5}{8} = 4 + \frac{1}{4} - 2 - \frac{5}{8}$

       $= 4 - 2 + \frac{1}{4} - \frac{5}{8}$

       $= 2 + \frac{1}{4} - \frac{5}{8}$

Now $\frac{1}{4} - \frac{5}{8} = \frac{2}{4} - \frac{5}{8}$

       $= -\frac{3}{8}$ A negative answer because $\frac{1}{4}$ is less than $\frac{5}{8}$.

This means that $4\frac{1}{4} - 2\frac{5}{8} = 2 - \frac{3}{8}$ Subtract the $\frac{3}{8}$ from 2.

       $= 1\frac{5}{8}$

An alternative method, that avoids negative fractions, is to write both numbers as improper fractions.

$4\frac{1}{4} - 2\frac{5}{8} = \frac{17}{4} - \frac{21}{8}$ $4 \times 4 + 1 = 17$ and $2 \times 8 + 5 = 21$

    $= \frac{34}{8} - \frac{21}{8}$ Change the quarters to eighths.

    $= \frac{13}{8}$

    $= 1\frac{5}{8}$

You can use either method.

Exercise 8G

Write your answers in their simplest form.

1 Subtract.

a $3\frac{5}{7} - 1\frac{2}{7}$ b $2\frac{5}{6} - \frac{1}{6}$ c $5\frac{9}{10} - 2\frac{3}{10}$ d $4\frac{8}{9} - 1\frac{2}{9}$

e $6\frac{4}{15} - 5\frac{2}{15}$ f $2\frac{7}{9} - 2\frac{4}{9}$ g $8\frac{11}{12} - 2\frac{5}{12}$ h $5\frac{9}{10} - 1\frac{3}{10}$

2 Subtract.

a $1\frac{5}{8} - \frac{1}{2}$ b $2\frac{1}{2} - 1\frac{1}{4}$ c $2\frac{7}{8} - 1\frac{5}{8}$ d $1\frac{7}{8} - \frac{1}{2}$

e $2\frac{3}{4} - 1\frac{3}{8}$ f $2\frac{7}{8} - 1\frac{1}{4}$ g $3\frac{3}{8} - 1\frac{1}{4}$ h $2\frac{7}{8} - 1\frac{3}{4}$

3 Subtract.

a $4\frac{1}{4} - 1\frac{3}{4}$ b $3\frac{1}{4} - 1\frac{1}{2}$ c $2\frac{1}{2} - \frac{5}{8}$ d $5\frac{1}{8} - 3\frac{1}{2}$

e $4\frac{1}{3} - 1\frac{1}{2}$ f $7 - 2\frac{5}{6}$ g $6\frac{1}{2} - 2\frac{3}{4}$ h $7\frac{1}{8} - 1\frac{5}{8}$

i $4\frac{1}{10} - 1\frac{1}{5}$ j $5\frac{1}{6} - 1\frac{2}{3}$ k $10\frac{1}{2} - 3\frac{3}{4}$ l $5\frac{1}{2} - 4\frac{2}{3}$

4 A flight is due to last $9\frac{1}{4}$ hours.

During the flight, Josie looks at her watch and sees that $3\frac{3}{4}$ hours have passed.
How much longer is it before the flight ends?

5 At birth, twins weighed $8\frac{3}{4}$ pounds and $7\frac{1}{2}$ pounds.
What is the difference between the amounts the twins weighed?

Activity: Illustrating calculations

This drawing illustrates the addition: $1\frac{3}{4} + 2\frac{5}{8} = 4\frac{3}{8}$.

 + =

$1\frac{3}{4}$ + $2\frac{5}{8}$ = $4\frac{3}{8}$

A Draw diagrams to illustrate these additions.

a $1\frac{1}{2} + 1\frac{7}{8}$ b $1\frac{5}{6} + 2\frac{2}{3}$

B Draw a diagram to illustrate $3\frac{1}{4} - 1\frac{7}{8}$.

Ready to progress?

 I can find simple equivalent fractions.

 I can find equivalent fractions, and compare fractions with different denominators.
I can write fractions in their simplest form.
I can add and subtract fractions with the same denominators.

 I can convert between mixed numbers and improper fractions.
I can add and subtract fractions with different denominators.
I can add two mixed numbers.
I can subtract one mixed number from another mixed number.

Review questions

1   Complete these equivalent fractions.

   a $\dfrac{2}{3} = \dfrac{\square}{12}$ b $\dfrac{4}{5} = \dfrac{20}{\square}$ c $\dfrac{7}{2} = \dfrac{\square}{10}$

2   Here are three fractions.

   $\dfrac{7}{10}$ $\dfrac{3}{4}$ $\dfrac{2}{3}$

   Which is the largest?

   Give a reason for your answer.

3   Here are four mixed numbers.

   $2\frac{7}{10}$ $1\frac{1}{4}$ $2\frac{1}{2}$ $1\frac{3}{5}$

   Copy the diagram and write each number in the correct box.

   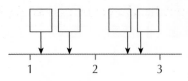

4   Add these fractions.

   Give each answer as a mixed number as simply as possible.

   a $\dfrac{5}{8} + \dfrac{7}{8}$ b $\dfrac{9}{10} + \dfrac{7}{10}$ c $\dfrac{5}{6} + \dfrac{5}{6}$

5   Here is a sequence.

   $\frac{2}{5}$, 1, $1\frac{3}{5}$, $2\frac{1}{5}$

   a   What is the rule for continuing the sequence?
   b   What is the next number in the sequence?

6 Look at these improper fractions.

$$\frac{9}{6} \quad \frac{4}{3} \quad \frac{24}{18} \quad \frac{18}{12} \quad \frac{8}{6} \quad \frac{12}{8} \quad \frac{25}{20} \quad \frac{16}{12}$$

    a Which ones are equivalent to $1\frac{1}{2}$?

    b Which ones are equivalent to $1\frac{1}{3}$?

    c One of the improper fractions is not equivalent to $1\frac{1}{2}$ or $1\frac{1}{3}$.

       Write it as a mixed number as simply as possible.

7 Work out the number that is halfway between the two numbers shown on each scale.

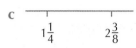

    a $\frac{1}{6} \qquad \frac{5}{9}$ **b** $\frac{1}{10} \qquad \frac{9}{20}$ **c** $1\frac{1}{4} \qquad 2\frac{3}{8}$

8 Add these numbers.

    a $\frac{3}{4} + \frac{3}{8}$ **b** $1\frac{1}{3} + 1\frac{1}{6}$ **c** $2\frac{5}{8} + 1\frac{1}{2}$ **d** $5\frac{1}{2} + 3\frac{1}{3}$

9 Subtract these numbers.

    a $5 - 3\frac{2}{5}$ **b** $4\frac{5}{8} - 1\frac{1}{4}$ **c** $2\frac{1}{2} - 1\frac{7}{8}$ **d** $6\frac{1}{5} - 2\frac{7}{10}$

10 Here is a sequence of numbers.

$$\frac{1}{4}, \frac{1}{2}, \frac{3}{4}, 1\frac{1}{4}, 2, 3\frac{1}{4}, 5\frac{1}{4}, \dots$$

    Each number after the first two is the sum of the two numbers before it.

    so $\frac{1}{4} + \frac{1}{2} = \frac{3}{4}$ and $\frac{1}{2} + \frac{3}{4} = 1\frac{1}{4}$ and $\frac{3}{4} + 1\frac{1}{4} = 2$.

    Work out the next two numbers in the sequence.

11 Work out the perimeter of this rectangle.

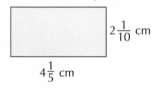

$2\frac{1}{10}$ cm

$4\frac{1}{5}$ cm

12 Jason is carrying two bags. He has one of mass $3\frac{1}{2}$ kg in one hand and one of mass $2\frac{2}{5}$ kg in the other hand.

    a What is the total mass of the two bags altogether?

    b What is the difference in mass between the two bags?

13 Work out the mode, median and range for this set of data.

    $14\frac{1}{2}$ kg $9\frac{1}{4}$ kg   15 kg $15\frac{1}{2}$ kg $14\frac{1}{2}$ kg $16\frac{3}{4}$ kg

14 Simplify this expression.

    $4\frac{1}{2}x + 3y + 2\frac{1}{2}x - 1\frac{1}{4}y$

Challenge

Fractional dissections

Task 1

This rectangle has 12 squares.
It is divided into three parts.

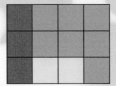

a Check that the red part is $\frac{1}{4}$, the yellow part is $\frac{1}{6}$ and the green part is $\frac{7}{12}$.

This shows that $\frac{1}{4} + \frac{1}{6} + \frac{7}{12} = 1$.

This is one way to write the whole rectangle as the sum of three fractions with different denominators (in this case 4, 6 and 12). We can call this a triple dissection of the rectangle.

b Draw a diagram to show that a different triple dissection of this rectangle is $\frac{3}{4} + \frac{1}{6} + \frac{1}{12}$.

c Find a third triple dissection of this rectangle.

Task 2

Now try drawing the triple dissections for each of these rectangles.
One is impossible. One has one solution. One has two solutions.

a   b    c

Task 3

Here is a rectangle with 18 squares.

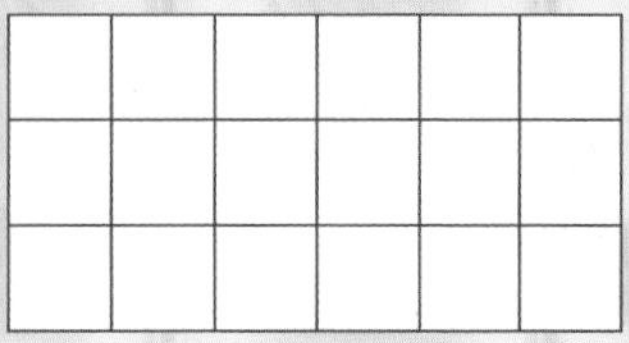

There are seven different triple dissections for this rectangle. Find them all.

Task 4

A unit fraction has a numerator of 1.

a This diagram shows one whole divided into six unit fractions.

What are they?

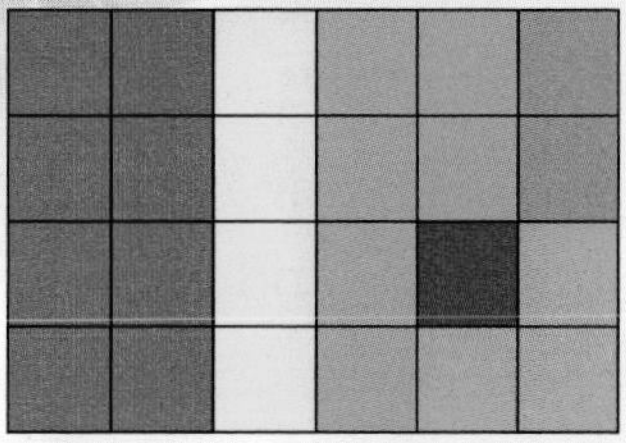

b This diagram shows one whole divided into seven unit fractions.

What are they?

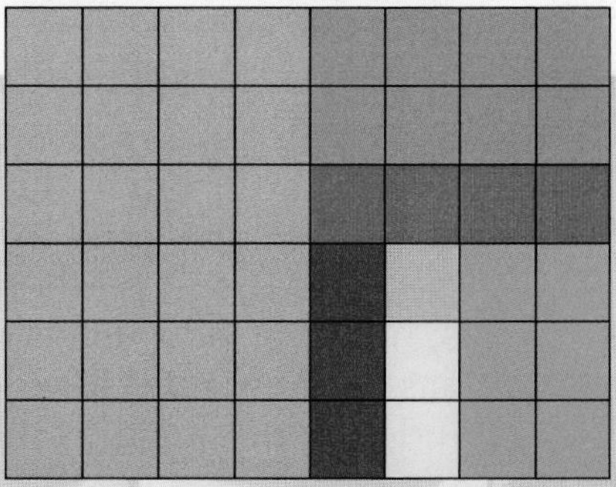

9

Angles

This chapter is going to show you:

- how to measure and draw angles
- how to calculate angles at a point, angles on a straight line and vertically opposite angles
- how to calculate angles in a triangle
- how to calculate angles in a quadrilateral
- how to recognise parallel, intersecting and perpendicular lines
- how to explain the geometrical properties of triangles and quadrilaterals.

You should already know:

- the names of the different types of angle
- the names of different triangles and quadrilaterals.

Introduction

Why does coloured light travel down glass-fibre optic tubes like these?

The answer is in angles. As it travels down the tube it is reflected back all the time from the sides instead of passing out through the glass. It has to hit them at a specific angle to do this, however, and this is called the critical angle. Fibre optics are now used for ultrafast telephone and broadband communications throughout the world. So that is one very important angle!

9.1 Measuring and drawing angles

Learning objectives

* To use a protractor to measure an angle
* To use a protractor to draw an angle

Key words	
acute angle	angle
degrees	obtuse angle
protractor	reflex angle
right angle	

When two lines meet at a point they form an **angle**.
An angle is measured in **degrees**.

To measure angles, you use a **protractor**.

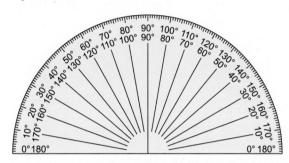

Notice that there are two scales on a protractor.

The outer scale goes from 0° to 180° and the inner one goes from 180° to 0°.

It is important that you use the correct scale.

When measuring or drawing an angle, always decide first whether it is an **acute angle** (less than 90°) or an **obtuse angle** (more than 90°).

The types of angle are shown below.

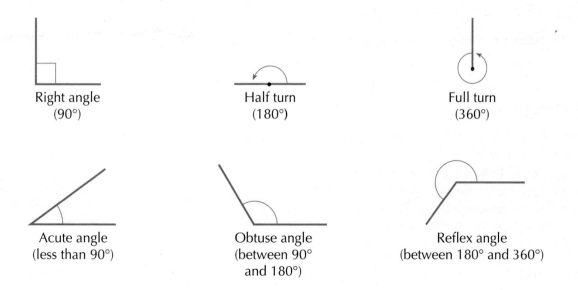

Right angle
(90°)

Half turn
(180°)

Full turn
(360°)

Acute angle
(less than 90°)

Obtuse angle
(between 90°
and 180°)

Reflex angle
(between 180° and 360°)

Example 1

Measure this angle.

First, decide whether the angle you are measuring is acute or obtuse.

This is an acute angle (less than 90°).

Place the centre of the protractor at the point of the angle, as in the diagram.

The two angles shown on the protractor scales are 60° and 120°.

Since you are measuring an acute angle, the angle is 60° (to the nearest degree).

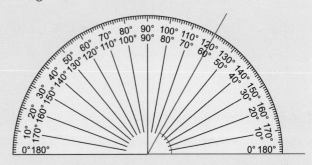

Example 2

Measure this angle.

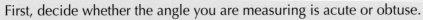

First, decide whether the angle you are measuring is acute or obtuse.

This is an obtuse angle (greater than 90°).

Place the centre of the protractor at the corner of the angle, as in the diagram.

The two angles shown on the protractor scales are 40° and 140°.

Since you are measuring an obtuse angle, the angle is 140° (to the nearest degree).

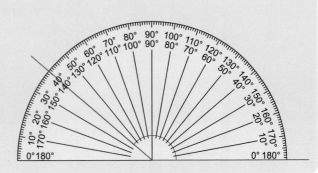

Example 3

Draw and label an angle of 70°.

First draw a line about 5 cm in length.

Place the middle of the protractor at one end of the line.

Put a mark on 70°, as it is an acute angle.

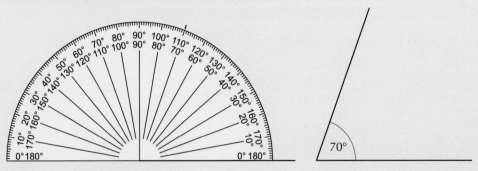

Then complete the angle.

Two other angles that you need to know about are:

- **right angles**, which are exactly 90°
- **reflex angles**, which are bigger than 180°.

Example 4

Measure this reflex angle.

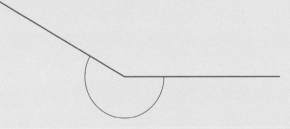

First, measure the inside or interior angle. This is an obtuse angle.

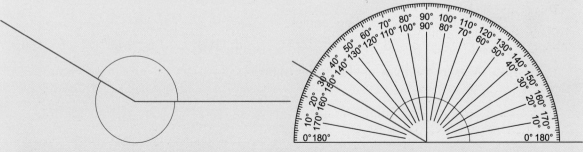

The two angles shown on the protractor scales are 30° and 150°.

Since you are measuring an obtuse angle, the angle is 150°.

You can find the size of the reflex angle by subtracting this angle from 360°.

The reflex angle is therefore 360° − 150°, which is 210° (to the nearest degree).

1 Measure each of these angles.
Give your answer to the nearest degree.

a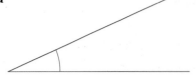

b

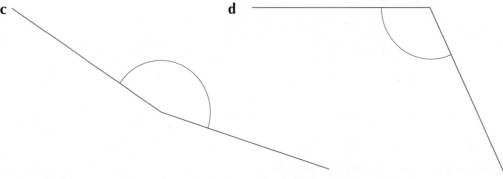
c d

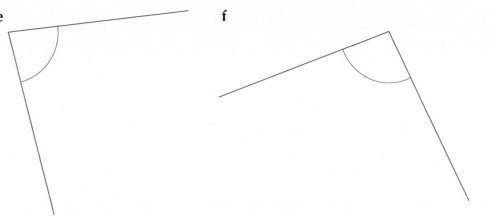
e f

2 Draw and label each of these angles.

    a 20°   **b** 35°   **c** 72°   **d** 100°   **e** 145°   **f** 168°

3 **a** Measure the three angles in this triangle.

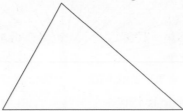

    b Add the three angles together.

4 Draw a triangle with an obtuse angle, similar to this one.

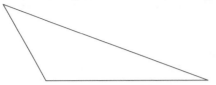

 a Measure the three angles in your triangle.

 b Add the three angles together.

 c You should now be able to complete this statement:

 In any triangle the sum of the three angles is always … .

5 Measure each of these reflex angles.

Give your answer to the nearest degree.

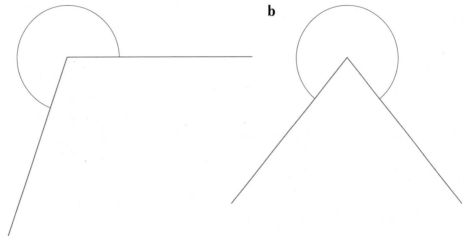

a

b

c

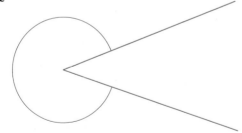

6 Draw and label each of these angles.

 a 220° **b** 258° **c** 300° **d** 347°

9.2 Calculating angles

Learning objectives

- To calculate angles at a point
- To calculate angles on a straight line
- To calculate opposite angles

You can **calculate** (work out) the unknown angles in a diagram from the information given.

Unknown angles are usually denoted by letters, such as $a, b, c, \ldots$.

Remember that diagrams are not usually drawn to scale.

Key words

angles at a point

angles on a straight line

calculate

opposite angles

right angles

vertically opposite angles

Right angles

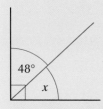

In the diagram, the square symbol means that the angle is 90° or a **right angle**.

Example 5

Calculate the size of the angle marked x.

48°

x

$x = 90° - 48°$

$x = 32°$

Angles at a point

Angles at a point add up to 360°.

Example 6

Calculate the size of the angle marked *a*.

The three angles add up to 360° so:

$a = 360° - 150° - 130°$

$a = 80°$

Angles on a straight line

Angles on a straight line add up to 180°.

Example 7

Calculate the size of the angle marked *b*.

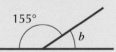

The two angles on a straight line add up to 180° so:

$b = 180° - 155°$

$b = 25°$

Vertically opposite angles

When two lines intersect, the **vertically opposite angles** are equal.

You will often see them simply called **opposite angles.**

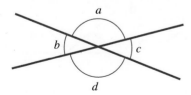

In this diagram:

- *a* and *d* are vertically opposite.
- *b* and *c* are vertically opposite.

    $a = d$ and $b = c$

Example 8

Calculate the sizes of the angles marked *d* and *e*.

Give reasons for your answers.

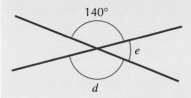

d = 140°   Opposite angles are equal.

Angles on a straight line = 180° so:

e = 180° − 140°

   = 40°

Exercise 9B

1. Work out the size of each unknown angle.

    a

    62°, *a*

    b

    43°, *b*

    c
    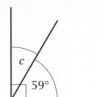
    c, 59°

    d
    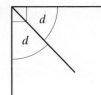
    d, *d*

2. Calculate the size of each unknown angle.

    a
    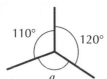
    110°, 120°, *a*

    b
    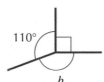
    110°, *b*

    c
    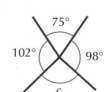
    75°, 102°, 98°, *c*

    d
    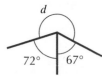
    d, 72°, 67°

3. Calculate the size of each unknown angle.

    a
    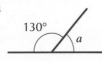
    130°, *a*

    b

    50°, *b*

    c
    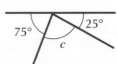
    75°, 25°, *c*

    d

    d, 49°

4. Calculate the size of each unknown angle.

    a
    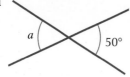
    a, 50°

    b

    138°, *b*

    c
    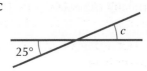
    c, 25°

    d

    d, *e*, 37°

5 Calculate the size of each unknown angle.

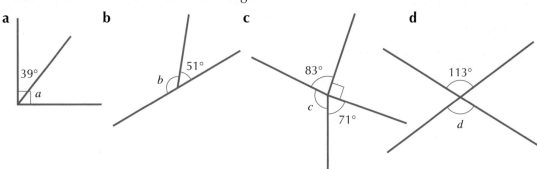

6 Choose three of these angles that would fit together to make a straight line.

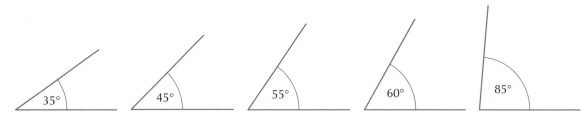

PS **7** Which of these angles, marked *a–f*, is not a multiple of 10°?

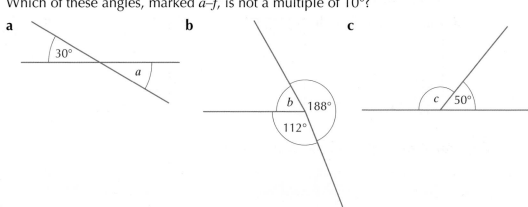

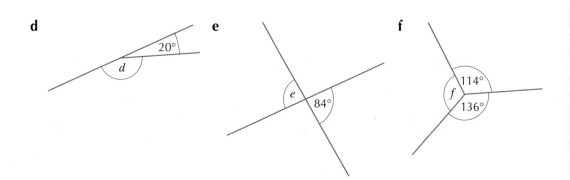

8 In the diagram, *x* and *y* lie on a straight line and the value of *y* is 10° more than the value of *x*.

Work out a pair of angles to make this statement true.

Reasoning: Unknown angles

Calculate the size of each unknown angle.

Explain your answers.

A

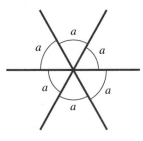

B

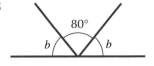

9.3 Angles in a triangle

Learning objective

- To know that the sum of the angles in a triangle is 180°

Key words	
isosceles	triangle

The angles in a **triangle** add up to 180°.

$a + b + c = 180°$

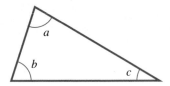

Example 9

Calculate the size of the angle marked c.

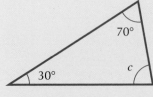

$c = 180° - 70° - 30°$

$c = 80°$

This is an **isosceles** triangle.

The two sides marked with dashes are the same length.

The two angles marked x are the same size.

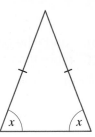

Example 10

Calculate the size of the unknown angles in this isosceles triangle.

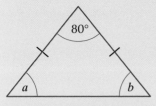

$180° - 80° = 100°$

The angles labelled a and b are the same, size.

$100° ÷ 2 = 50°$

So $a = b = 50°$

You can also use the angles inside a triangle to calculate an angle outside it.

Example 11

Calculate the sizes of the angles marked a and b.

Give reasons for your answers.

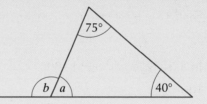

$a = 180° - 75° - 40°$

So $a = 65°$ Angles in a triangle = 180°

$b = 180° - 65°$

So $b = 115°$ Angles on a line = 180°

Exercise 9C

1   Calculate the size of the unknown angle in each diagram.

a

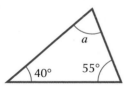

b

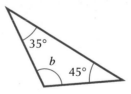

c

d

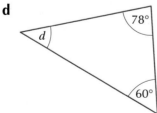

e

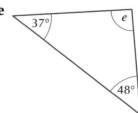

2 Calculate the size of the unknown angle in each diagram.

a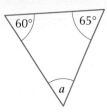

b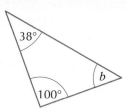

c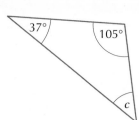

d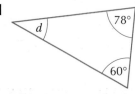

e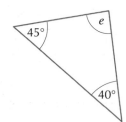

f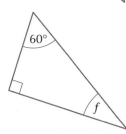

3 Calculate the sizes of the unknown angles in each isosceles triangle.

a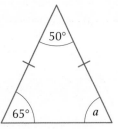

b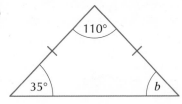

c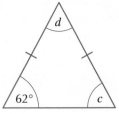

d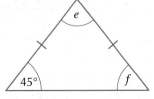

e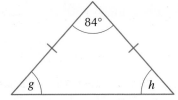

4 Calculate the sizes of the unknown angles in each diagram.

a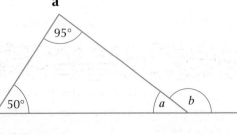

b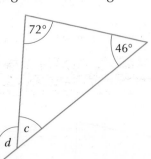

c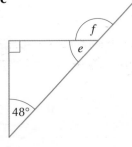

MR **5** One angle in an isosceles triangle is 42°.

Calculate the possible sizes of the other two angles.

Use diagrams to explain your answer.

6 Calculate the size of the unknown angle in each diagram.

a

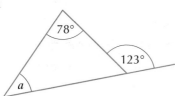

b

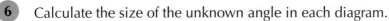

c

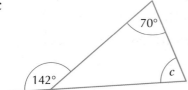

d

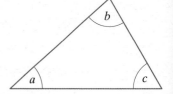

MR **7** In this triangle, the value of *b* is 10° more than the value of *a*.

The value of *c* is 10° more than the value of *b*.

What are the sizes of the three angles?

PS **8** Calculate the size of the unknown angle in each diagram.

Give reasons for your answers.

a

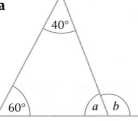

b

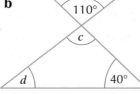

c

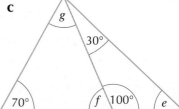

Problem solving: Calculating angles

Calculate the size of each unknown angle.

A

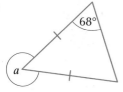

B

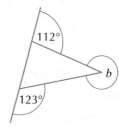

C

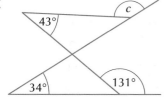

D

9.4 Angles in a quadrilateral

Learning objective

* To know that the sum of the angles in a quadrilateral is 360°

A **quadrilateral** is any shape with four straight sides.

Draw a large quadrilateral similar to the one on the right.

Use a protractor to measure each of the four angles.

Now add up the four angles. What do you notice?

You should find that your answer is close to 360°.

Now draw a different quadrilateral and find the sum of the four angles.

How close were you to 360°?

The angles in a quadrilateral add up to 360°.

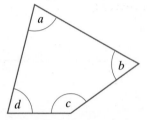

So, in the diagram; $a + b + c + d = 360°$.

Example 12

Calculate the sizes of the angles marked a and b on the diagram.

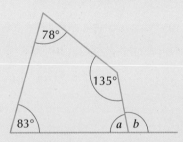

The angles in a quadrilateral add up to 360°.

So $a = 360° - 135° - 78° - 83°$

$\quad = 64°$

The angles on a straight line add up to 180°.

So $b = 180° - 64°$

$\quad = 116°$

Exercise 9D

1 Calculate the size of each angle marked by a letter in each quadrilateral.

a
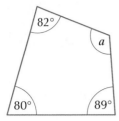

b
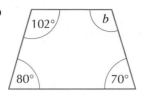

c
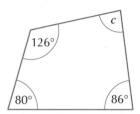

d
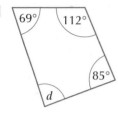

e
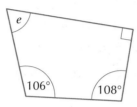

f
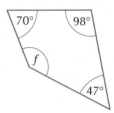

2 Calculate the size of each angle marked by a letter in each quadrilateral.

a
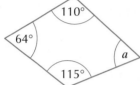

b
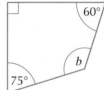

c
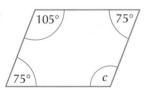

d
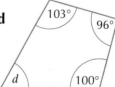

3 Calculate the size of each angle marked by a letter in each quadrilateral.

a
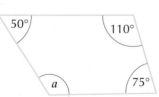

b
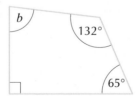

c

d
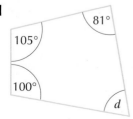

e
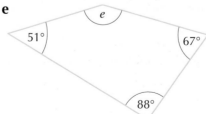

4 Calculate the size of each angle marked by a letter in each quadrilateral.

Give a reason for each of your answers.

a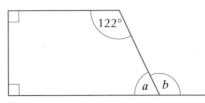

b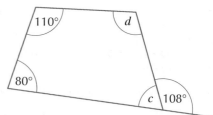

5 Calculate the size of each angle marked by a letter in each quadrilateral.

a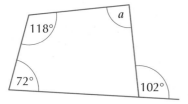

b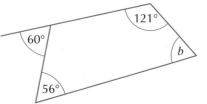

 6 The diagram shows a kite.

a Make a sketch of the kite and draw on it a line that divides it into two equal parts (its line of symmetry).

b What does this tell you about the angles marked p and q?

c Use this information to work out the size of the angles marked p and q.

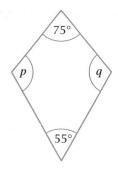

 7 Can a quadrilateral have **exactly** three right angles?

Give a reason for your answer.

Reasoning: Angles in a quadrilateral

Copy these diagrams.

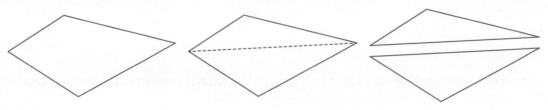

Explain to a partner how the diagrams show that the angles in a quadrilateral add up to 360°.

9.5 Properties of triangles and quadrilaterals

Learning objectives

- To understand the properties of parallel, intersecting and perpendicular lines
- To understand and use the properties of triangles
- To understand and use the properties of quadrilaterals

Describing lines

A ————————————————————— B

This line has point A at one end and point B at the other, so you can describe it as the line AB.

Any two lines either are **parallel** or **intersect**.

Parallel lines never meet. You can show lines are parallel by putting arrows on them.

These two lines intersect at a point X.

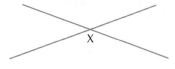

These two lines intersect at right angles. The lines are **perpendicular**.

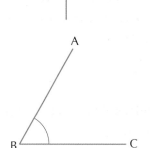

Describing angles

The angle at B can be written as:

∠B or ∠ABC or angle ABC.

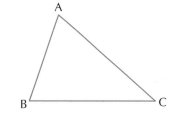

Describing triangles and quadrilaterals.

This triangle can be described as triangle ABC.

Each corner is called a **vertex**.

The triangle has:

- three **vertices**, A, B and C
- three angles, ∠A, ∠B and ∠C
- three sides, AB, AC and BC.

In some shapes some or all of the sides are the same size or may be parallel to each other, or some or all angles the same. These are called their **geometrical properties**.

The quadrilateral can be described as quadrilateral ABCD.

It has:

- four vertices, A, B, C and D
- four angles, ∠A, ∠B, ∠C and ∠D
- four sides, AB, BC, CD and AD.

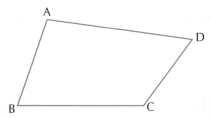

Types of triangle

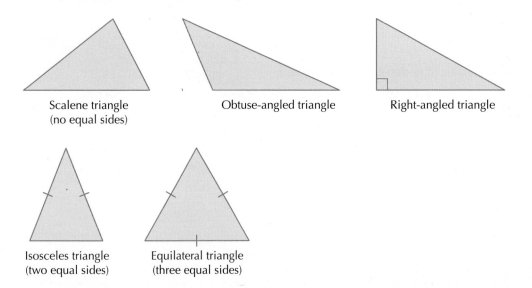

Scalene triangle
(no equal sides)

Obtuse-angled triangle

Right-angled triangle

Isosceles triangle
(two equal sides)

Equilateral triangle
(three equal sides)

Example 13

Describe the geometrical properties of the isosceles triangle ABC.

AB = AC

$\angle ABC = \angle ACB$

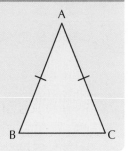

You can use this flow chart to identify triangles.

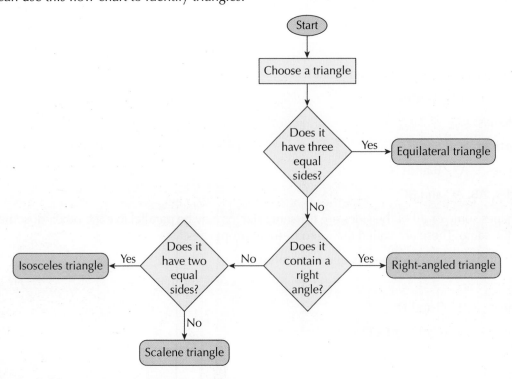

Types of quadrilateral

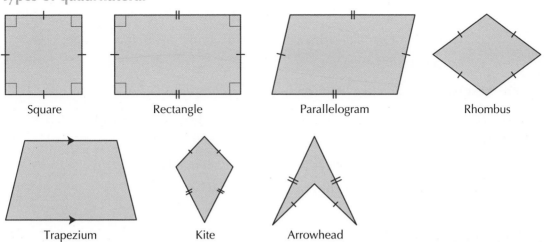

Square Rectangle Parallelogram Rhombus

Trapezium Kite Arrowhead

Example 14

Describe the geometrical properties of the parallelogram ABCD.

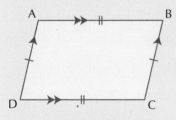

AB = CD and AD = BC.

AB is parallel to CD.

AD is parallel to BC.

Exercise 9E

1 Use the flow chart to identify and name these triangles.

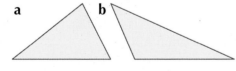

a b c d e

2 Describe the geometrical properties of the equilateral triangle ABC.

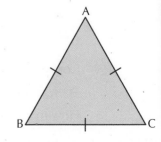

3 Which quadrilaterals have the following properties?

    a Four equal sides   **b** Two different pairs of equal sides

    c Two pairs of parallel sides   **d** Only one pair of parallel sides

    e Adjacent sides equal

4 Explain the difference between:

    a a square and a rhombus   **b** a rhombus and a parallelogram

    c a trapezium and a parallelogram.

(MR) **5** A line that joins two vertices of a shape is called a **diagonal**.

This quadrilateral ABCD has two diagonals AC and BD.

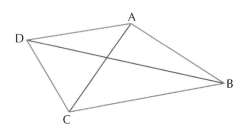

Name the quadrilaterals in this diagram in which the diagonals:

    a are equal in length   **b** bisect each other

    c are perpendicular to each other.

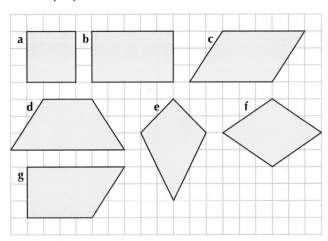

6 Describe the geometrical properties of the parallelogram ABCD.

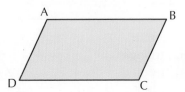

7 Copy this square onto a piece of card.

Then draw in the two diagonals and cut out the four triangles.

How many different triangles or quadrilaterals can you make with:

    a four of the triangles   **b** three of the triangles

    c two of the triangles?

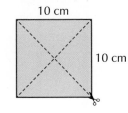

8   Copy this 3 by 3 grid and draw as many different triangles as you can.

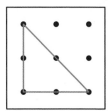

Use square dotted paper to record your triangles.

Below each one, write down what type of triangle it is.

Here is an example.

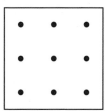

A right-angled triangle

Challenge: How many quadrilaterals?

How many distinct quadrilaterals can be constructed on this 3 by 3 pin-board?

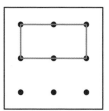

Use square dotted paper to record your quadrilaterals.

Below each one, write down what type of quadrilateral it is.

Here are two examples.

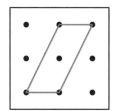

A rectangle   A parallelogram

Ready to progress?

I can draw and measure angles.
I can calculate angles at a point, angles on a straight line, vertically opposite angles and angles in a triangle.
I can recognise parallel, intersecting and perpendicular lines.
I can describe and use the properties of different triangles.

I can describe and use the properties of different quadrilaterals.

Review questions

1   Measure these angles.

a
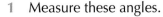

b

c
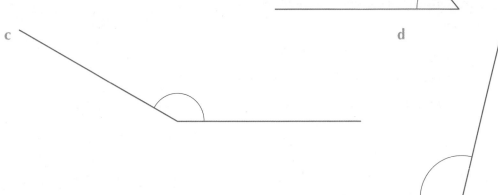

d

2   Calculate the size of the unknown angles in each diagram.

Give reasons for your answers.

a

b

c

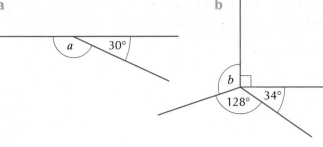

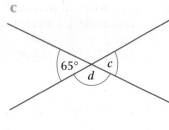

3 Calculate the size of the unknown angles in each triangle.

a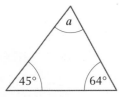

b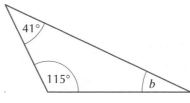

c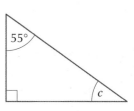

d

e

f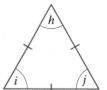

4 State whether the following statements are true or false.

   a A triangle can have three acute angles.

   b A triangle can have three obtuse angles.

   c A triangle can have two acute angles and one obtuse angle.

   d A triangle can have one acute angle and two obtuse angles.

MR 5 Nabeel measures the four angles in this quadrilateral. These are his answers.

∠A = 30°   ∠B = 160°   ∠C = 25°
∠D = 155°

Explain why his answers must be wrong.

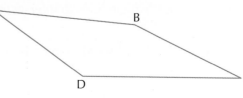

MR 6 The diagram shows triangle PQR.

Calculate the sizes of the angles marked *a*, *b* and *c*.

Give a reason for each answer.

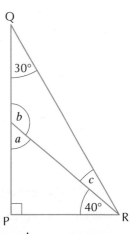

MR 7 Ella wrote down these statements for the geometrical properties of this kite ABCD.

Which of the statements are correct?

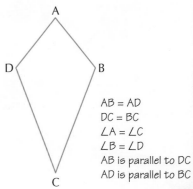

AB = AD
DC = BC
∠A = ∠C
∠B = ∠D
AB is parallel to DC
AD is parallel to BC

Activity
Constructing triangles

You need to be able to use a ruler, a protractor and compasses to draw shapes exactly, from the information you are given. This is called constructing a shape.

When constructing a shape you must draw lines accurately to the nearest millimetre and angles to the nearest degree.

Example: How to construct a triangle if you know two angles and one side.

Construct the triangle XYZ.

- Draw a line YZ 8.3 cm long.

- Draw an angle of 42° at Y.

- Draw an angle of 51° at Z.

- Extend both angle lines to intersect at X to complete the triangle.

The completed, full-sized triangle is given below.

Nowadays many architects and draughtsmen use computer-aided design (CAD) software packages instead of drawing by hand. Use the internet to find out more about these packages.

Example: How to construct a triangle if you know two sides and one angle.

Construct the triangle ABC.

- Draw a line BC 7.5 cm long.
- Draw an angle of 50° at B.
- Draw the line AB 4.1 cm long.
- Join AC to complete the triangle.

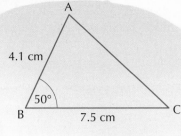

The completed, full-sized triangle is given below.

1 Construct each of these triangles. Remember to label all lines and angles.

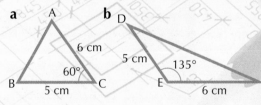
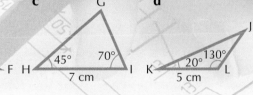

2 a Construct the triangle PQR.

  b Measure the size of ∠P and ∠R to the nearest degree.

  c Measure the length of the line PR to the nearest millimetre.

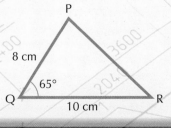

3 Construct the triangle ABC with ∠A = 100°, ∠B = 40° and AB = 8 cm.

10

Coordinates and graphs

This chapter is going to show you:

- how to use coordinates in all four quadrants
- how to draw a variety of graphs
- how to recognise lines of the form $x = a$, $y = b$
- how to recognise the graphs of $y = x$, $y = -x$ and $y = ax$
- how to interpret and draw graphs that show real-life problems.

You should already know:

- how to plot coordinates in the first quadrant.

About this chapter

Graphs can save lives. If the doctor thinks you have a heart problem, you will be linked up to an electrocardiogram machine that will turn the rhythm of your heartbeat into a graph on a screen. This makes it easy to see instantly if there are any problems. It also helps to monitor very ill people, or those having operations, as any problem with their heartbeat can be seen on the graph. Graphs of all types make it easier to interpret data visually and see what is happening.

10.1 Coordinates

Learning objective

- To understand and use coordinates to locate points in all four quadrants

You can use **coordinates** to locate a point on a grid.

The grid consists of two **axes**, called the **x-axis** and the **y-axis**. They are perpendicular (at right angles) to each other.

The two axes meet at a point called the **origin**, which is labelled 0 on both axes.

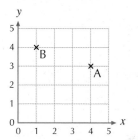

The point A on the grid is 4 units across and 3 units up.

So the coordinates of A are (4, 3). You can write this as A(4, 3).

The first number, 4, is the **x-coordinate** of A and the second number, 3, is the **y-coordinate** of A. The x-coordinate is always written first.

When you plot a point on a grid, you should use a small cross (×) or a small, neat dot (•).

The coordinates of the origin are (0, 0) and the coordinates of the point B are (1, 4).

The grid can be extended to include negative numbers and points can be plotted in all four **quadrants**.

Example 1

Write down the coordinates of the points A, B, C and D.

The coordinates of the points on the grid are:

A(4, 2), B(–2, 3), C(–3, –1), D(1, –4).

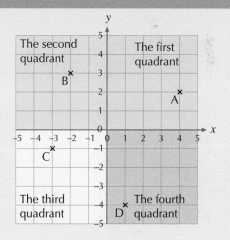

Exercise 10A

1 Write down the coordinates of the points P, Q, R, S and T.

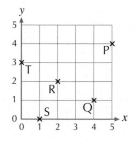

2 **a** Make a copy of the grid in Question 1.

Then plot the points A(1, 1), B(1, 5) and C(4, 5).

b The three points are the vertices of a rectangle.

Plot point D to complete the rectangle.

c Write down the coordinates of D.

(MR) **3** Ailsa and Bernice use a very simple code.

They write the letters of the alphabet in a 5 by 5 grid, using the same square for X and Y.

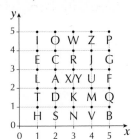

Then they use coordinates to send each other messages.

a What is this message?

(2, 3) (3, 4) (1, 4) (3, 3) (2, 5) (4, 3) (5, 4) (2, 5) (1, 5) (3, 1) (5, 4) (1, 2)
(2, 5) (1, 2) (1, 1) (1, 4) (2, 2) (1, 5) (2, 1) (2, 4) (2, 5)

b Another friend, Carla, finds the code and sends a message. When Ailsa decodes the message it reads:

B N N T V V X/Y Q R N K S V U.

Bernice realises that Carla has got all the coordinates the wrong way round.

What should the message be?

4 Write down the coordinates of the points A, B, C, D, E, F, G and H.

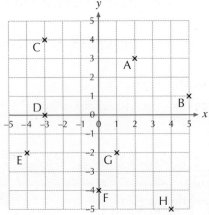

5 **a** Copy the grid in Question 4.

Plot the points P(–4, 3), Q(–2, –2), R(0, 1), S(2, –2) and T(4, 3).

b Join the points in the order given. What letter have you drawn?

6 **a** Copy the grid in Question 4.

Plot the points W(3, 4), X(3, −2) and Y(−3, −2).

b The points form three vertices of a square WXYZ.

Plot the point Z and draw the square.

c What are the coordinates of the point Z?

d Draw in the diagonals of the square. What are the coordinates of the point of intersection of the diagonals?

  7 In a game of 'Connect 4', players take turns to place counters on a grid. The first player to get four counters in a line, horizontally, vertically or diagonally, is the winner.

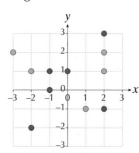

Jake and Rashid are playing the game.

Jake has blue counters and Rashid has orange counters.

It is Jake's turn to play.

a Where could Jake play his counter to stop Rashid winning on his next go?

b Explain why Jake can definitely win on his next go.

  8 Here is a sequence of coordinates.

(2, 3), (4, 7), (6, 11), (8, 15), (10, 19)

a Describe the sequence formed by the first number in each coordinate pair, 2, 4, 6, 8, 10, ….

b Describe the sequence formed by the second number in each coordinate pair, 3, 7, 11, 15, 19, ….

c Work out the 10th term in each sequence and then write down the full coordinate pair.

d Work out the 100th coordinate pair in this sequence.

e Work out the 100th coordinate pair in the sequence (3, 5), (7, 8), (11, 11), (15, 14), (19, 17), …

Investigation: Spot the rule

A **a** Draw a coordinate grid with both axes numbered from −8 to 8.

b Plot the points (0, 2) and (6, 8) and join them to make a straight line.

c Write down the coordinates of other points that lie on the line.

B Can you spot a rule that connects the x-coordinate and the y-coordinate?

C The rule you have found is given by the formula $y = x + 2$.

Extend the line into the third quadrant. Does your rule still work?

10.2 Graphs from relationships

Learning objectives

- To work out coordinates that fit a simple relationship
- To draw a graph for a simple relationship

Key words

| graph | relationship |

Think about the **relationship**: y is one more than x or $y = x + 1$.

You can show this on an arrow diagram.

y is one more than x		$y = x + 1$
x		y
1	→	2
2	→	3
3	→	4
4	→	5
5	→	6

If you put the numbers together to form ordered pairs, you get:

(1, 2), (2, 3), (3, 4), (4, 5), (5, 6)

You could choose to use more that just these five starting points, but the relationship between the coordinates will stay the same.

You can use these ordered pairs as coordinates, and plot them on a pair of axes, as shown on this **graph**.

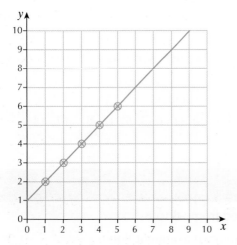

Note that the first number is always counted along (→) from the origin, towards the right, and the second number is counted up (↑) from the origin. You can join all the points with a straight line.

Exercise 10B

1 Copy each relationship diagram, then:

   i complete the arrow diagram   **ii** write in the coordinates alongside

   iii plot the coordinates and draw the graph.

a   *y* is the same as *x* $y = x$

x *y*	Coordinates
$0 \rightarrow 0$	(0, 0)
$1 \rightarrow 1$	(1, 1)
$2 \rightarrow$	(2,)
$3 \rightarrow$	(3,)
$4 \rightarrow$	(4,)
$5 \rightarrow$	(5,)

b   *y* is 2 more than *x* $y = x + 2$

x *y*	Coordinates
$0 \rightarrow 2$	(0, 2)
$1 \rightarrow 3$	(1, 3)
$2 \rightarrow$	(2,)
$3 \rightarrow$	(3,)
$4 \rightarrow$	(4,)
$5 \rightarrow$	(5,)

c   *y* is *x* multiplied by 2 $y = 2x$

x *y*	Coordinates
$0 \rightarrow 0$	(0, 0)
$1 \rightarrow 2$	(1, 2)
$2 \rightarrow$	(2,)
$3 \rightarrow$	(3,)
$4 \rightarrow$	(4,)
$5 \rightarrow$	(5,)

d   *y* is 2 less than *x* $y = x - 2$

x *y*	Coordinates
$1 \rightarrow -1$	(1, −1)
$2 \rightarrow 0$	(2, 0)
$3 \rightarrow$	(3,)
$4 \rightarrow$	(4,)
$5 \rightarrow$	(5,)
$6 \rightarrow$	(6,)

e   *y* is 3 more than *x* $y = x + 3$

x *y*	Coordinates
$0 \rightarrow 3$	(0, 3)
$1 \rightarrow 4$	(1, 4)
$2 \rightarrow$	(2,)
$3 \rightarrow$	(3,)
$4 \rightarrow$	(4,)
$5 \rightarrow$	(5,)

f   *y* is *x* multiplied by 3 $y = 3x$

x *y*	Coordinates
$0 \rightarrow 0$	(0, 0)
$1 \rightarrow 3$	(1, 3)
$2 \rightarrow$	(2,)
$3 \rightarrow$	(3,)
$4 \rightarrow$	(4,)

2 Using values of *x* from 0 to 5, and your own arrow diagram, draw a graph for each relationship.

   a   *y* is 4 more than *x* ($y = x + 4$)   **b**   *y* is 1 more than twice *x* ($y = 2x + 1$)

   c   *y* is 1 less than twice *x* ($y = 2x - 1$)   **d**   *y* is 3 more than twice *x* ($y = 2x + 3$)

3 Draw a coordinate grid. Label the x-axis from 0 to 5 and the y-axis from 0 to 10.

   a On the grid, draw the graphs of:

     i $y = x + 1$ **ii** $y = x + 2$ **iii** $y = x + 3$ **iv** $y = x + 5.$

   b What do you notice?

   c Add the graph of $y = x + 7$ to your grid, without calculating the coordinates first.

   d Add the graph of $y = x - 2$ to your grid, without calculating the coordinates first.

Challenge: $y = a - x$

A Look at the relationship $y = 5 - x.$

   a Draw a set of coordinate axes, both numbered from −2 to 6.

   b Work out the coordinates for the relationship $y = 5 - x$, for x-values 0, 1, 2, 3, 4 and 5.

   c Draw the graph.

   d Did this surprise you?

B **a** On the same set of axes, draw the graphs for the relationships:

     i $y = 3 - x$ **ii** $y = 6 - x$ **iii** $y = 2 - x.$

   b What do you notice in each case?

C Draw a sketch of the relationship $y = 100 - x$, without working out all the coordinates.
Explain how you knew where to draw the graph.

10.3 Graphs for fixed values of x and y

Learning objective

- To recognise and draw line graphs with fixed values of x and y

Key words	
coordinate	equation
relationship	

When you use **coordinates**, the first number inside the brackets is the x-coordinate and the second number is the y-coordinate. You can write a general coordinate pair as (x, y).

What do you notice about the coordinates (0, 3), (1, 3), (2, 3), (3, 3), (4, 3)? The second number, the y-coordinate, is always 3. In other words, $y = 3$.

Look what happens when you plot it on a graph.

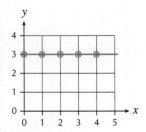

However long you draw the line, every set of coordinates will have the y-value of 3, for example, (−7, 3), (−1, 3), (106, 3).

This is the graph of the **relationship** $y = 3$. The **equation** of the graph is $y = 3$.

Look at the graphs of $y = 2$ and $y = 5$, shown below.

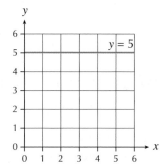

You should see that when the value of y is fixed, the graph is always a horizontal line.

If you do the same for a fixed x-value, such as $x = 2$, you will draw a vertical line, as shown. The equation of this graph is $x = 2$.

This is the graph of $x = 2$.

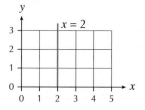

Exercise 10C

1 Work out the relationship between each pair of points on the diagram, then write down the equation of the straight line that goes through them.

   a A and B **b** C and D **c** E and F

   d G and H **e** I and D **f** J and D

   g K and A **h** G and F

2 Look at the coordinate grid.

Write down the letters that are on each line.

   a $x = 1$ **b** $y = 1$ **c** $y = 6$

   d $y = 2$ **e** $x = 3$ **f** $x = 2$

   g $y = 4$ **h** $x = 5$ **i** $x = 6$

   j $y = 3$

3 Draw a coordinate grid and label each axis from 0 to 7.

Draw each of these graphs on the same coordinate grid. Label each graph.

a $y = 1$ **b** $y = 4$ **c** $y = 6$

d $x = 1$ **e** $x = 3$ **f** $x = 5$

4 Draw a coordinate grid and label each axis from 0 to 8.

Draw each pair of lines on your grid.

Write down the coordinates of the points where they cross.

a $y = 1$ and $x = 3$ **b** $y = 4$ and $x = 1$ **c** $x = 5$ and $y = 6$

5 Here are eight sets of coordinates.

    A(2, 3), B(3, 5), C(7, 3), D(2, 5), E(3, 7), F(7, 4), G(3, 4), H(7, 7)

Try to write down the equation of the straight line that goes through each pair of points.

Then plot the points on the graphs to check your answers.

a A and C   **b** B and D   **c** C and F   **d** A and D

e E and H   **f** F and G   **g** B and G   **h** C and H

(PS) **6** Draw a suitable set of axes, then sketch the graph of:

a $y = -3$ **b** $x = -5$ **c** $y = -8$ **d** $x = -10$.

Investigation: Areas of rectangles

The lines $x = 2$, $x = 5$, $y = 1$ and $y = 6$ are drawn on this coordinate grid.

They enclose a rectangle with an area of $3 \times 5 = 15$ square units.

A **a** Copy the grid and draw at least two more pairs of $x = ?$ lines and $y = ?$ lines.

   b Work out the area of the rectangle they enclose, each time.

B Write down a rule for working out the area without drawing the lines.

C Use your rule to work out the areas of the rectangles enclosed by these lines, without drawing them.

a $x = 1$, $x = 8$, $y = 2$ and $y = 5$ **b** $x = 2$, $x = 8$, $y = 3$ and $y = 8$

c $x = -5$, $x = 5$, $y = 0$ and $y = 7$ **d** $x = -7$, $x = -1$, $y = -2$ and $y = 3$

e $x = -5$, $x = -2$, $y = -8$ and $y = -4$

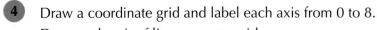

10.4 Graphs of the form $y = ax$

Learning objective

- To recognise and draw lines of the form $y = ax$

Think again about the graph of the relationship $y = x$.

y is the same as x		$y = x$
x	y	Coordinates
$0 \rightarrow 0$		$(0, 0)$
$1 \rightarrow 1$		$(1, 1)$
$2 \rightarrow 2$		$(2, 2)$
$3 \rightarrow 3$		$(3, 3)$
$4 \rightarrow 4$		$(4, 4)$
$5 \rightarrow 5$		$(5, 5)$

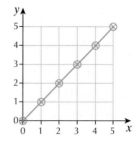

The equation of this **straight-line graph** is $y = x$, because the x-coordinate is always the same as the y-coordinate.

Similarly, the straight-line graph in which the x-coordinate has the same numerical value as the y-coordinate, but has a different sign, has the equation $y = -x$.

If the sign changes, for example, from $y = x$ to $y = -x$ the graph is still a straight line but it slopes a different way.

Example 2

Use x-values of -4, 0 and 4 to work out some coordinates (x, y) of points that lie on the line $y = x - 2$. Draw the line for values of x from -4 to 4.

Substitute the x-values into the equation and write down the coordinate pairs.

This gives $(-4, -6)$, $(0, -2)$ and $(4, 2)$.

Plot these coordinates and draw the line.

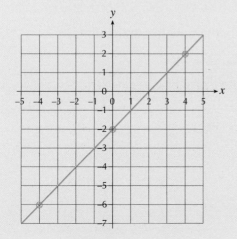

When you are asked to plot a line from a given equation of a straight line, how many points do you need to calculate, to be sure you are drawing the line correctly?

The short answer is two but you should always plot at least three. Then, if all three points lie on the same straight line, you can be almost certain that you have drawn the line correctly.

Exercise 10D

1 **a** Draw a set of axes, labelling both axes from 0 to 12.

   b On your set of axes, draw graphs of these equations.

   i $y = x$ **ii** $y = 2x$ **iii** $y = 3x$ **iv** $y = 4x$ **v** $y = 5x$

   c What do you notice?

   d Draw the graph $y = 7x$ on your diagram without calculating the coordinates of any points.

   e Now draw the graph of $y = 8x$ on your diagram.

2 **a** Draw a set of axes, labelling both x and y from −5 to 5.

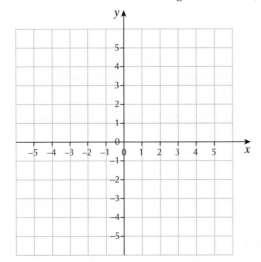

   b Fill in the missing numbers of these coordinates for the relationship $y = -x$. Notice that one of them has been done for you.

   (1, ?), (2, ?), (3, ?), (4, ?), (5, ?), (−1, 1), (−2, ?), (−3, ?), (−4, ?), (−5, ?)

   c Plot these coordinates on your grid and join them with a straight line.

   d Label the line $y = -x$.

3 **a** Draw a set of axes, labelling x from −4 to 4 and y from −16 to 16.

   b On your set of axes, draw graphs of:

   i $y = -x$ **ii** $y = -2x$ **iii** $y = -3x$ **iv** $y = -4x$

4 Where do the lines $y = x$ and $y = -x$ intersect?

5 Here are ten sets of coordinates.

A(4, 6), B(1, 5), C(5, 5), D(1, 3), E(5, 3),

F(–2, 2), G(4, 1), H(3, 0), I(–1, –1), J(1, –1)

Try to write down the equation of the straight line that goes through each pair of points, below.

Then plot the points on the graphs to check your answers.

a A and D **b** B and F **c** C and I
d E and J **e** G and H **f** F and J
g B and D **h** D and E

Investigation: Areas of parallelograms

The lines $x = 2$, $x = 4$, $y = x + 4$ and $y = x + 1$ are drawn on this coordinate grid.

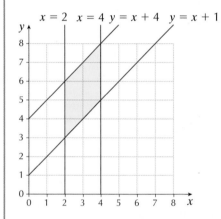

By counting squares you can work out the area of the parallelogram as 6 square units.

A **a** Draw:

- at least two more pairs of $x = ?$ lines
- atleast pairs of $y = x + a$ lines, where a is an integer bigger than 0.

b Work out the area of the parallelogram they enclose, in each case.

B Write down a rule for working out the area without drawing the lines.

C Use your rule to work out the areas of the parallelograms enclosed by these lines, without drawing them.

a $x = 1$, $x = 8$, $y = x + 2$ and $y = x + 5$

b $x = 3$, $x = 5$, $y = x + 3$ and $y = x + 9$

c $x = -2$, $x = 3$, $y = x + 1$ and $y = x - 4$

d $x = -7$, $x = -1$, $y = x$ and $y = x + 9$

e $x = -5$, $x = -2$, $y = x - 2$ and $y = x - 6$

10.5 Graphs of the form $x + y = a$

Learning objective

- To recognise and draw graphs of the form $x + y = a$

This table shows pairs of values for x and y. Each pair adds up to 4.

x	y	Total	Coordinates
1	3	4	(1, 3)
2	2	4	(2, 2)
−1	5	4	(−1, 5)
6	−2	4	(6, −2)

The coordinates have been plotted on this grid and joined with a straight line.

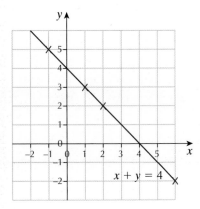

Because the values of x and y in each coordinate pair add up to 4, this line is called $x + y = 4$.

Notice, too, that the line $x + y = 4$ goes through (0, 4) on the y-axis and (4, 0) on the x-axis.

All lines of the form $x + y = a$ always pass through the points (0, a) and (a, 0).

Exercise 10E

1   Draw a table of values, like the one above, for x and y when x and y add up to 6.

Remember to include some negative values.

Copy this grid, plot the coordinates and join up the points.

Label the line $x + y = 6$.

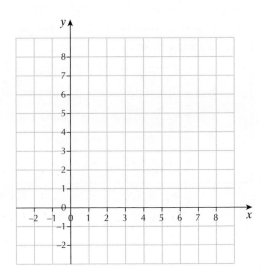

2 Use a table of values to find coordinate pairs. Copy the grid, below, and then draw the graph of these equations.

a $x + y = 2$ **b** $x + y = 5$ **c** $x + y = -1$

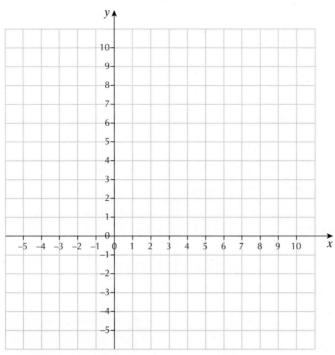

MR 3 Explain why the lines $x + y = 4$ and $x + y = 10$ will never meet.

PS 4 Which of these lines is the same as $y = -x$?

(There may be more than one answer.)

a $y = x$ **b** $y + x = 0$ **c** $x = -y$ **d** $y - x = 0$ **e** $y = x + 0$

5 16 points are marked on the grid.

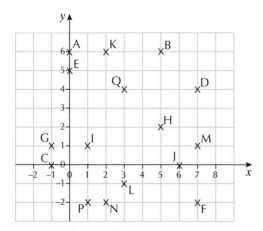

Write down the equation of the line that passes through both points, in each pair.

a A and J   **b** K and M   **c** Q and H   **d** E and F

e I and L   **f** C and P   **g** G and N   **h** B and D

207 **10.5** Graphs of the form $x + y = a$

10.6 Graphs from the real world

Learning objective

- To learn how graphs can be used to represent real-life situations

- To draw and use real-life graphs

Key word

conversion graph

When you use a recipe book, you will see that the ingredients may be given in grams and kilograms, or in ounces and pounds (lb).

There may be a table, like this one.

Kilograms (kg)	1	2	3	4	5
Pounds (lb)	2.2	4.4	6.6	8.8	11

This information can also be represented as a set of coordinates.

   (1, 2.2), (2, 4.4), (3, 6.6), (4, 8.8), (5, 11)

The graph on the right relates pounds (lb) to kilograms.

This is an example of a **conversion graph**.

You can use it to work out the number of kilograms for any number of pounds, or the number of pounds for any number of kilograms.

Conversion graphs are usually straight-line graphs.

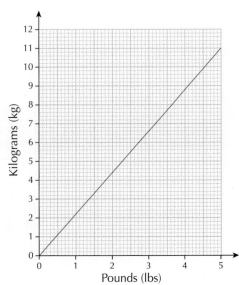

Exercise 10F

1 Use the graph to answer these questions.

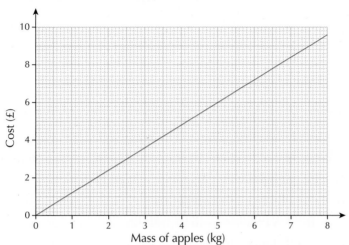

a Work out the cost of each quantity of apples.

   i 3 kg   **ii** 7 kg

b What quantity of apples can be bought for:

   i £6   **ii** £4.80?

2 The graph below shows the distance travelled by a car during an interval of 5 minutes.

a Work out the distance travelled during the second minute of the journey.

b Work out the time taken to travel 3 km.

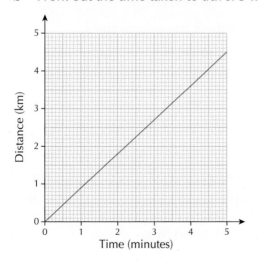

3 This is a kilometre–mile conversion graph.

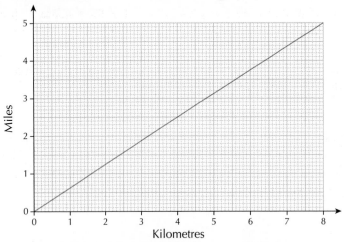

a Express each of these distances in kilometres.

   i 3 miles   **ii** 4.5 miles   **iii** 1 mile

b Express each of these distances in miles.

   i 2 km   **ii** 4 km   **iii** 6 km

(FS) **4** **a** One month, the exchange rate between the pound and the euro was €1 to £0.90. Copy and complete the table below to show how many pounds you would get for the given numbers of euros.

Euros (€)	1	5	10	15	20
Pounds (£)	0.90	4.50			

b Use the data from this table to draw a conversion graph from pounds to euros.

c Use your graph to convert each of these amounts to pounds.

   i €7   **ii** €16   **iii** €17.50

d Use your graph to convert each of these amounts to euros.

   i £9   **ii** £12   **iii** £10.80

5 **a** Copy and complete the following table for the approximate comparison of gallons and litres.

Gallons	1	5	10	15	20
Litres	4.5	22.5			

b Use the data from this table to draw a conversion graph from gallons to litres.

c Use your graph to work out an approximate conversion of each capacity to gallons.

   i 15 litres   **ii** 30 litres   **iii** 80 litres

d Use your graph to work out an approximate conversion of each capacity to litres.

   i 8 gallons   **ii** 14 gallons   **iii** 17 gallons

e A car travels, on average, 200 miles on 25 litres of petrol.

   Work out approximately how many miles per gallon this is.

f A car's petrol tank holds 11 gallons. Petrol is £1.38 per litre.

   Approximately how much would it cost to fill the tank with petrol?

6 A box weighs 2 kg. Packets of juice, each weighing 425 g, are packed into it.

   a Draw a graph to show the mass of the box plus the mass of the packets of juice on the horizontal axis, and the number of packets of fruit juice put into the box on the vertical axis.

   b Work out, from the graph, the number of packets of juice for which the total mass of the box and packets is as close to 5 kg as possible.

Challenge: Graphs with fixed charges

A This graph shows how CityCabs works out how much to charge for a taxi ride.

   There is a fixed charge of £2.50 and then a charge of 50p per kilometre.

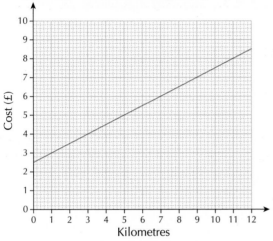

   a Why is this graph different to all those you used in Exercise 10F?

   b How much does a 10 km taxi ride cost with CityCabs?

   c Another taxi firm, AceCars, has a fixed charge of £1 plus 75p a kilometre.

     Copy the graph above and draw a line to show how much AceCars charges.

   d For what distance do the two firms charge the same amount?

B Draw a graph to show the cost of gas from a supplier who charges a fixed fee of £18 plus 3p per unit of gas. Draw the horizontal axis from 0 to 500 units and the vertical axis from £0 to £35.

Ready to progress?

I can plot coordinates in all quadrants.

I can recognise and draw lines such as $x = 3$ and $y = -1$.
I can read values from conversion graphs.

I can recognise and draw the lines of the form $y = x$, $y = x + a$ and $y = ax$.
I can recognise and draw the lines of the form $y + x = a$.

Review questions

1 a The point M is halfway between points A and B.

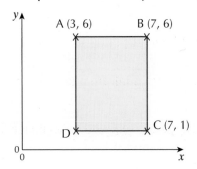

What are the coordinates of point M?

  b Shape ABCD is a rectangle.
     What are the coordinates of point D?

2 a Write down the next two numbers in the sequence below.

       1   5   9   13   17   ☐   ☐

  b This is a sequence of coordinates.
     (1, 2) (5, 6) (9, 10) (13, 14) (17, 18)
     Write down the next two coordinates in the sequence.

  c Work out the 25th coordinate in the sequence.

FS 3 A music club sells music downloads over the internet.

     They allow each member up to 10 downloads per week.

     The first five downloads cost £1 each then the next five cost 50p each.

Their charges are shown in this graph.

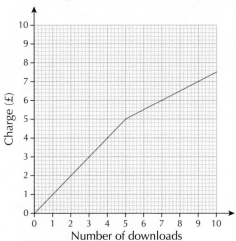

a   Use the graph to work out the missing values from this table.

Number of downloads	Charge (£)
4	
9	

b   A second music club also sells music downloads.

Their charge is £0.80 per download.

Copy the graph and draw a line on it to show this information.

c   Complete this sentence.

Downloads are cheaper with the first company if you buy more than ☐ downloads.

 4   The fractions $\frac{2}{3}$ and $\frac{4}{5}$ are plotted as coordinates.

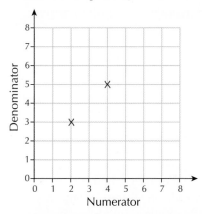

a   Join the points and extend the straight line.
b   Write down one other fraction that lies on this line.
c   What is the equation of the line?
d   Which of these fractions lie on the line?

   i $\frac{10}{11}$ ii $\frac{23}{24}$ iii $\frac{398}{399}$ iv $\frac{401}{400}$

e   Explain why all fractions that are plotted below the line $y = x$ will be improper ones.

Challenge
Global warming

Our world is getting warmer.

Higher temperatures have many effects on our world, including the melting of sea ice at the North Pole.

Use the graphs and answer the questions here to work out what might happen to sea ice levels in the future.

Sea ice melting

The red line on the graph shows the area of Arctic sea ice each year since 1978 and the blue line shows the average over that time. Use the average blue line to answer questions 1 to 5.

1 Estimate by how many million square kilometres the area of Arctic sea ice has decreased between 1978 and 2013.

2 On average, approximately how many square kilometres of Arctic sea ice are being lost each year?

3 If this average yearly loss continues from 2013 onwards, estimate the area of Arctic sea ice in 2050.

4 There are estimated to be 25 000 polar bears in the Arctic in 2013. The number of bears is expected to drop by 2000 for every half a million square kilometres of sea ice lost. When the number of bears reaches 12 000 they will become an endangered species. Approximately when will this happen?

5 If sea ice continues to melt at the current yearly average how long will it take for it all to melt?

6 Using the actual yearly area of sea ice graph work out the difference between the maximum area and minimum area of sea ice between 1978 and 2013.

11

Percentages

This chapter is going to show you:

- how to interpret percentages as fractions or decimals
- how to work out a fraction or a percentage of a quantity
- when and how you can work out using a percentage of a quantity without using a calculator
- how to work out the result of a simple percentage change
- how to solve simple problems involving percentage changes.

You should already know:

- how to write a quarter and a tenth as decimals or percentages
- how to simplify fractions
- how to work out a simple percentage of a whole number.

About this chapter

Few people can resist a good sale. The percentages taken off prices tell you instantly how much they have been reduced and help you judge straight away if you might be getting a good bargain. A reduction of £5 is a good deal when the original price was £10 (50% off), but it's less attractive when the starting price is £500 – a reduction of just 1%! Becoming comfortable working with percentages will help you to become a better bargain hunter, and enable you to compare lots of other kinds of important data as well such as the interest you will get on bank savings accounts.

11.1 Fractions, decimals and percentages

Learning objective

• To understand the equivalence between a fraction, a decimal and a percentage

Keywords	
decimal	fraction
per cent (%)	percentage

Fractions, **decimals** and **percentages** can all be used to compare quantities or measurements.

This pie chart shows the favourite colours of a group of children.

The red sector is a quarter of the whole circle.

You can write that as $\frac{1}{4}$ or 0.25 or 25%.

These all mean the same thing.

Remember that **per cent** means 'for every 100'.

So 25% is 25 parts out of 100 in the whole, or $\frac{25}{100}$.

As a fraction, this can be simplified to $\frac{1}{4}$.

As a decimal, this can be expressed as 0.25.

Favourite colours

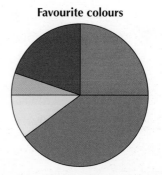

Example 1

The blue sector is 40% of the pie chart.

What fraction is that?

$40\% = \frac{40}{100} = \frac{2}{5}$

Example 2

The yellow sector is 0.1 of the pie chart.

What percentage is that?

$0.1 = \frac{1}{10} = 10\%$

 Hint Remember that:

$\frac{1}{10} = 0.1$

$\frac{1}{100} = 0.01$

You should know simple equivalences such as these.

Example 3

The green sector is 5% of the pie chart.

What percentage is the purple sector?

The total of the four sectors that you already know is 25% + 40% + 10% + 5% = 80%.

The whole pie chart is 100% so the purple sector must be 100% − 80% = 20%.

1 Change these fractions to percentages.

    a $\dfrac{1}{2}$ **b** $\dfrac{1}{4}$ **c** $\dfrac{3}{10}$ **d** $\dfrac{9}{10}$ **e** $\dfrac{3}{4}$

2 Write these decimals as percentages.

    a 0.5   **b** 0.8   **c** 0.05   **d** 0.08   **e** 0.77

3 Write these percentages as fractions.

Give your answers as simply as possible.

    a 20%   **b** 30%   **c** 5%   **d** 65%   **e** 95%

4 Copy and complete this table.

The first row has been done for you.

Percentage	Fraction	Decimal
20%	$\dfrac{1}{5}$	0.2
80%		
		0.35
4%		
	$\dfrac{9}{25}$	

5 $\dfrac{1}{3}$ is $33\dfrac{1}{3}\%$.

Write $\dfrac{2}{3}$ as a percentage.

(MR) 6 This pie chart shows the most popular colours chosen by a group of children to paint a pattern.

Three of the sectors of this pie chart represent 10%, 20% and 30%.

Colours to paint a pattern

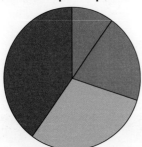

    a What percentage does the fourth sector represent?

    b What fractions of the whole are the four sectors?

    c What percentage of the pie chart is not red?

    d What colour is 0.3 of the pie chart?

7 Match each fraction with a percentage.
One has been done for you.

$\frac{3}{5}$ 70%

$\frac{4}{5}$ 60%

$\frac{7}{10}$ 74%

$\frac{17}{20}$ 80%

$\frac{37}{50}$ 85%

8 $\boxed{\frac{1}{2} + \frac{1}{4} = \frac{3}{4}}$

    a Write the fractions as percentages to make a new addition.

    b Write the fractions as decimals to make a new addition.

9 $\boxed{20\% + 75\% = 95\%}$

    a Rewrite this as an addition of decimals.

    b Rewrite this as an addition of fractions.

10 $\boxed{\frac{1}{4} = 25\% \qquad \frac{1}{8} \text{ is half of } \frac{1}{4}}$

    a Write $\frac{1}{8}$ as a percentage.

    b Write $\frac{3}{8}$, $\frac{5}{8}$ and $\frac{7}{8}$ as percentages.

(MR) **11** Percentages can be larger than 100%.

$\boxed{1 = 100\% \qquad 1.5 = 150\% \qquad 2 = 200\%}$

Write these decimal numbers as percentages.

    a 2.5   **b** 1.2   **c** 1.9   **d** 1.75   **e** 1.88

12 Write these percentages as mixed numbers.
Remember that a mixed number is a whole number plus a fraction.

    a 150%   **b** 125%   **c** 130%   **d** 160%   **e** 275%

Investigation: Looking into percentages

A Here is a sequence of percentages.

    10%, 20%, 30%, 40%, ..., ..., ..., ..., 90%

  a Copy the sequence and fill in the missing numbers.

  b Write each percentage as a fraction, as simply as possible.

  c Which percentages give the fractions that have the smallest denominator?

B Repeat part **A** with this sequence of percentages.

    5%, 15%, 25%, ..., ..., ..., ..., ..., ..., 95%

11.2 Fractions of a quantity

Learning objective

* To find a fraction of a quantity

Keyword

quantity

You can work out a fraction of a number or a **quantity** by using multiplication and division.

Example 4

There are 360 animals in a farm.

$\frac{1}{5}$ are cows and $\frac{3}{8}$ are sheep.

a How many cows are there?

b How many sheep are there?

> **a** $360 \div 5 = 72$ Divide by 5 to work out $\frac{1}{5}$.
>
> There are 72 cows.
>
> **b** $360 \div 8 = 45$ To work out $\frac{3}{8}$ first work out $\frac{1}{8}$ by dividing by 8.
>
> $45 \times 3 = 135$ Then $\frac{3}{8}$ of 360 = $\frac{1}{8}$ of 360 × 3.
>
> There are 135 sheep.

Exercise 11B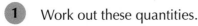

1   Work out these quantities.

    a $\frac{1}{3}$ of £96   **b** $\frac{2}{3}$ of £96

2   Work out these quantities.

    a $\frac{1}{10}$ of £600   **b** $\frac{3}{10}$ of £600   **c** $\frac{7}{10}$ wof £600   **d** $\frac{9}{10}$ of £600

3   Work out these quantities.

    a $\frac{2}{3}$ of 120 cm   **b** $\frac{3}{5}$ of 120 cm   **c** $\frac{5}{8}$ of 120 cm   **d** $\frac{11}{20}$ of 120 cm

(PS) **4**   A marathon is approximately 26 miles.

    a   How far is half a marathon?

    b   Janice says: 'When I have run 20 miles I shall have completed more than three-quarters of the marathon.'

       Is this correct?

       Give a reason for your answer.

5 Copy the questions and answers below.

Draw an arrow from each part of the question to the correct answer.

$\frac{3}{4}$ of 72   49

$\frac{2}{5}$ of 150   54

$\frac{7}{8}$ of 64   56

$\frac{7}{20}$ of 140   60

6 The complete angle at the centre of a circle is 360°.

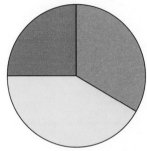

a One-third of this circle is coloured blue.

What is the angle at the centre of the blue sector?

b $\frac{5}{12}$ of this circle is coloured yellow.

What is the angle at the centre of the yellow sector?

7 Work out each quantity.

a $\frac{1}{12}$ of 2 hours.

Give your answer in minutes.

b $\frac{5}{6}$ of 2 days.

Give your answer in hours.

c $\frac{2}{3}$ of 2 minutes.

Give your answer in seconds.

(MR) **8** Tom has £600.

He spends $\frac{3}{5}$ of it on a bed.

He spends $\frac{3}{4}$ of the remainder on curtains.

Show that he has £60 left.

(PS) **9** Sam has a large bag of apples.

She gives away two-thirds of them.

She has 6 left.

How many did she have at the start?

11.3 Percentages of a quantity

Learning objective

* To find a percentage of a quantity

You have learnt how to find a fraction of a quantity. You can find a percentage of a quantity in a similar way.

Example 5

There are 450 people in a village. 60% are over 18 years old.

How many people is that?

$60\% = \frac{60}{100} = \frac{3}{5}$

$\frac{3}{5}$ of 450 = (450 ÷ 5) × 3 = 90 × 3 = 270

270 people are over 18 years old.

Example 6

A woman earns £3600. She has to pay 23% of this in income tax.

How much tax must she pay?

Here are two different methods.

Method 1

$23\% = \frac{23}{100}$ and this fraction cannot be simplified.

$\frac{23}{100}$ of 3600 is (3600 ÷ 100) × 23 = 36 × 23 = 828

She must pay £828.

Method 2

$23\% = 20\% + 1\% + 1\% + 1\%$

20% of $3600 = \frac{1}{5}$ of $3600 = 720$

1% of $3600 = \frac{1}{100}$ of $3600 = 36$

So 23% of $3600 = 720 + (3 \times 36) = 720 + 108 = 828$

She must pay £828.

You can use either method. If you do not have a calculator the second one could be easier.

Exercise 11C

1 Work out 1% of each amount.

   a £700   **b** £7000   **c** £760   **d** £723   **e** £7   **f** £74

2 Find these amounts.

   a 50% of 320 kg   **b** 25% of 48 m   **c** 20% of 45 litres   **d** 10% of 60 cm

   e 5% of 500 g   **f** 2% of £1000   **g** 75% of 640 people   **h** 30% of 410 km

3 **a** Work out 10% of 32 kg.

   b Use your answer to part **a** to find these amounts.

   i 20% of 32 kg   **ii** 30% of 32 kg   **iii** 5% of 32 kg   **iv** 90% of 32 kg

4 **a** Find: **i** 25% of £28   **ii** 10% of £28.

   b Use your answers to part **a** to work these out.

   i 35% of £28   **ii** 15% of £28   **iii** 30% of £2   **iv** 5% of £28

   v 12.5% of £28

5 Work out 63% of each quantity.

   a £1   **b** £2   **c** £10   **d** £20

6 Work out these percentages of 640 kg.

   a 50%   **b** 25%   **c** 35%   **d** 90%   **e** 99%

(PS) 7 38% of £49.00 is £18.62.

   Use this fact to work out 62% of £49.00.

8 Work out these amounts.

   a 9% of £300   **b** 19% of £400   **c** 32% of £2000   **d** 91% of £3000

(FS) 9 The cost of a holiday for a couple is £1320.

   They must make a first payment of 30%.

   a How much is the first payment?

   b How much is left to pay?

(PS) 10 At a conference, 25% of the people attending are men.

   There are 30 men.

   How many people are there at the conference altogether?

Financial skills: Buying furniture

Here is a notice in a furniture store.

A Adele buys some furniture for £2700.

 a She makes an initial payment of 20%.
  How much did she pay?

 b She pays the remainder in 10 monthly payments.
  How much is each monthly payment?

> **Easy payments on furniture**
> Initial payment of just 20%
> Pay the remainder in
> 10 monthly installments

B a Complete this table to show the initial and the monthly payments for each of these items.

Item	Table	Chair	Sideboard	Cabinet
Cost	£800	£120	£1400	£500
Initial payment				
Monthly payments				

 b David buys a table and four chairs. Work out his total monthly payment.

11.4 Percentages with a calculator

Learning objectives

- To use a calculator to find a percentage of a quantity
- To know when it is appropriate to use a calculator

Keyword

deposit

Sometimes you can work out a percentage easily, without using a calculator.

If the calculation is complicated it is more efficient to use a calculator.

It is easy to work out 25% of £48 without using a calculator.

If you need to work out 27% of £49, it is easier to use a calculator.

Can you explain why?

Example 6

In an election, 850 people vote. 28% vote for Ms White.

How many people vote for Ms White?

 Write 28% as a decimal and multiply by 850. Use a calculator to do this.

 28% of 850 = $0.28 \times 850 = 238$

 238 people vote for Ms White.

How would you do Example 6 without using a calculator? Look back at section 11.3 if you need to.

Exercise 11D

1 **a** Work out these percentages without using a calculator.

     i 20% of 70 kg   **ii** 75% of 240 m   **iii** 15% of 600 people

  b Now use a calculator to work out the percentages in part **a**.

    Check that you get the same answers.

2 Work out:

  a 13% of £29.00   **b** 39% of 8200 km   **c** 72% of 9500 people

  d 93% of 6200 years   **e** 42% of 65.5 cm   **f** 88% of £88.

3 **a** Work out:

    i 17% of 4300 people   **ii** 54% of 4300 people   **iii** 29% of 4300 people.

  b Show that the three answers in part **a** add up to 4300. Explain why.

4 **a** Work out:

    i 64% of 380 kg   **ii** 32% of 380 kg   **iii** 16% of 380 kg   **iv** 8% of 380 kg.

  b The questions and answers in part **a** form a sequence.

    What is the next term in the sequence?

5 In an election, 17 600 people voted.

The Red party gained 23% of the votes. The Blue party gained 36%.

The Yellow party gained 19%.

How many votes did each party get?

6 A politician is talking to a meeting of 350 people.

He says: 'I know that 95% of the people in this room agree with me.'

How many people is that?

7 **a** Write 1.5% as a decimal.

  b A concert hall charges an extra 1.5% if you pay for tickets with a credit card. Jason buys a ticket for £68.

    How much will he be charged for paying with a credit card?

8 This information was found on a website.

> 15.3% of the population of England live in Greater London.
>
> 4.9% of the population of England live in the North East.
>
> The population of England is 53.0 million.

Work out the population of Greater London and of the North East.

Give your answers in millions, correct to one decimal place (1 dp).

9 In the general election in the UK, in 2010, 29.6 million people voted.

This table shows the percentages of voters that voted for the three main parties.

Conservative	36%
Labour	29%
Liberal Democrat	23%

    a Work out how many people voted for each party. Give your answers correct to one decimal place (1 dp).

    b How many of the people who voted did not vote for one of the main parties? Give your answer in millions, correct to one decimal place.

10 The members of a club are voting about a change in the rules.

65% must be in favour for the change to take place.

The club has 327 members.

How many must vote in favour for the change to take place?

  11   **a** Use a calculator to work out 32% of 76 g.

    b Find a simple way of working these out, without using your calculator.

      i 16% of 76 g   **ii** 32% of 38 m   **iii** 16% of £38

Financial skills: Don't lose your deposit

When you book a holiday, or order something you want to buy, you often have to pay a **deposit**.

The deposit will not be returned if you change your mind about taking the holiday or buying the item you have ordered.

A Mr Brown books a holiday for his family. The holiday costs £3250.

He pays a deposit of 15%.

Work out the deposit.

B Ms Green is getting new glasses. The cost is £286.

She is asked to pay a deposit of 40%.

How much is that?

C Sam orders a new car.

The car costs £12 456.

She adds metallic paint for £475 and alloy wheels for £395.

She is asked to pay a deposit of 30%. How much is that?

D Three friends are going on holiday together. The cost for each person is £789.

They must pay a deposit of 35%.

    a Work out the total deposit for all three.

    b They must pay the rest a month before the holiday starts.

      How much is that?

11.5 Percentage increases and decreases

Learning objective

• To work out the result of a simple percentage change

Keywords

decrease

increase

reduction

In a sale, prices are often reduced by a certain percentage.

When the value of something **increases** or **decreases**, the change is often described in terms of a percentage. This is the value of the increase or decrease as a percentage of the original price or value.

You add it on for an increase. You subtract it for a decrease. A decrease is often called a **reduction**.

Example 7

Here is a sign in a shop window.

The original price of a dress is £135.

In the sale the price is reduced by 30%.

What is the sale price?

SALE
NOW ON
Selected
prices
reduced
by 30%

    The reduction is 30% of £135.

    30% of 135 = 0.3 × 135 = 40.5

    The reduction is £40.50.

    The sale price is £135 − £40.50 = £94.50.

If, instead of a reduction, the price had been increased by 30%, then the new price would be £135 + £40.50 = £175.50.

For an increase, you calculate the percentage in the same way and then add it to the original value.

Exercise 11E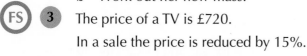

1   A tree is 5.60 m high. In a year the height increases by 10%.

    a   Work out the increase in height.

    b   Work out the new height.

2   A woman's mass is only 32 kg and she is trying to increase it.

    She successfully increases her mass by 12%.

    a   Work out the increase in her mass.

    b   Work out her new mass.

(FS) **3**   The price of a TV is £720.

    In a sale the price is reduced by 15%.

    a   Work out the reduction.

    b   Work out the new price.

FS **4** The price of a car is decreased by 3%.

The original price was £14 800.

a Work out the decrease in price.

b Work out the new price.

5 The population of a village has increased by 45% over the last ten years.

Ten years ago the population of the village was 360 people.

Work out the population now.

FS **6** The price of a washing machine is £440.

Work out the new price after an increase of:

a 5%   b 10%   c 15%.

FS **7** In a sale, prices are reduced. Work out the sale price of each of these items.

a	A jacket	Original price £85.00	Reduction 40%
b	A pair of trainers	Original price £63.50	Reduction 20%
c	A bag	Original price £44.00	Reduction 70%

8 Census figures show that in 2001 the population of England and Wales was 52.4 million.

In the next ten years the population increased by 7%.

What was the population of England and Wales in 2011?

PS **9** This is an extract from a newspaper article.

GAS AND ELECTRICITY PRICES INCREASE
A fuel company has announced that domestic gas bills will rise by 16% and electricity bills will rise by 18%.

The Watsons' gas bill last year was £625.

Their electricity bill was £441.

a Work out the expected bills for the Watsons for gas and electricity after the increases.

b What is the total increase in their bills for gas and electricity?

FS **10** A woman earns £36 600 per year.

She is given a pay rise of 4%.

a Work out her new salary.

b She is paid $\frac{1}{12}$ of her salary each month.

How much extra will she earn each month?

Financial skills: Add on the tax

VAT is a tax that is added to goods and services.

If you buy something, or have work done by someone, VAT is probably included in your bill.

The rate of VAT can vary.

In January 2011 the rate of VAT in the UK increased from 17.5% to 20%.

A The cost of a computer game before adding VAT is £38.

20% VAT must be added to this.

a How much is the VAT?

b What is the price including VAT?

B a Write 17.5% as a decimal.

b The cost of fitting a new kitchen, before adding VAT, is £8200.

If the rate of VAT is 17.5% work out the tax.

c Work out the cost including VAT.

C When the rate of VAT went up from 17.5% to 20%, prices increased.

The cost of a camera before VAT is added is £354.

a If the rate of VAT is 17.5%, what is the price of the camera including VAT?

b If the rate of VAT is 20%, what is the price of the camera including VAT?

c What is the increase in the price of the camera because of the increase in the VAT?

Ready to progress?

I can interpret percentages as fractions or decimals.
I can work out a fraction or a percentage of a quantity.
I can work out some percentages of quantities without using a calculator.

I can work out the result of a simple percentage change.
I can solve simple problems involving percentage changes.

Review questions

1 Write these fractions as percentages.

   a $\frac{3}{4}$ b $\frac{3}{10}$ c $\frac{3}{20}$ d $\frac{3}{50}$

2 Write each percentage as a fraction, as simply as possible.

   a 70%   b 60%   c 4%   d $12\frac{1}{2}$%   e 35%

3 Write each percentage as a decimal.
   a 90%   b 9%   c 0.9%

4 Here are five numbers.

   0.65   69%   0.8 $\frac{2}{3}$ $\frac{3}{4}$

   a Write down the largest number.   b Write down the smallest number.

5 Work out these quantities.

   a $\frac{2}{3}$ of 60 cm   b $\frac{3}{4}$ of 60 cm   c $\frac{4}{5}$ of 60 cm   d $\frac{5}{6}$ of 60 cm

6 There are 600 people in a concert hall. $\frac{2}{5}$ of them are teenagers. $\frac{3}{8}$ of the teenagers are girls. How many teenage girls are there in the concert hall?

7 Work out these quantities.
   a 60% of 750 kg   b 15% of 40 cm   c 30% of 1.5 litres   d 99% of £17.00

8 Work out these percentages of 7.5 kg.
   a 12%   b 72%   c 92%   d 2%

9 This pie chart shows the proportions of people in the crowd at a hockey game. The percentage of the crowd who are men is 25%.

   a Estimate, to the nearest ten per cent, the percentage of the crowd that are women.
   b There are 2300 people in the crowd.
      Estimate the number of women.

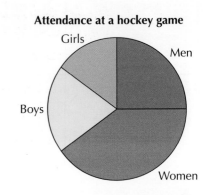

Attendance at a hockey game

Girls

Men

Boys

Women

(PS) **10** This information was found on a website.

> Modern bronze is typically
> 88% copper and 12% tin

A small bronze statue has a mass of 160 g.

Work out the masses of copper and tin in the statue.

(FS) **11** Arthur is given £417.

He decides to donate 20% to charity.

a How much does he donate?   **b** How much does he have left?

(FS) **12** Max pays a bill of £726 with a credit card.

There is a charge of 2% for doing this.

a What is the charge, in pounds?

b What is the total amount he has to pay?

c If Max pays a bill of £N, which of these expressions gives the credit card charge?
$2N$ $0.2N$ $0.02N$ $0.2 + N$ $0.02 + N$

13 Jan draws a rectangle. The sides are 16 cm and 24 cm long.

a Work out the area of the rectangle.

b Lou draws another rectangle. Each side is 25% longer than Jan's.
Work out:
i the lengths of the sides of Lou's rectangle   **ii** the area of Lou's rectangle.

c Show that the area of Lou's rectangle is more than 50% greater than the area of Jan's rectangle.

(FS) **14** The price of a second-hand car is £4900. In a sale, the price is reduced by 5%.
Work out the sale price of the car.

(FS) **15** Josie's salary is £22 400 a year. She gets a pay rise of 7%.

Work out her salary after the increase.

16 On Friday a website gets 150 hits.

On Saturday the number of hits increases by 40%.

a Work out the number of hits on Saturday.

b On Sunday the number of hits is 40% fewer than on Friday.
Work out the number of hits on Sunday.

c Draw a bar chart to show the number of hits each day.

(FS) **17** Here are three sale notices.

Which one gives the greatest reduction?

Explain your answer.

Prices reduced to 70%

Prices slashed by 30%

Prices down by one-third

Financial skills

Income tax

Most people who earn money have to pay income tax.
You can earn a certain amount before you have to pay tax.
This is called your tax allowance.
You pay a percentage of anything over your tax allowance as income tax.
This percentage is called the tax rate.

Peter earns £20 000 in one year. His tax allowance is £10 000. The tax rate is 20%.

1 Copy and complete these sentences.

   a Peter pays tax on £20 000 – £10 000 = £…

   b Peter's tax bill is 20% of … = £…

2 Work out the tax Peter will pay if he earns £30 000 in one year.

3 a Copy and complete this table for Peter. Fill in the answers from questions 1 and 2.

Income	£15 000	£20 000	£25 000	£30 000	£35 000
Tax					

   b Use the table to draw a graph that shows how much tax Peter pays. Draw axes like this.

     Plot five points and join them with a straight line that starts at 10 000 on the 'income' axis.

4 Use your graph to find out how much tax Peter will pay if he earns £27 500 in one year.

5 One year Peter pays £2400 income tax. Use the graph to find out how much he earned.

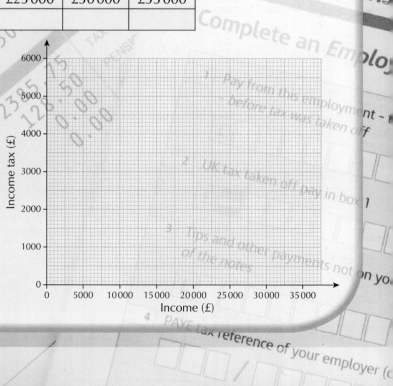

6 One year Peter did not pay any income tax. What can you say about the amount he earned?

7 Peter earns £16 000. He says: 'If I earn twice as much, I shall pay twice as much income tax.'

Is this true? Give a reason for your answer.

8 Suppose the tax allowance for Peter is increased from £10 000 to £15 000 and the tax rate is changed from 20% to 25%.

  a Show that if Peter earns £20 000 he will pay £1250 income tax.

  b Draw a new table, like the one in question 3, to show the tax Peter pays.

  c Draw a line, on the same graph as the previous one, to show how much tax Peter pays in this case.

  d Decide whether Peter pays more tax or less tax under this new system.

12

Probability

This chapter is going to show you:

- how to use the correct words to describe probability
- how to work with a probability scale
- how to work out theoretical probabilities in different situations
- how to use experimental probability to make predictions.

You should already know:

- some basic ideas about chance and probability
- how to collect data from a simple experiment
- how to record data in a table or chart.

About this chapter

In October 2012 the mayor of New York had a tricky decision to make. Hurricane Sandy, a violent and destructive storm, was heading across the Atlantic towards the east coast of the USA. But where exactly would its main force hit? What effect would it have on New York?

As it approached, scientists calculated and recalculated the probability of it devastating the city. Eventually, with the storm just hours away, the mayor ordered the compulsory evacuation of 375 000 people and so saved many lives.

Assessing the probability of what might happen like this is vital for scientists trying to prevent natural events such as storms and earthquakes from turning into disasters for the people who might be in their way.

12.1 Probability words

Learning objective

- To learn and use the correct words about probability

Key words

at random	chance
event	outcome
probability	probability scale
random	

Look at the pictures. Which one has the greatest **chance** of happening where you live today?

In **probability**, when something, such as rolling a dice, happens, it is called an **event**. The possible results are called the **outcomes** of the event. For example, rolling a dice has six possible outcomes: a score of 1, 2, 3, 4, 5, or 6.

You can use probability to decide how likely it is that different outcomes will happen.

Here are some words you will hear, when talking about whether something may happen: very likely, unlikely, certain, impossible, an even chance, very unlikely, likely.

The two complete opposites here are impossible and certain, with an even **chance** (evens) in the middle, and so these can be given in the order:
impossible, very unlikely, unlikely, evens, likely, very likely, certain.

These words can be shown on a **probability scale**.

Impossible   Very   Unlikely   Evens   Likely   Very   Certain
unlikely   likely

There are lots of other words you can use when describing probability, such as: 50–50 chance, probable, uncertain, good chance, poor chance.

If you flip a coin or throw a dice the outcome is **random**, which means that the outcome cannot be predicted. If you take a coloured ball from a bag, without looking at it, you are 'taking the ball **at random**'.

Example 1

Which is the more likely outcome: flipping tails on a coin or rolling a number less than 5 on a dice?

A coin can only land two ways (heads or tails), so there is an even chance of landing on tails.

On a dice there are four numbers less than 5 and two numbers that are not, so there is more than an even chance of rolling a number less than 5. So, rolling a number less than 5 is more likely than getting tails when a coin is flipped.

Example 2

Match each of these outcomes to a position on a probability scale.

a It will snow in the winter in London.

b You will come to school in a helicopter.

c The next person to walk through the door will be male.

d When a normal dice is thrown the score will be 8.

    a It usually snows in the winter, but not always, so this event is very likely.

    b Unless you are very rich this is very unlikely to happen.

    c As the next person to come through the door will be either male or female, this is an evens chance.

    d An ordinary dice can only score from 1 to 6 so this is impossible.

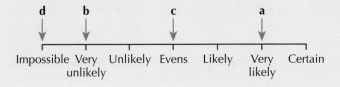

Impossible Very   Unlikely Evens   Likely   Very   Certain
               unlikely   likely

Exercise 12A

1 Match the events to the probability outcomes.

Events

  A You are younger today than you were last year.

  B You will score an odd number on an ordinary dice.

  C Most people in your class went to sleep last night.

  D Someone in your class will have a pet dog.

  E Someone in your class will have a pet snake.

  F Someone in you class will have a birthday this month.

  G Someone in your class will have three sisters.

  a certain

  b impossible

  c fifty-fifty chance

  d very unlikely

  e likely

  f very likely

  g unlikely

2 A shape is picked at random from one of these two grids. Copy and complete these sentences.

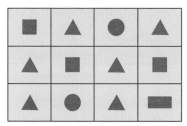

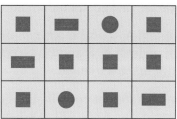

a Picking a … from grid … is impossible.

b Picking a … from grid … is likely.

c Picking a … from grid … is unlikely.

d Picking a … from grid … is very unlikely.

e Picking a … from grid … is fifty-fifty.

3 You pick one of these cards at random.

Put these outcomes in order of how likely they are, with the least likely first.

A The number on the card will be a factor of 24.

B The number on the card will be a multiple of 2.

C The number on the card will be a multiple of 5.

D The number on the card will be a square number.

E The number on the card will be a multiple of 3.

(MR) **4** Bag A contains 10 red marbles, five blue marbles and five green marbles.
Bag B contains eight red marbles, two blue marbles and no green marbles.

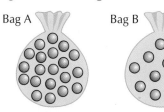

A girl wants to pick a marble at random from a bag.

Which bag should she choose to have the better chance of picking:

a a red marble   b a blue marble   c a green marble?
Explain your answers.

(MR) **5** A coin has been flipped five times and has landed 'heads' each time. If it is flipped again, is the chance of scoring another head likely, unlikely or fifty-fifty? Explain your answer.

(PS) **6** You have five rods with lengths, in metres (m), as shown.

A —— 2 m   B —— 3 m   C —— 4 m   D —— 5 m   E —— 6 m

Three rods are picked at random and, if it is possible, are made into a triangle.

For example if A, C and D are chosen they make a triangle. If A, B and E are picked they do not make a triangle.

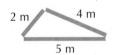

There are 10 different combinations of the three rods that can be picked from the five rods, for example, ABC, ABE, DCE. Work out the 10 different combinations.

Which is more likely, that the three rods chosen will make a triangle or the three rods chosen will not make a triangle?

Investigation: Pick a number

It is claimed that if you ask people to pick a single-digit number (1–9) it is most likely to be 7. Carry out a survey by asking at least 30 people to pick a number from 1 to 9 inclusive.

Record the results. Do your results support the claim?

12.2 Probability scales

Learning objectives

- To learn about and use probability scales from 0 to 1
- To work out probabilities based on equally likely outcomes

Key words	
biased	equally likely
fair	probability fraction

You know that probability is the way of describing and measuring the chance or likelihood that an outcome of an event will happen. Probability can be shown on a probability scale.

The following outcomes are shown on the probability scale below.

a The probability that a new-born baby will be a girl.

b The probability that a person is right-handed.

c The probability that someone in your class will have four sisters.

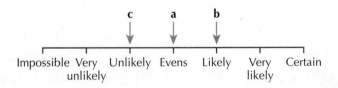

To measure probability as a value, rather than in words, you need to use a scale from 0 to 1.

Probabilities are written as fractions or decimals, and sometimes as percentages, as in the weather forecasts.

The numerical probability scale looks like this.

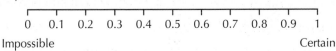

The probability of an outcome happening is written as:

$$P(\text{outcome}) = \frac{\text{number of ways the outcome can happen}}{\text{total number of all possible outcomes}}$$

The P stands for 'the probability of'. The outcome is shown inside the brackets.

When you toss a **fair** coin, there are two possible outcomes: Head (H) or Tail (T).

When a coin, a dice or a spinner is described as fair it means each outcome is **equally likely**. Sometimes, a dice may not be fair, so that one outcome is more likely than the rest.

That means that it is **biased**.

However, with a fair coin each outcome is equally likely to happen. So:

$$P(H) = \frac{1}{2} \text{ and } P(T) = \frac{1}{2}$$

This is the **probability fraction** for the event.

The probability can also be given as P(H) = 0.5 or P(H) = 50%.

Note that decimals are often used and you will see percentages used often, too, especially on weather forecasts.

When you throw a fair dice, there are six equally likely outcomes: 1, 2, 3, 4, 5, 6.

So, for example:

$$P(6) = \frac{1}{6}$$

$$P(1 \text{ or } 2) = \frac{2}{6} = \frac{1}{3}$$

Probability fractions can be simplified, but sometimes it can be better to leave them unsimplified, especially if you are comparing probabilities.

Exercise 12B

1 Here are two grids.

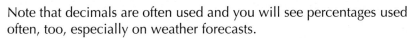

Grid 1   Grid 2

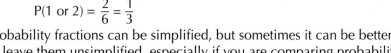

a A shape is chosen at random from grid 1. What is the probability it will be:
     i a triangle   **ii** a circle   **iii** a square   **iv** a rectangle   **v** a hexagon?

b A shape is chosen at random from grid 2. What is the probability it will be:
     i a triangle   **ii** a circle   **iii** a square   **iv** a rectangle   **v** red?
Give your answers as fractions in their simplest form.

2 A bag contains 10 red marbles, five blue marbles and five green marbles.
If a marble is chosen at random from the bag, what is the probability it will be:

     a a red marble   **b** a blue marble   **c** a green marble?

Give your answers as fractions in their simplest form.

3 Cards numbered 1 to 10 are placed in a box.

A card is drawn at random from the box.

Find the probability that the card drawn will be:

a a 5   **b** an even number   **c** a number in the 3 times table

d a 4 or an 8   **e** a number less than 12   **f** an odd number.

Give your answers as decimals.

4 Adam picks a card at random from a normal pack of 52 playing cards.

Find each of the following probabilities.

Give your answers as fractions with a denominator of 52.

a P(a Jack)   **b** P(a Heart)   **c** P(a picture card)

d P(Ace of Spades)   **e** P(a 9 or a 10)   **f** P(Ace)

g How can you tell easily that the probability of choosing a picture card is higher that the probability of choosing an ace?

5 A bag contains five red discs, three blue discs and two green discs.

Linda takes out a disc at random.

Find the probability that she takes out:

a a red disc   **b** a blue disc   **c** a green disc

d a yellow disc   **e** a red or blue disc.

6 Syed is using a fair, eight-sided spinner in a game.

What is the probability that he scores:

a 0   **b** 1   **c** 2   **d** 3?

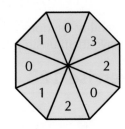

7 Sandhu rolls a fair dice. Calculate:

a P(3)   **b** P(odd number)   **c** P(5 or 6)

d P(even number)   **e** P(6)   **f** P(1 or 6).

8 Mr Evans has a box of 25 calculators, but five of them do not work very well.

What is the probability that the first calculator taken out of the box at random does not work very well?

Write your fraction as simply as possible.

9 At the start of a tombola, there are 300 tickets inside the drum.

There are 60 winning tickets available.

What is the probability that the first ticket taken out of the drum is a winning ticket? Write your fraction as simply as possible.

10 Emma and Nazir are playing a game with spinners.

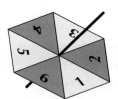 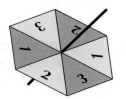

Emma's spinner   Nazir's spinner

a Who has more chance of spinning a three?

Explain your answer.

b Suggest a way in which they could change the spinners, so that they both have the same chance of scoring a three.

Activity: Lower or higher?

Work in pairs.

You will need a pack of cards numbered 1 to 10 for this experiment.

A One of you shuffles the pack, deals out five cards, face down, then puts the rest to one side.

1 Turn over the first card.

2 Ask your partner to predict if the second card will be lower or higher.

3 Turn over the second card.

4 If your partner was correct, ask them to predict if the third card will be lower or higher than the second card. If they were wrong their game is ended.

5 Repeat step 4 until your partner guesses incorrectly, or until all five cards have been played.

6 Play the game 10 times and record how many times your partner managed to predict correctly up to the fifth card.

7 Swap over and repeat the activity.

B If the whole class have done the activity discuss any strategies you used to predict the numbers.

C a Are there some numbers that make it certain your prediction will be correct?

  b Are there some numbers that make it likely your prediction will be correct?

  c Are there some numbers that make it hard to predict what the next one will be?

  d Does it get easier to make correct predictions after you see the first couple of cards?

12.3 Experimental probability

Learning objectives

- To understand experimental probability
- To understand the difference between theoretical probability and experimental probability

Key words

experimental probability

theoretical probability

trial

So far, you have used equally likely outcomes to calculate probabilities.

A probability that is calculated in this way is called a **theoretical probability**.

Sometimes, you can find a probability only by carrying out a series of experiments and recording the results in a frequency table. Then you will use these results to estimate the probability of an outcome.

A probability found in this way is called an **experimental probability**.

To find an experimental probability, you must repeat the experiment a number of times. Each separate experiment carried out is called a **trial**.

$$\text{Experimental probability of an outcome} = \frac{\text{number of times the outcome occurs}}{\text{total number of trials}}$$

It is important to remember that when you repeat an experiment, the experimental probability will be slightly different each time. The experimental probability of an event is an estimate for the theoretical probability.

As the number of trials increases, the value of the experimental probability gets closer to the theoretical probability.

Example 3

Ten coins are spun at the same time. Six of them land on 'heads'.

What is the experimental probability of spinning a head in this case?

The experimental probability of scoring a head = $\frac{6}{10} = \frac{3}{5}$.

Example 4

An electrician wants to estimate the probability that a new light bulb lasts for less than 1 month.

He fits 20 new bulbs and 3 of them fail within 1 month.

What is his estimate of the probability that a new light bulb fails?

3 out of 20 bulbs fail within 1 month, so his experimental

probability = $\frac{3}{20}$.

Example 5

A dentist keeps a record of the number of fillings she gives her patients over 2 weeks.

These are her results, for 150 patients.

Number of fillings	Number of patients
None	80
1	54
More than 1	16

Estimate the probability that a patient does not need a filling.

Experimental probability $= \frac{8}{150} = \frac{8}{15}$

Example 6

A company manufactures items for computers.

The numbers of faulty items are recorded in this table.

Number of items produced	Number of faulty items	Experimental probability
100	8	0.08
200	20	
500	45	
1000	82	

a Complete the table.

b Which is the best estimate of the probability of an item being faulty? Explain your answer.

a

Number of items produced	Number of faulty items	Experimental probability
100	8	0.08
200	20	0.1
500	45	0.09
1000	82	0.082

b The last result (0.082) is the best estimate, as it is based on more results.

Exercise 12C

1 Working in pairs, toss a coin 50 times. Record your results in a frequency table, like this one.

	Tally	Frequency
Head		
Tail		

a Use your results to find the experimental probability of scoring a head.

b What is the experimental probability of scoring a tail?

c If possible, combine your results with those of the rest of the class.

Is the value of the combined results for the experimental probability of getting a head closer to the theoretical probability of $\frac{1}{2}$ than your value?

2 Working in pairs, throw a dice 100 times.

Record your results in a frequency table, like this one.

Score	Tally	Frequency
1		
2		
3		
4		
5		
6		

a Find the experimental probability of getting 6.

b Find the experimental probability of getting an even score.

c If possible, combine your results with those of the rest of the class.

Is the value of the combined results for the experimental probability of getting a six closer to the theoretical probability of $\frac{1}{6}$ than your value?

3 Working in pairs, drop a drawing pin 50 times.

Copy this frequency table.

Use your table to record your results.

	Tally	Frequency
Point up		
Point down		

a What is the experimental probability that when the drawing pin is dropped it will land point up?

b Is your answer greater or less than an evens chance?

c Explain what would happen if you repeated the experiment.

d If possible, combine your results with those of the rest of the class.

What is the experimental probability of the drawing pin landing point down now, when it is dropped?

4 **a** Working in pairs, take four playing cards, one of each suit (♣, ♦, ♥, ♠). Shuffle them.

Look at the suit of the top card and record it in a frequency table like this one.

Suit	Tally	Frequency
Clubs ♣		
Diamonds ♦		
Hearts ♥		
Spades ♠		
	Total	

Shuffle the four cards after every turn.

Complete the table for 100 turns.

b Find your experimental probability of the top card being a Heart.

c Find your experimental probability of the top card being a black suit.

d If possible, combine your results with those of the rest of the class.

What are the experimental probabilities of:

- the top card being a Heart and

- the top card being a black card

now?

 5 A girl wishes to test whether a dice is biased. She rolls the dice 60 times. The results are shown in the table below.

Score	1	2	3	4	5	6
Frequency	6	12	10	9	15	8

a Do you think the dice is biased?

Give a reason for your answer.

b How could she improve the experiment?

c From the results, estimate the probability of rolling a 2.

d From the results, estimate the probability of rolling a 1 or a 4.

Activity: Spin the spinner

A 1 Make a six-sided spinner from card and a cocktail stick.

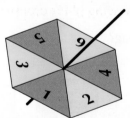

2 Weight it by sticking a small piece of a sticky pad below one of the numbers on the card. This will make the spinner unfair or biased.

3 Roll the spinner 60 times and record the scores in a frequency table.

4 Find the experimental probability for each score.

5 Remove the sticky pad.

Roll the spinner another 60 times and record the scores in a frequency table.

B Compare your results for the spinner with and without the sticky pad with what you would expect from a fair, six-sided spinner.

Ready to progress?

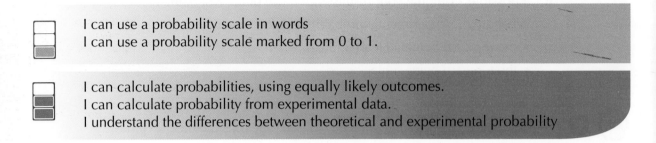

I can use a probability scale in words
I can use a probability scale marked from 0 to 1.

I can calculate probabilities, using equally likely outcomes.
I can calculate probability from experimental data.
I understand the differences between theoretical and experimental probability

Review questions

1 a Adam puts three white counters and two black counters in a bag.

He is going to take out one counter without looking.

What is the probability that the counter will be black?

b Adam puts the counter back in the bag and then puts more black counters in the bag.

He is going to take one counter without looking.

The probability that the counter will be black is now $\frac{3}{4}$.

How many more black counters did Adam put in the bag?

2 In each box of cereal there is a free gift of part of a toy train.

There are four parts to the train.

You cannot tell which part will be in any box. Each part is equally likely.

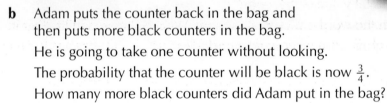

Engine   Small wagon   Big wagon   Caboose

a Xanda needs an engine to complete her train.

Her brother Micha needs a big wagon and a caboose.

They buy one box of cereal.

   i   What is the probability that the part is the engine?

   ii What is the probability that the part is a big wagon or a caboose?

b Their mother opens the box.

She tells them the part is not an engine.

   i   Now what is the probability that the part is the engine?

   ii Now what is the probability that the part is a big wagon or a caboose?

3 Katie buys a bag of sweets.

On the bag is a list of the sweets inside.

She takes a sweet from the bag at random.

Sweet Goody Bag
Contents
2 Humbugs
6 Lemon drops
7 Mojos
5 Pear drops

   a   What is the probability that she will get a lemon drop?

   b   Write the missing sweet from the sentence below.

   The probability that Katie will get a … is $\frac{1}{4}$.

4 **a**   On a 12 × 12 grid draw the three different rectangles that have whole number sides and an area of 12 cm².

   b   A student is asked to draw a rectangle with whole-number sides and an area of 12 cm².

   What is the probability that she draws a rectangle with a perimeter that is greater than 15 cm?

5 The word MATHEMATICS is made from Scrabble® tiles.

$M_3\ A_1\ T_1\ H_4\ E_1\ M_3\ A_1\ T_1\ I_1\ C_3\ S_1$

   a   What is the total value of the word?

   b   A letter from the word is picked at random. What is the probability that it:

     i   is a vowel   **ii**   is a letter in the word STATISTICS   **iii**   has a value more than 1?

6 There are some cubes in a bag. The cubes are either red (R) or black (B).

The probability that a cube taken at random from the bag is red is $\frac{1}{4}$.

   a   A pupil takes one cube out of the bag. It is red.

   What is the smallest number of black cubes there could be in the bag?

   b   Then the pupil takes another cube out of the bag. It is also red.

   From this new information, what is the smallest number of black cubes there could be in the bag?

   c   A different bag has blue (B), green (G) and yellow (Y) cubes in it. There is at least one of each of the three colours.

   The probability that a cube taken at random from the bag is blue is $\frac{3}{4}$.

   There are 20 cubes in the bag.

   What is the greatest number of yellow cubes there could be in the bag? Show your working.

 7 I need to score 6 or more to win a game. I can choose to roll 1 dice or 2 dice.

Which option should I choose? Explain your answer.

Financial skills
School Easter Fayre

Westfield Community School is having an Easter Fayre to raise money.

These are two of the games.

Find the Easter Bunny

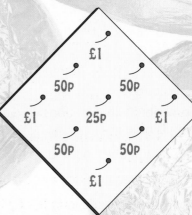

Class 9J have made a large board with 10 squares across and 10 squares down.

Each square has a window cut into it.

Players pay £1.50 to open the window on a square.

Behind each window is a prize.

There are 60 crème eggs, 30 packets of hot cross buns, 9 chocolate Easter eggs and 1 large Easter Bunny as prizes.

Throw a ring

Class 10F are running a game in which players throw rings at a board from 20 feet away and try to get the ring on one of the hooks. If they get their ring on a hook they win that amount of money.

You can buy five rings for £1.25.

There are 25 students in the form. To work out the chances of winning, each student threw 20 rings at the board.

These are the results.

	Number of rings
Miss	340
25p	90
50p	60
£1	10

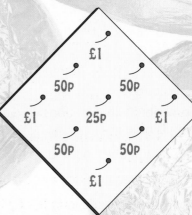

Use the information on Find the Easter Bunny to answer these questions.

1 Crème eggs cost 40p each, packets of hot cross buns cost 90p each, chocolate Easter eggs cost £2.25 each and the Easter Bunny cost £5.99.
   If all the squares are opened how much money will the class make?

2 At the start of the game what is the probability of winning:

   a a crème egg   **b** a packet of hot cross buns
   c a chocolate Easter egg   **d** the Easter Bunny?

3 After half the squares are opened there are still 25 crème eggs, 20 packets of hot cross buns, 4 chocolate Easter eggs and the Easter Bunny left as prizes.
   What is the probability now of winning:

   a a crème egg   **b** a packet of hot cross buns
   c a chocolate Easter egg   **d** the Easter Bunny?

4 Later in the day the Easter Bunny still hasn't been won and the probability of winning it is now $\frac{1}{10}$. How many squares are there still to be opened? Explain your answer.

Use the information about 'Throw a ring' to answer these questions.

5 What is the experimental probability of winning a prize of:

   a 25p   **b** 50p   **c** £1?

6 Tom buys five rings. He misses with his first four rings. Is he more likely to win or lose with his last ring? Explain your answer.

7 The class expect 500 rings to be thrown through the day. Show that they expect to make £62.50.

8 Will the class make exactly £62.50 if 500 rings are thrown?

9 Tim threw five rings and made a profit of 75p. Work out all the possible scores he could have had with these five rings. Explain your answer.

13

Symmetry

This chapter is going to show you:

- how to recognise shapes that have reflective symmetry
- how to use line symmetry
- how to recognise and use rotational symmetry
- how to reflect shapes in a mirror line
- how to use coordinates to reflect shapes in all four quadrants
- how to tessellate a shape.

You should already know:

- how to recognise symmetrical shapes
- how to plot coordinates.

About this chapter

If you drew one side of an animal, such as a pet dog or cat, could someone draw the other side without looking at the animal? They probably could, because, for most animals, one side of the body reflects the other, like a mirror image. Their legs are the same length, their feet and ears are the same size. Their bodies are symmetrical. There are many other examples of symmetry all around us – in leaves, flowers, feathers. Symmetry is essential in the living world.

13.1 Line symmetry

Learning objectives

- To recognise shapes with reflective symmetry
- To draw lines of symmetry on a shape

Key words

line of symmetry

mirror line

reflect

reflective symmetry

If you can fold a 2D shape along a line, so that one half of the shape fits exactly over the other half, the fold line is a **line of symmetry**.

You can use a mirror or tracing paper to check whether a shape has a line of symmetry.

Some shapes have no lines of symmetry.

A line of symmetry is also called a **mirror line** because the shapes on each side **reflect** each other.

This property is called **reflective symmetry**.

Example 1

Describe the symmetry of this shape.

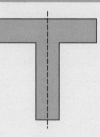

This T-shape has one line of symmetry, as shown.

Put a mirror on the line of symmetry and check that the image in the mirror is half the T-shape.

Trace the T-shape and fold the tracing along the line of symmetry to check that both halves of the shape fit exactly over each other.

Example 2

Describe the symmetry of this shape.

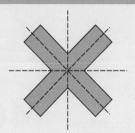

This cross has four lines of symmetry, as shown.

Check that each line drawn here is a line of symmetry.

Use either a mirror or tracing paper.

Example 3

Describe the symmetry of this shape.

This L-shape has no lines of symmetry.

You can use tracing paper or a mirror to check.

Exercise 13A

1 Copy each shape and draw its lines of symmetry.
Write below each shape the number of lines of symmetry it has.

a

Isosceles triangle

b

Equilateral triangle

c

Square

d

Rectangle

e

Parallelogram

f

Kite

2 Write down the number of lines of symmetry for each shape.

a   **b** 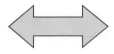 **c**   **d**

e   **f**   **g**   **h**

3 Write down the number of lines of symmetry for each of these road signs.

a   **b**   **c**

d   **e**   **f**

(PS) **4** Here are three identical rectangles.

Put the three rectangles together to make a shape that has:

a no lines of symmetry   **b** exactly one line of symmetry

c exactly two lines of symmetry.

MR **5** Here is a sequence of symmetrical shapes.

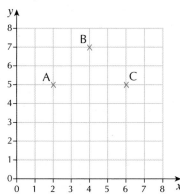

    a There is one line of symmetry that works for all these shapes.

       Draw this in for each one and look carefully at the shapes formed.

    b Try to draw the next two shapes in the sequence.

    c Explain how the sequence is formed.

PS **6** The points A(2, 5), B(4, 7) and C(6, 5) are shown on the grid.

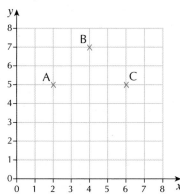

    Copy the grid onto squared paper and plot the points A, B and C.

    a Plot a point D so that the four points have no lines of symmetry.

    b Plot a point E so that the four points have exactly one line of symmetry.

    c Plot a point F so that the four points have exactly four lines of symmetry.

7 Design a logo for a new sports and leisure centre that is due to open soon.

    Your logo should have four lines of symmetry.

Investigation: Symmetrical squares

Two squares can be put together along their sides to make a shape that has line symmetry.

One symmetrical
arrangement for two squares

Three squares can be put together along their sides to make two different shapes that have line symmetry.

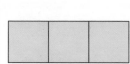

Two symmetrical arrangements
for three squares

A Investigate how many different symmetrical arrangements there are for four squares.

B What about five squares?

13.2 Rotational symmetry

Learning objectives

- To recognise shapes that have rotational symmetry
- To find the order of rotational symmetry for a shape

A 2D shape has **rotational symmetry** if it can be rotated so that it looks exactly the same in a new position.

The **order of rotational symmetry** is the number of different positions in which the shape looks the same, as it is rotated through one complete turn (360°).

A shape has no rotational symmetry if it has to be rotated through one complete turn to look exactly the same. Such a shape has rotational symmetry of order 1.

To find the order of rotational symmetry of a shape, it is a good idea to use tracing paper.

- First, trace the shape.
- Then rotate the tracing paper until the tracing again fits exactly over the shape.
- Count the number of times that the tracing fits exactly over the shape, until you return to the starting position.
- The number of times that the tracing fits is the order of rotational symmetry.

Example 4

Describe the symmetry of this shape.

This shape has rotational symmetry of order 3.

Example 5

Describe the symmetry of this shape.

This shape has rotational symmetry of order 4.

Example 6

Describe the symmetry of this shape.

This shape has no rotational symmetry.

Therefore, it has rotational symmetry of order 1 as it fits on top of itself only once.

Exercise 13B

1 Copy each of these capital letters and write down its order of rotational symmetry.

a **H** b **M** c **N**

d **S** e **W** f **X**

2 Write down the order of rotational symmetry for each shape.

a  b   c

d   e   f

MR 3 Copy and complete the table below for each of these regular polygons.

a b c d e

Shape	Number of lines of symmetry	Order of rotational symmetry
a Equilateral triangle		
b Square		
c Regular pentagon		
d Regular hexagon		
e Regular octagon		

What do you notice?

4 These patterns are from Islamic designs.

Write down the order of rotational symmetry for each pattern.

a 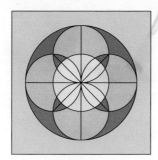 b  c

PS **5** Here are four identical right-angled triangles.

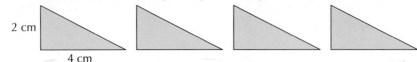

2 cm

4 cm

Copy the four triangles and put them together to make a shape that has rotational symmetry of:

a order 1 **b** order 2 **c** order 4.

Activity: Rotational patterns

A Make eight copies of this shape, on square dotty paper.

B Cut them out and arrange them to make a pattern with rotational symmetry of order 8.

C Design your own pattern that has rotational symmetry of order 8.

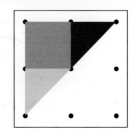

13.3 Reflections

Learning objectives

- To understand how to reflect a shape
- To use coordinates to reflect shapes in all four quadrants

Key words

| image | object |
| reflect | reflection |

The diagram shows an L-shape **reflected** in a mirror.

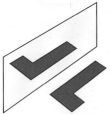

You can use a mirror line to draw the **reflection**, like this.

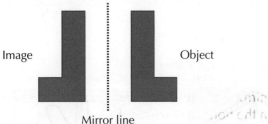

Image

Object

Mirror line

The **object** is reflected in the mirror line to give the **image**.

The mirror line becomes a line of symmetry. So, if the paper is folded along the mirror line, the object will fit exactly over the image.

Note that the image is the same distance from the mirror line as the object is.

Example 7

Reflect this shape in the mirror line.

Notice that the image is the same size as the object, and that the mirror line becomes a line of symmetry.

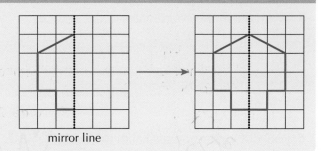

mirror line

Example 8

Describe the reflection in this diagram.

Triangle A'B'C' is the reflection of triangle ABC in the mirror line.

Notice that the line joining A to A' is at right angles to the mirror line and the three points on the object and image are at the same distance from the mirror line.

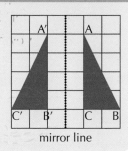

mirror line

Example 9

Reflect the rectangle in the two mirror lines.

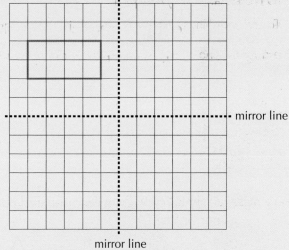

mirror line

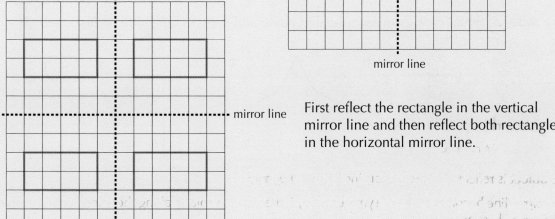

mirror line

mirror line

First reflect the rectangle in the vertical mirror line and then reflect both rectangles in the horizontal mirror line.

Example 10

a Write down the coordinates of the vertices of triangle P.

b Reflect P in the *x*-axis. Label the new triangle Q.

c Write down the coordinates of the vertices of triangle Q.

d Reflect Q in the *y*-axis. Label the new triangle R.

e Write down the coordinates of the vertices of triangle R.

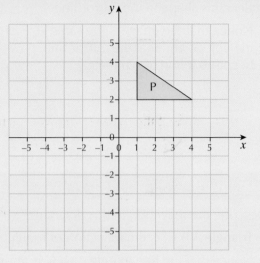

a (1, 4), (4, 2), (1, 2)

b and d See the diagram.

c (1, −4), (4, −2), (1, −2)

d (−1, −4), (−4, −2), (−1, −2)

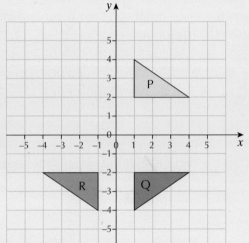

Exercise 13C

1 Copy each diagram onto squared paper and draw its reflection in the dotted mirror line.

a 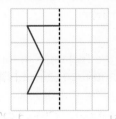   b 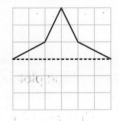   c 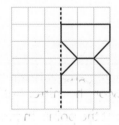   d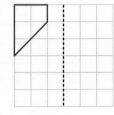

2 Copy each shape onto squared paper and draw its reflection in the dotted mirror line.

a 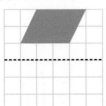 b 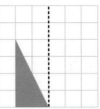 c 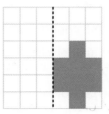 d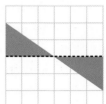

3 Reflect the shape in the two mirror lines.

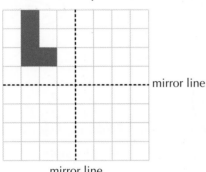

mirror line

mirror line

4 a Copy the diagram onto squared paper and reflect the triangle in the series of parallel mirror lines.

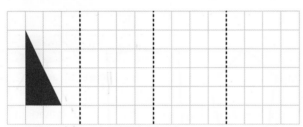

b Use a series of parallel mirror lines to make up your own patterns.

5 The points A(1, 2), B(2, 5), C(4, 4) and D(6, 1) are shown on the grid.

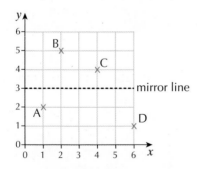

a Copy the grid onto squared paper and plot the points A, B, C and D. Draw on the mirror line.

b Reflect the points in the mirror line and label them A′, B′, C′ and D′.

c Write down the coordinates of the image points.

d The point E(12, 6) is reflected in the mirror line. What are the coordinates of E′?

6

a Copy the grid onto squared paper and draw the triangle ABC.

Write down the coordinates of A, B and C.

b Reflect the triangle in the *x*-axis. Label the vertices of the image A′, B′ and C′.

What are the coordinates of A′, B′ and C′?

c Reflect triangle A′B′C′ in the *y*-axis. Label the vertices of this image A″, B″ and C″.

What are the coordinates of A″, B″ and C″?

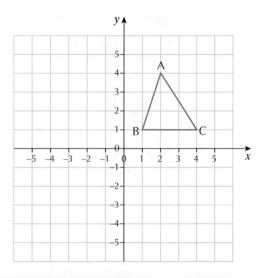

Activity: Using ICT software

Use ICT software packages, such as Logo or Cabri Geometry, to reflect shapes.

13.4 Tessellations

Learning objective

- To understand how to tessellate shapes

Key word

tessellation

A **tessellation** is a pattern made by fitting the same shapes together without leaving any gaps.

When drawing a tessellation, use a square or a triangular grid, as in the examples below.

To show a tessellation, you should generally draw up to about ten repeating shapes.

Example 11

These are two different shapes that each makes a tessellation on a square grid.

Example 12

This shape tessellates on a triangular grid.

Exercise 13D

1 Make a tessellation with each shape. Use a square grid.

a   b  c  d

2 Make a tessellation with each shape. Use a triangular grid.

a   b   c   d

3 Here is a tessellation that uses curves.

Design a different tessellation that uses curves.

4 Any quadrilateral will tessellate.

This is an example of an irregular quadrilateral.

Make an irregular quadrilateral tile cut from card.

Then use your tile to show how it tessellates.

Activity: Tessellation poster

Work in pairs or groups.

A Design a tessellation of your own.

B Make an attractive poster to show all your different tessellations.

Ready to progress?

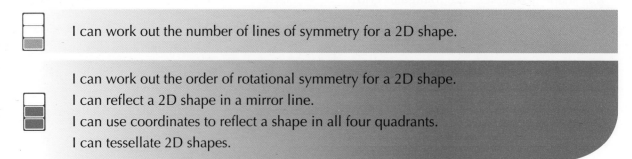

I can work out the number of lines of symmetry for a 2D shape.

I can work out the order of rotational symmetry for a 2D shape.
I can reflect a 2D shape in a mirror line.
I can use coordinates to reflect a shape in all four quadrants.
I can tessellate 2D shapes.

Review questions

1   These are examples of symmetry from nature.

Write down the number of lines of symmetry for each one.

a   butterfly   b   flower   c   starfish   d   snowflake

2   Write down the order of rotational symmetry for each of these artistic patterns.

a   b   c   d

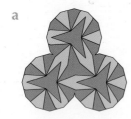
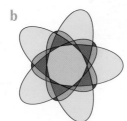

 3   Copy this table.

a   Write the name of each shape in the correct cell.

Number of lines of symmetry	Order of rotational symmetry			
	1	2	3	4
0				
1				
2				
3				
4				

a   isosceles triangle   b   equilateral triangle   c   square   d   rectangle
e   parallelogram   f   rhombus   g   kite

4   Copy this square grid and reflect the triangle in the two mirror lines.

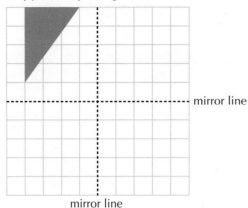

········· mirror line

mirror line

5   On the right is a square grid with two rectangles.

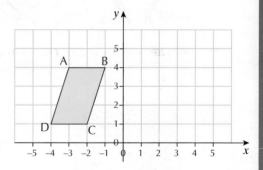

You can use the grid and the two rectangles
to make a pattern.

This pattern has no lines of symmetry.

a   Copy the grid and use the two rectangles to make a pattern
     that has exactly one line of symmetry.

b   Copy the grid and use the two rectangles to make a pattern
     that has exactly two lines of symmetry.

c   Copy the grid and use the two rectangles to make a pattern that has rotational
     symmetry of order 2.

6   a   Copy this grid onto squared paper and
          draw the parallelogram ABCD.

     b   Write down the coordinates of A, B, C
          and D.

     c   Reflect the parallelogram in the y-axis.
          Label the vertices of the image A', B', C'
          and D'.

     d   What are the coordinates of A', B', C'
          and D'?

 7   This is a tessellating mosaic tiling
        pattern, similar to those found in
        Roman villas.

     a   How many different shapes can
          you find?

     b   Draw the shapes that are
          tessellated here on a triangular
          grid.

Activity
Landmark spotting

Look at the symmetry of these famous landmarks.

1 How many lines of symmetry does each landmark have?

   Draw sketches of the landmarks to show the lines of symmetry.

2 Some of the buildings will have a different number of lines if the picture was taken directly from above. We call this the aerial view.

   How many lines of symmetry would a picture of the Eiffel Tower have from an aerial view?

   Draw a sketch to show the lines of symmetry.

   Explain why it may not be possible to do this for the aerial views of the other buildings.

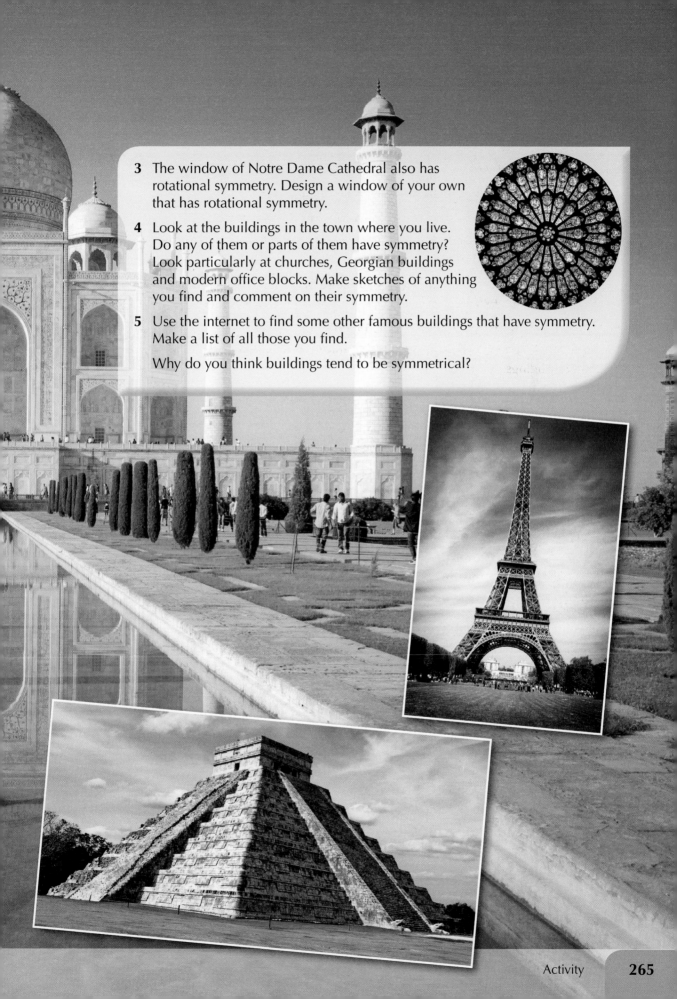

3 The window of Notre Dame Cathedral also has rotational symmetry. Design a window of your own that has rotational symmetry.

4 Look at the buildings in the town where you live. Do any of them or parts of them have symmetry? Look particularly at churches, Georgian buildings and modern office blocks. Make sketches of anything you find and comment on their symmetry.

5 Use the internet to find some other famous buildings that have symmetry. Make a list of all those you find.

Why do you think buildings tend to be symmetrical?

14

Equations

This chapter is going to show you:

- how to solve simple equations
- how to set up equations to solve simple problems.

You should already know:

- how to write and use expressions
- how to substitute numbers into expressions to work out their value
- how to write and use simple formulae.

About this chapter

Algebra is the branch of mathematics where we use letters to stand for numbers. When you wrote formulae in Chapter 7 you were using algebra. You also used algebra in Chapter 10, when you learnt about graphs.

An understanding of algebra helps you in studying mathematics and many other subjects that use mathematics.

Algebra started developing when the ancient Babylonians first worked out rules for doing calculations.

In the third century AD, a Greek mathematician called Diophantus wrote a book about solving equations, which is what you will be doing in this chapter.

Modern algebra started with the work of the Arabic mathematician Al-Khwarizmi (780–850AD). He called his method *al-jabr*, which is Arabic for 'restoration' or 'completion'. From *al-jabr* we get the English word 'algebra'.

14.1 Finding unknown numbers

Learning objective

• To find missing numbers in simple calculations

Key words

| algebra | unknown number |

In Chapter 7 you learnt how to use **algebra** to write expressions in which letters represent **unknown numbers**. You are going to use those skills in this chapter.

Nat thinks of a number.

He doubles it and then adds 7.

Suppose Nat's number is n.

If you double n you get $2n$. If you then add 7 the result is $2n + 7$.

Now Nat says that the answer is 19.

Can you guess the value of n that makes $2n + 7$ equal to 19?

You should be able to see that it is $n = 6$ because $2 \times 6 + 7 = 19$.

Example 1

Molly thinks of a number.

She subtracts 5 and then multiplies by 3.

The answer is 24.

a Call Molly's number m. Write down an expression to show what Molly did.

b Find the value of m that makes the expression equal to 18.

  a If you subtract 5 from m you get $m - 5$.

  If you multiply this by 3 you get $3(m - 5)$.

  The brackets show that you do the subtraction first.

  b Now you want to find the value of m that makes $3(m - 5) = 18$.

  By guessing, you should see that $m = 11$.

  Check: $11 - 5 = 6$ and $3 \times 6 = 18$.

Example 2

a Work out the value of the letter a if $a + 4 = 20$.

b Work out the value of the letter b if $2b + 4 = 20$.

  a $a + 4 = 20$ What number do you add to 4 to make 20? The answer is 16.

  So $a = 16$.

  b $2b + 4 = 20$ In this case the answer is 8 because $2 \times 8 + 4 = 20$.

  So $b = 8$.

Example 3

In this number wall, the number in each brick is the sum of the numbers in the two bricks below it.

Work out the values of a, b and c.

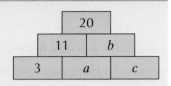

The top number is always the sum of the two numbers below it.

$11 + b = 20$, so b must be 9.

In the same way, $11 = 3 + a$ so $a = 8$.

Finally, $a + c = b$, so $8 + c = 9$.

Therefore $c = 1$.

Exercise 14A

1 Work out the number that each letter represents.

    a $5 + x = 7$ **b** $6 + y = 12$ **c** $5 + d = 19$ **d** $9 + g = 31$

    e $a + 9 = 13$ **f** $r + 8 = 11$ **g** $w + 12 = 36$ **h** $t + 7 = 22$

2 Work out the number that each letter represents.

    a $5x = 15$ **b** $9y = 18$ **c** $5z = 25$ **d** $6w = 18$

    e $2v = 12$ **f** $2u = 28$ **g** $3t = 36$ **h** $4r = 80$

3 Work out the number that each letter represents.

    a $a - 2 = 6$ **b** $a - 7 = 9$ **c** $c - 3 = 11$ **d** $d - 1 = 9$

    e $8 - e = 7$ **f** $12 - f = 9$ **g** $20 - g = 13$ **h** $15 - h = 2$

4 In this number wall, the number in each brick is the sum of the numbers in the two bricks below it.

Work out the values of a, b and c.

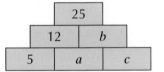

5 Work out the values of d, e and f in this number wall.

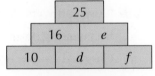

6 Work out the values of g, h and i in this number wall.

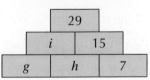

7 Jason thinks of a number. He multiplies it by 5. Then he adds 3.

    a Call Jason's number j.

       Write down an expression to show what Jason did.

    b Find the value of j, if the answer is 13.

    c Find the value of j, if the answer is 23.

    d Find the value of j, if the answer is 38.

8 Nina thinks of a number.

She adds 6 then multiplies by 2.

a Call Nina's number k.

Write down an expression to show what Nina did.

b Find the value of k, if the answer is 18.

c Find the value of k, if the answer is 24.

d Find the value of k, if the answer is 40.

Investigation: Bricks in a number wall

A This number wall has four rows and three missing numbers.

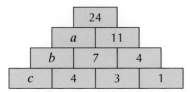

Work out the values of a, b and c.

B Make up a number wall of your own, with letters for missing numbers.

You must include at least one number in each row.

Make sure it is possible to solve your number wall.

Give it to someone else to solve.

C Now try making up a number wall with more than three letters.

14.2 Solving equations

Learning objectives

- To understand what an equation is
- To solve equations involving one operation

Key words

| equation | solve |

At the start of the previous section Nat was thinking of a number, n.

After multiplying by 2 and adding 7 he got the expression $2n + 7$.

Nat's answer was 19 so you can write $2n + 7 = 19$.

This is an **equation**.

There is only one value of n that makes $2n + 7$ equal to 19. It is $n = 6$.

Finding the value of n is called **solving** the equation.

Example 4

Solve these equations.

a $x + 17 = 53$ **b** $5y = 45$ **c** $\frac{z}{3} = 9$

   a $x + 17 = 53$ This means 'a number + 17 = 53'.

   You could try to guess the answer, but it is easier do it by subtraction.

   $x = 53 - 17$ The number is $53 - 17$.

   $\quad = 36$

   b $5y = 45$ This means '5 × a number = 45'.

   $y = 45 \div 5 = 9$ The number is $45 \div 5$.

   c $\frac{z}{3}$ means $z \div 3$.

   $\frac{z}{3} = 9$ This means 'a number divided by 3 = 9'.

   $z = 3 \times 9 = 27$ Multiply 9 by 3 to find the answer.

Example 5

a Write down an expression for the perimeter of this triangle, in centimetres.

b The perimeter of the triangle is 100 cm. Write an equation to express this fact.

c Solve the equation.

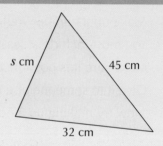

   a The perimeter is $s + 45 + 32 = s + 78$ cm.

   b The perimeter is 100 cm so the equation is $s + 78 = 100$.

   c Solving the equation means finding the value of s.

   $s + 78 = 100$

   Then $s = 100 - 78$

   $\qquad = 22$

Example 6

a Write down an expression for the area of this rectangle.

b The area of the rectangle is 63 cm². Write an equation involving y.

c Solve the equation.

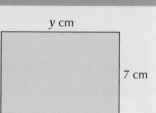

   a The area is $7 \times y = 7y$ cm².

   b The area is 63 cm² so the equation is $7y = 63$.

   c $\quad 7y = 63$

   Then $y = 63 \div 7$

   $\qquad = 9$

Exercise 14B

1 Solve these equations.

   a $x + 3 = 11$ **b** $x + 5 = 13$ **c** $x + 14 = 39$ **d** $x - 7 = 12$

   e $m - 1 = 15$ **f** $k + 6 = 33$ **g** $n - 8 = 20$ **h** $x - 9 = 0$

   i $a + 8 = 25$ **j** $b - 11 = 60$ **k** $c + 9 = 40$ **l** $d - 24 = 19$

2 Solve these equations.

   a $3x = 12$ **b** $2m = 18$ **c** $4x = 16$ **d** $5t = 25$

   e $2x = 24$ **f** $4m = 44$ **g** $2m = 30$ **h** $7x = 35$

   i $5m = 100$ **j** $3k = 39$ **k** $8x = 120$ **l** $2t = 5$

3 Solve these equations.

   a $\dfrac{a}{2} = 6$ **b** $\dfrac{b}{5} = 8$ **c** $\dfrac{x}{12} = 2$ **d** $\dfrac{y}{4} = 20$

   e $\dfrac{k}{3} = 15$ **f** $\dfrac{m}{8} = 2$ **g** $\dfrac{r}{10} = 10$ **h** $\dfrac{s}{25} = 6$

4 **a** Write down an expression for the perimeter of this triangle.

   b Suppose the perimeter of the triangle is 37 cm.

     i Write down an equation involving f.

     ii Solve the equation to find the value of f.

   c Suppose the perimeter of the triangle is 45 cm.

     i Write down an equation involving f.

     ii Solve the equation.

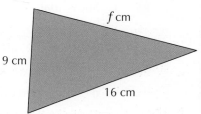

5 **a** Write down an expression for the area of this rectangle.

   b Suppose the area of the rectangle is 88 cm².

     i Write down an equation involving r.

     ii Solve the equation.

   c Suppose the area of the rectangle is 120 cm².

     i Write down an equation involving r.

     ii Solve the equation.

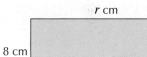

6 **a** Write down an expression for the sum of the angles in this quadrilateral.

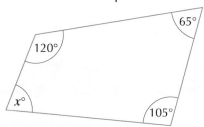

   b The angles in a quadrilateral add up to 360°.

     Write down an equation involving x.

   c Solve your equation to find the value of x.

7 For each diagram:

   i write down an equation   **ii** solve it to work out the value of x.

a

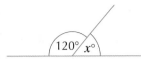

b

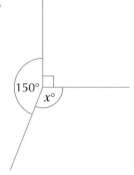

c

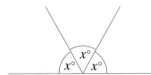

d

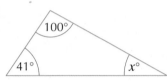

8 **a** Show that an expression for the number in the top brick of this number wall is $x + 48$.

   b Suppose the number in the top cell is 54.

      i Write down an equation involving x.

      ii Solve the equation to find the value of x.

   c Suppose the number in the top cell is 65.

      i Write down an equation involving x.

      ii Solve the equation to find the value of x.

   d Suppose the number in the top cell is 90.

      i Write down an equation involving x.

      ii Solve the equation to find the value of x.

9 **a** Work out an expression for the number in the top brick of this number wall. Write it as simply as possible.

   b Suppose the number in the top cell is 50.

      i Write down an equation involving y.

      ii Solve the equation.

   c Suppose the number in the top cell is 100.

      i Write down an equation involving y.

      ii Solve the equation.

   d Suppose the number in the top cell is 86. Work out the value of y.

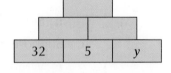

Challenge: Another brick in another wall

Work out the value of x in this number wall.

> **Hint:** Try to find an equation.

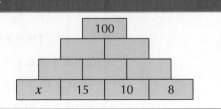

14.3 Solving more complex equations

Learning objective

- To solve equations involving two operations

Key words

| inverse | operation |

Each of the equations you solved in the last section had an **operation**, such as addition, subtraction or multiplication.

You have seen the equation $2n + 9 = 17$ before.

It involves two operations, first multiplication and then addition.

Example 7

Solve these equations.

a $4a - 9 = 35$ **b** $3a + 8 = 41$ **c** $3(k + 2) = 27$ **d** $\dfrac{d}{4} - 6 = 14$

a $4a - 9 = 35$

$\quad 4a = 35 + 9$ First add 9 to both sides.

$\quad 4a = 44$

$\quad a = 44 \div 4$ Now divide both sides by 4.

$\quad a = 11$

You can see that to 'undo' a subtraction you do an addition.

To 'undo' a multiplication you do a division.

These are **inverse** operations.

b $3a + 8 = 41$

$\quad 3a = 33$ First subtract 8 from both sides.

$\quad a = 33 \div 3$ Now divide both sides by 4.

$\quad a = 11$

Here, to 'undo' an addition, you do a subtraction.

c $3(k + 2) = 27$

$\quad k + 2 = 9$ First divide both sides by 3. $27 \div 3 = 9$

$\quad k = 7$ Then subtract 2 from both sides. $9 - 2 = 7$

In this case, because of the brackets, you do the division first.

The inverse of 'multiply by 3' is 'divide by 3'.

The inverse of 'add 2' is 'subtract 2'.

d $\dfrac{d}{4} - 6 = 14$

$\quad \dfrac{d}{4} = 20$ First add 6 to both sides. $14 + 6 = 20$

$\quad d = 80$ Then multiply both sides by 4. $20 \times 4 = 80$

The inverse of 'divide by 4' is 'multiply by 4'.

Example 8

a Work out an expression involving x for the number in the top box of this number wall.

b The top number is 21. Write an equation and solve it to find the value of x.

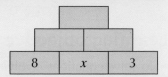

a The expressions on the second row are $x + 8$ and $x + 3$.

The expression in the top box is $x + 8 + x + 3$.

This simplifies to $2x + 11$.

b The equation is $2x + 11 = 21$.

$2x = 21 - 11$ First subtract 11 from both sides.   'Subtract 11' is the inverse of 'add 11'.

$2x = 10$

$x = 10 \div 2$ Then divide by 2.   'Divide by 2' is the inverse of 'multiply by 2'.

$x = 5$

Example 9

In this pentagon, four of the sides are the same length.

a Write an expression for the perimeter of the pentagon, in terms of a.

b Suppose the perimeter of the rectangle is 98 cm. Write down an equation involving a.

c Solve the equation to find the value of a.

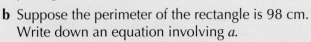
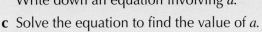

a cm a cm

a cm a cm

30 cm

a The perimeter is $a + a + a + a + 30 = 4a + 30$ cm.

b If the perimeter is 98 cm, then $4a + 30 = 98$.

c $4a + 30 = 98$

$\quad\quad 4a = 68$ Subtract 30 from both sides. $98 - 30 = 68$

$\quad\quad\ a = 17$ Divide both sides by 4. $68 \div 4 = 17$

Exercise 14C

1 Solve each equation.

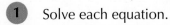

a $3x + 2 = 11$	**b** $2m - 7 = 1$	**c** $4x - 5 = 19$	**d** $5t + 3 = 18$
e $2x + 5 = 13$	**f** $4m - 5 = 15$	**g** $2m - 17 = 13$	**h** $7x - 2 = 19$
i $5m - 2 = 28$	**j** $3k + 4 = 31$	**k** $8x - 5 = 75$	**l** $2t + 2 = 48$

2 Solve each equation.

a $2(x + 1) = 10$	**b** $3(y - 4) = 21$	**c** $4(z + 4) = 40$	**d** $2(w - 3) = 30$
e $2(k + 7) = 50$	**f** $10(f - 8) = 70$	**g** $9(g + 4) = 99$	**h** $2(w - 25) = 14$

3 Solve each equation.

a $\dfrac{x}{3} + 4 = 10$ **b** $\dfrac{x}{5} - 1 = 2$ **c** $\dfrac{x}{4} - 3 = 2$ **d** $\dfrac{m}{3} - 2 = 1$

e $\dfrac{m}{5} + 4 = 7$ **f** $\dfrac{m}{7} + 3 = 5$ **g** $\dfrac{m}{4} + 2 = 8$ **h** $\dfrac{k}{6} + 1 = 25$

i $\dfrac{k}{5} + 5 = 20$ **j** $\dfrac{k}{3} + 12 = 16$ **k** $\dfrac{k}{2} + 5 = 37$ **l** $\dfrac{x}{7} - 3 = 8$

4 Solve these equations.

a $3x + 4 = 19$ **b** $3(x + 4) = 30$ **c** $\dfrac{m}{4} + 3 = 12$ **d** $5n - 7 = 23$

e $5(t - 7) = 55$ **f** $\dfrac{y}{5} - 17 = 3$ **g** $9x + 37 = 100$ **h** $2(x - 21) = 88$

i $4s + 15 = 135$ **j** $10(d + 4) = 90$ **k** $2a - 12 = 19$ **l** $\dfrac{c}{12} + 30 = 32$

 5 For each of these number walls:

   i use the number in the top brick to write an equation involving x

   ii solve the equation to find the value of x.

Part **a** has been done for you.

a 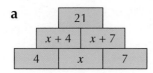   **b** 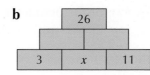   **c**

   i $2x + 11 = 21$

   ii $2x = 10 \rightarrow x = 5$

d 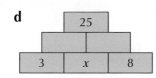   **e** 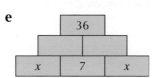   **f**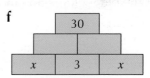

g 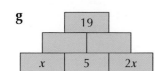   **h** 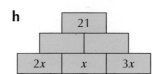   **i**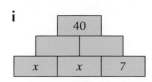

 6 For each of these number walls:

   i use the number in the top brick to write an equation involving x.

   ii solve the equation to find the value of x.

a 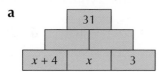   **b**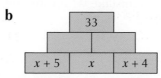

7 **a** Write down an expression for the perimeter of this hexagon.

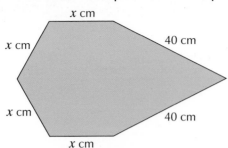

b The perimeter of the hexagon is 152 cm.

Write down an equation for this.

c Solve your equation and find the value of x.

8 In this octagon, six sides are the same length.

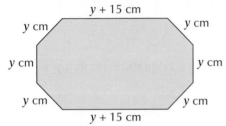

a Write down an expression for the perimeter of the octagon.

b The perimeter of the hexagon is 214 cm.

Write down an equation for this.

c Solve your equation and find the value of y.

d Work out the lengths of the two longest sides of the octagon.

 9 This is a page from Emma's exercise book.

1. $3x + 7 = 22$
Subtract 7 $3x = 18$
Divide by 3 $x = 6$
Check $3 \times 6 + 7 = 15 + 7 = 22$ ✓

2. $\frac{x}{5} - 8 = 2$
Add 8 $\frac{x}{5} = 10$
Multiply by 5 $x = 2$
Check $2 \times 5 - 8 = 10 - 8 = 2$ ✓

3. $\frac{x}{2} - 5 = 6$
Multiply by 2 $x - 5 = 12$
Add 5 $x = 17$
Check $17 - 5 = 12, 12 \div 2 = 6$ ✓

4. $3(x + 6) = 18$
Subtract 6 $3x = 12$
Divide by 3 $x = 4$

She has made a mistake when solving each equation. Write down a correct solution to each problem.

Equations can be written in different ways.

For example, the equation $2n + 7 = 25$ can be written as:

$$7 + 2n = 25$$
or $\quad 25 = 2n + 7$
or $\quad 25 = 7 + 2n.$

Here are some equations written in unusual ways.

Try to solve them.

a $9 + 4n = 3$ **b** $13 = 3f - 20$ **c** $2(10 + g) = 38$

d $56 = 3w - 31$ **e** $7 + 7c = 77$ **f** $3(r + 2) - 27 = 0$

14.4 Setting up and solving equations

Learning objective

* To use algebra to set up and solve equations

Many real-life problems can be solved by first setting up an equation.

Example 10

The cost of renting a hostel is £25 per night plus £30 per person staying.

a Write an expression for the cost, in pounds, for x people.

b The bill for a group of people for one night is £415.

Write an equation for this, in terms of x.

c Solve the equation to find how many people were in the group.

  a The cost in pounds is $30x + 25$.

    This is the number of people $\times 30 + 25$.

    This could also be written as $25 + 30x$.

  b The equation is $30x + 25 = 415$.

    Do not put a £ sign in the equation.

  c $30x + 25 = 415$

         $30x = 390$ First subtract 25 from both sides. $415 - 25 = 390$

           $x = 13$ Then divide both sides by 30. $390 \div 30 = 13$

    There are 13 people in the group.

Example 11

Kate thinks of a number.

First she subtracts 13, then she multiplies by 4.

a Call Kate's number k. Write an expression for her answer.

b Write an equation to show this.

My answer is 72.

c Solve the equation to find Kate's initial number.

   a After subtracting 13 from her number, Kate has $k - 13$.

     She then multiplies this by 4 to get $4(k - 13)$.

     The expression for Kate's answer is $4(k - 13)$.

   b Kate's answer is 72.

     The equation for Kate's answer is $4(k - 13) = 72$.

   c $4(k - 13) = 72$

       $k - 13 = 18$ First divide both sides by 4. $72 \div 4 = 18$

           $k = 31$ Then add 13 to both sides. $18 + 13 = 31$

     Kate's initial number is 31.

Exercise 14D

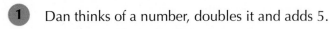

1 Dan thinks of a number, doubles it and adds 5.

   a Use d to represent Dan's number.

     Write down an expression for the answer.

   b

My answer is 59.

   Write down an equation and solve it to find Dan's initial number.

2 Mike has *m* coloured pencils.

Jon has 12 fewer pencils than Mike.

   a   Write down an expression, in terms of *m*, for the total number of pencils.

   b   They have 48 pencils altogether.

       Write an equation and solve it to find the value of *m*.

   c   How many pencils does each boy have?

3 Josie is 24 years older than her son Tom.

   a   If her son is *t* years old, write down an expression for Josie's age.

   b   Their total age is 122 years.

       Write an equation, in terms of *t*, to show this.

   c   Solve the equation to find the value of *t*.

   d   How old is Josie?

4 Marie thinks of a number. She adds 14 then multiplies by 6.

   a   Call Marie's number *m*.

       Write down an expression for her answer.

   b

My answer is 120.

       Write down an equation in terms of *m*.

   c   Work out Marie's original number.

5 This is the plan of the floor of a room. The lengths are in metres.

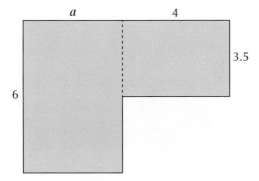

   a   Work out an expression for the area of this shape.

   b   The area is 29 m². Write an equation to show this.

   c   Solve the equation to find the value of *a*.

 Hint   Find the area of each rectangle.

6 On Monday k cm of snow fell.

The snowfall on Tuesday was 5 cm less than on Monday.

On Wednesday there was twice as much snow as on Tuesday.

a Write an expression, in terms of k, for the number of centimetres of snow on Wednesday.

b In fact there were 30 cm of snow on Wednesday. Write an equation for this.

c Solve the equation to find the value of k.

d How many centimetres of snow fell altogether on the three days?

7 On Monday, at work, Suzie sent m emails.

On Tuesday she sent three times as many emails as she did on Monday.

On Wednesday she sent 18 fewer than she did on Tuesday.

a Write down an expression, in terms of m, for the number she sent on Wednesday.

b Suzie sent 21 emails on Wednesday. Write down an equation and use it to work out the value of m.

c How many emails did Suzie send on Tuesday?

8 Flopsie has c carrots.

Mopsie has four fewer carrots than Flopsie.

Cottontail has twice as many carrots as Mopsie.

a If Cottontail has 14 carrots, write down an equation involving c.

b How many carrots does Flopsie have?

9 There are y girls in a school.

The number of girls is 28 less than the number of boys.

There are 1176 students altogether.

a Write down an equation, in terms of y, based on this information.

b Work out the number of girls and the number of boys in the school.

10

Harry

Alfie

Think of a number, subtract 3 and then multiply by 4. Tell me your answer.

52

96

a Set up an equation and work out the number Alfie thought of.

 Hint Choose a letter for Alfie's number.

b Set up an equation and work out the number Harry thought of.

11 Buns cost £*b* each. Coffees cost £1.79 each.

    a Ravi buys four buns and six coffees. Write down an expression for the total cost, in pounds.

    b The cost for Ravi is £19.34. Write down an equation to show this.

    c Work out the cost of one bun.

12 Set up and solve an equation to work out how many goals Robert Percy scored last season.

13 Louis has £8. He buys five ice-creams that cost *c* pounds each. He gets 75p change. Set up and solve an equation to work out the cost of one ice-cream.

Challenge: Changing temperatures

In Europe temperatures are measured in degrees Celsius (°C).

In the USA temperatures are measured in degrees Fahrenheit (°F).

This is a formula for degrees Fahrenheit in terms of degrees Celsius.

$$F = 1.8C + 32$$

A Change 40 °C to degrees Fahrenheit by putting *C* equal to 40 in the formula.

B To change 212 °F to degrees Celsius you need to solve this equation.

$$212 = 1.8C + 32$$

  Solve the equation.

C Change these temperatures to degrees Celsius.

    a 59 °F   **b** 140 °F   **c** 167 °F   **d** 32 °F   **e** 932 °F

Ready to progress?

I can solve simple number puzzles.

I can solve simple equations that involve one operation.

I can solve simple equations that involve two operations.
I can set up and solve an equation for a simple real-life problem.

Review questions

1 Solve these equations.

   a $5 + y = 16$ **b** $4e = 28$ **c** $f - 20 = 6$

   d $3z = 48$ **e** $\dfrac{m}{2} = 10$ **f** $\dfrac{r}{3} = 6$

2 a Show that an expression for the volume of this cuboid is $8x$ cm³.

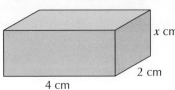

x cm

2 cm

4 cm

   b Suppose the volume of the cuboid is 12 cm³.

     i Write down an equation involving x.

     ii Solve the equation.

   c Suppose the volume of the cuboid is 17.6 cm³.

     i Write down an equation involving x.

     ii Solve the equation.

3 a Write an expression for the sum of the angles of this triangle, in terms of x.

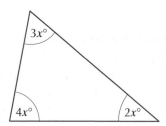

$3x°$

$4x°$ $2x°$

   b The angles of a triangle add up to 180°.
      Write an equation for x.

   c Solve the equation to find the value of x.

   d Work out the angles of the triangle.

4 Solve these equations.

    a $4x + 7 = 23$ **b** $3s - 9 = 12$ **c** $2(c + 5) = 18$

    d $2y - 19 = 21$ **e** $4(k - 3) = 32$ **f** $\frac{t}{2} + 3 = 7$

5 A pattern is made from matchsticks.

   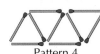

Pattern 1   Pattern 2   Pattern 3   Pattern 4

An expression for the number of matches in pattern p is $2p + 1$.

    a Show that this expression has the correct value if p is 4.

    b A particular pattern has 175 matches.

        Write down an equation involving p to express this.

    c Solve the equation to work out the value of p.

6 The mean of two numbers, a and b is $\dfrac{a + b}{2}$.

    a Use this expression to work out the mean of 7 and 15.

    b The mean of 5 and x is 9.

        Write down an equation to express this fact.

    c Solve the equation to find the value of x.

7 Two taxi firms use these formulae to work out how much to charge (C pounds) for a journey of k kilometres.

        Cosycabs: $C = 2.8 + 2.5k$

        Tixitaxi: $C = 3.2 + 2.4k$

    a The charge for Tom's journey home with Cosycabs is £30.80.

        Use this fact to write down an equation involving k.

    b Solve the equation and work out how far Tom travelled.

    c Jessie travelled home with Tixicabs and also paid £30.80.

        Write down an equation involving k based on Jessie's journey.

    d Work out how far Jessie travelled.

8 I think of a number, multiply it by 2 then add 11.

The answer is 69.

    a If the original number is n, write down an equation involving n.

    b Solve the equation to find the original number.

Challenge
Number puzzles

Here is a common type of number puzzle.

Each letter stands for a different number.

A	B	C	A	22
B	C	D	A	23
C	C	C	C	20
D	B	A	D	26
23	16	25	27	

The row and column totals are given.

The task is to find the value of each letter.

Using equations can help you do this.

Start by looking for a row or column with just one letter.

A	B	5	A	22
B	5	D	A	23
5	5	5	5	20
D	B	A	D	26
23	16	25	27	

Row 3 has just C. The total is 20 so you can write:

$4C = 20 \rightarrow C = 20 \div 4 = 5$

Now look for a row or column with just one other letter.

Column 2 has just B.

$2B + 10 = 16$
$\rightarrow 2B = 16 - 10 = 6$
$\rightarrow B = 6 \div 2 = 3$

Now you know B and C.

Row 1 has just one letter.

$2A + 8 = 22$
$\rightarrow 2A = 22 - 8 = 14$
$\rightarrow A = 14 \div 2 = 7$

Column 1 gives $D + 15 = 23$
$\rightarrow D = 23 - 15 = 8$

You should check that all the row and column totals are correct.

A	3	5	A	22
3	5	D	A	23
5	5	5	5	20
D	3	A	D	26
23	16	25	27	

7	3	5	7	22
3	5	D	7	23
5	5	5	5	20
D	3	7	D	26
23	16	25	27	

Solve these number squares. Use equations to help you.

1

A	A	B	23
C	C	B	43
C	A	B	33
35	25	39	

2

A	B	C	32
A	C	A	31
A	B	B	38
36	33	32	

3

A	A	A	B	22
B	C	A	A	31
C	B	A	C	40
D	D	A	D	29
38	38	8	38	

4

A	B	C	D	35
C	A	C	C	42
D	D	C	B	29
D	B	C	A	35
34	32	40	35	

5

A	B	C	D	51
D	D	D	D	56
A	D	A	C	52
D	B	B	A	45
50	48	51	55	

6

A	B	C	D	22
C	B	A	D	22
D	B	A	D	25
C	C	C	D	17
23	11	26	26	

7

A	A	B	C	D	47
B	A	B	C	C	46
E	E	E	E	E	35
C	C	A	D	D	42
E	E	A	A	E	45
43	47	47	43	35	

8 Now make your own puzzle.
Make sure it is possible to solve it.
Give it to someone else to solve.

15

Interpreting data

This chapter is going to show you:

- how to read data from a pie chart in which the data is given as percentages
- how to read data from pie charts when the sectors are simple fractions of the whole
- how to use the mean and range to compare sets of data
- how to carry out and interpret a statistical survey.

You should already know:

- how to draw a simple chart
- how to work out the mean and range of a set of data
- how to draw tally charts.

About this chapter

The daily news is full of statistical data about everyone's lifestyles, society and the world around them.

How can you make sense of it all?

One of the most important ways is to use different types of charts and graphs to organise and interpret data and to understand what they can – and cannot – tell you.

To analyse data, you have to select the right tools and know what they can do. Just as importantly, you need to assess what the graphs and charts other people present to you really mean and whether they interpret information in the most useful way, or lead you to false conclusions.

15.1 Pie charts

Learning objectives

- To read data from pie charts in which the data is given as percentages

Key words

percentage	pie chart
sector	

Sometimes you will see **pie charts** showing **percentages**. The simplest of these are split into 10 **sectors**, with each sector representing 10%, like the ones shown below.

Example 1

The pie chart shows the favourite drinks of some Year 7 pupils.

What does it tell you?

You can see that:

Favourite drinks

- tea occupies 1 sector,

  hence 10% of the pupils chose tea as their favourite

- milk occupies 3 sectors,

  hence 30% of the pupils chose milk as their favourite

- cola occupies 4 sectors,

  hence 40% of the pupils chose cola as their favourite

- coffee occupies 2 sectors,

  hence 20% of the pupils chose coffee as their favourite.

Example 2

The pie chart shows how Britain got rid of its dangerous waste products in 1985.

a What percentage of dangerous waste was burnt?

b For every kilogram of dangerous waste being chemically treated, how many kilograms were land-filled?

Disposal of waste, 1985

  a Burning is represented by half a sector.

    Half of 10% is 5%.

    So 5% of dangerous waste was burnt.

  b Chemical treatment is represented by one sector.

    Land-fill is represented by 7.5 sectors.

    So the sector for land-fill is 7.5 times the size of the sector for chemical treatment.

    Hence, for every 1 kg of chemically treated waste, there will be 7.5 kg of land-fill.

Example 3

The two pie charts show what percentage of trains in Britain and Spain are on time or late.

Use the pie charts to compare how many are on time and how many are late in the two countries.

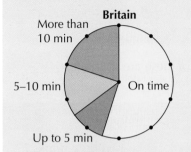

Hint Remember that each division represents 10% (so half a sector will be 5%).

From the pie charts you can create tables interpreting the data.

Lateness: Britain	Percentage
On time	55
Up to 5 minutes late	10
Between 5 and 10 minutes late	15
More than 10 minutes late	20

Lateness: Spain	Percentage
On time	85
Up to 5 minutes late	10
Between 5 and 10 minutes late	5
More than 10 minutes late	0

Now you can see that:

- a higher percentage of trains in Spain are on time
- the same percentage of trains are up to 5 minutes late in both countries
- a higher percentage of trains in Britain are over 5 minutes late.

Exercise 15A

1 The pie chart shows the percentages of cars of five colours in a car park.

What percentage of the cars were:

   a red   **b** blue   **c** green

   d yellow   **e** black?

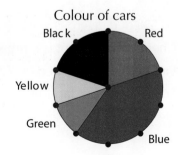

Colour of cars

2 The pie chart shows the types of pet owned by the pupils in a class, as percentages.

What percentage of the pets were:

a dogs **b** cats **c** birds
d fish **e** gerbils?

Pets

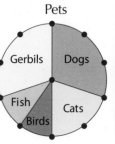

3 The pie chart shows the percentages of various school subjects that pupils chose as their favourite.

What percentage of the pupils said their favourite subject was:

a maths **b** English **c** geography
d history **e** PE?

Favourite subject

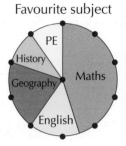

4 The pie chart shows the percentage of various television soap operas that pupils chose as their favourite.

What percentage of the pupils said their favourite soap opera was:

a EastEnders **b** Hollyoaks
c Coronation Street **d** Neighbours?

Favourite show

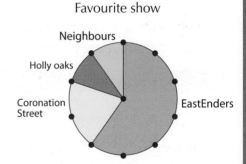

5 The pie chart shows the percentages of various age groups living in Oslo, in Sweden.

What percentage of the people in Oslo were aged:

a under 16 **b** 16–25 **c** 26–40
d 41–60 **e** over 60?

Age groups in Oslo

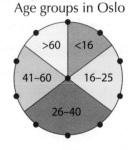

6 The pie chart shows the percentages of various age groups living in Monaco.

What percentage of the people in Monaco were aged:

a under 16 **b** 16–25 **c** 26–40
d 41–60 **e** over 60?

Age groups in Monaco

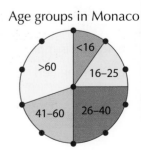

7 The chart shows the distribution of ages in an Indian village. What percentage of the people in the Indian village were aged:

Age groups in an Indian village

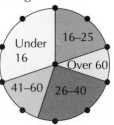

a under 16   b 16–25   c 26–40

d 41–60   e over 60?

 8 Use the information in questions 5, 6 and 7 to decide whether each statement is true or false.

a There is a greater percentage of under 16s in Oslo than in Monaco.

b There is a greater percentage of over 60s in Oslo than in Monaco.

c There is a greater percentage of people aged 16–40 in Oslo than in Monaco.

d There are equal percentages of people aged 41–60 in Oslo and Monaco.

e There is a smaller percentage of under 16s in Oslo than in the village in India.

f There is a smaller percentage of over 60s in the village in India than in Monaco.

g There is a smaller percentage of people aged 41–60 in the village in India than in Monaco.

 9 Use the information in questions 5, 6 and 7 to decide whether each statement is true, false or you cannot tell.

a In Monaco one–quarter of the people are aged 26–40.

b In the Indian village there are twice as many people aged over 60 than aged 16–25.

c In Oslo more than half of the people are aged 40 or less.

d In Oslo and Monaco, there are the same number of people aged 41–60.

Problem solving: True or false?

The pie charts show the favourite sports of class A and class B.

Here are some statements that may apply to class A or class B.

In each case decide whether the statement is true for class A, true for class B, true for both or true for neither.

a Football is the most popular sport.

b Rugby is more popular than netball.

c Running and netball are equally popular.

d There are odd numbers of pupils.

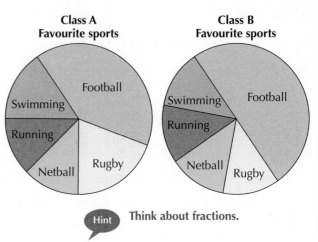

Hint Think about fractions.

290 15 Interpreting data

15.2 Comparing mean and range

Learning objectives

- To use the mean and range to compare data
- To make sensible decisions by comparing the mean and range of two sets of data

Key words	
data	mean
range	

When you compare the **mean** of two sets of **data**, you are comparing an average, which is a value that represents the whole set of data.

For example, in a group of pupils:

- the mean height of the boys = 1.55 m
- the mean height of the girls = 1.48 m.

For this data, you can say that, *on average*, boys are taller than girls.

When you compare the **range** of two sets of data, you are comparing how far the data is spread out, or which set of data is more consistent.

Now, in the example above, suppose you are told that:

- the range of the height of boys = 0.3 m
- the range of the height of girls = 0.5 m.

For this data you can say that the boys' heights are more consistent because the height difference between the shortest and tallest boys is 0.3 m, compared to a difference of 0.5 m between the shortest and tallest girls.

Example 4

You are organising a ten-pin bowling match. You have one team place to fill.

These are the last five scores for Noah and Ava.

Noah	122	131	114	162	146
Ava	210	91	135	99	151

Who would you pick to be in the team?

Give reasons.

The mean for Noah is 135 and the range is 48.

The mean for Ava is 137.2 and the range is 119.

You could pick Ava as she has the greater mean score.

This means that she has higher scores, on average.

You could pick Noah as his range of scores is smaller.

This tells you that he is more consistent, which means that he has higher scores most of the time.

Example 5

A teacher thinks that the girls in her class are absent more often than the boys.

There are 10 boys in the class. These are the numbers of days they were absent over last term.

5 0 3 4 6 3 0 8 6 5

There are 12 girls in the class. These are the numbers of days they were absent over last term.

2 1 0 0 5 3 1 2 3 50 2 3

Is she correct? Give reasons for your answer.

The mean for the boys is 4 and the range is 8.

The mean for the girls is 6 and the range is 50.

Using these results, the teacher is correct because, on average, the girls are absent for more days than the boys.

If you do not include the girl who was absent 50 times because she was in hospital, however, the mean for the girls becomes 2 and the range 5.

If you ignore this girl because she is a special case, you could say the teacher is wrong as the rest of the girls are absent less often than the boys.

Exercise 15B

1 You have been asked to choose someone to play darts for your team. You ask Ryan and Ali to throw ten times each.

These are their scores.

Ryan	32	16	25	65	12	24	63	121	31	11
Ali	43	56	40	31	37	49	49	30	31	24

  a Work out the mean for Ryan.   **b** Work out the range for Ryan.

  c Work out the mean for Ali.   **d** Work out the range for Ali.

  e Who would you choose? Give a reason for your answer.

2 You have to catch a bus regularly. You can catch bus A or bus B.

On the last ten times you caught these buses, you noted down, in minutes, how late they were.

Bus A	1	2	4	12	1	3	5	6	2	9
Bus B	6	5	5	6	2	4	4	5	6	7

  a Work out the mean for bus A.   **b** Work out the range for bus A.

  c Work out the mean for bus B.   **d** Work out the range for bus B.

  e Which bus should you catch? Give a reason for your answer.

3 Each day I buy a bag of biscuits from a school canteen. I can buy them from canteen A or canteen B. I made a note of how many biscuits there were in each bag I bought from each canteen, over the last four weeks.

Canteen A	12	11	14	10	13	12	9	12	15	12
Canteen B	5	18	13	15	10	15	17	8	11	13

a Work out the mean for Canteen A. **b** Work out the range for Canteen A.

c Work out the mean for Canteen B. **d** Work out the range for Canteen B.

e Which canteen should I use? Give a reason for your answer.

 4 You have been asked to choose someone for a quiz team. These are the last ten quiz scores (out of 20) for Lily and Josh.

Lily	1	19	2	12	20	13	2	6	5	10
Josh	8	7	9	12	13	8	7	11	7	8

Who would you choose for the quiz team? Give a reason for your answer.

 5 Grace and Harry take the same two tests.
The table gives information about their scores.

	Mean	Range
Grace	16.5	7
Harry	14.0	10

a The teacher wants to give Grace and Harry some feedback.

Use the information to compare their scores.

b Can you work out their scores on each test?

Grace and Harry retake the tests one week later.

This table shows their new scores.

c Grace says that she has improved.

Give a reason to support this.

	Test 1	Test 2
Grace	25	15
Harry	16	12

d Harry says that he has improved.

Give a reason to support this.

Activity: Mean fingers

Work in pairs.

A a Use a ruler to measure the length of the fingers on each hand, as accurately as you can.

 b Repeat this for both of you.

 c Calculate the mean and the range of the lengths of your fingers, for each of you.

 d Comment on your results.

B a Try to compare your results with those of others in your class.

 b Compare the results for boys and girls. What do you notice?

15.3 Statistical surveys

Learning objective

* To use charts and diagrams to interpret data

Statistical surveys are used to collect data.

You can obtain data by carrying out:

* a survey

* an **experiment**.

You can record data on:

* a **questionnaire**

* a data-collection form or sheet.

As you saw in Chapter 6, you can use a **tally** chart and a **frequency** table to record the data.

There are several ways to present the data, to make it easier to interpret. You could use bar charts, pie charts and line graphs.

Exercise 15C

1   **a**   Ask a sample of 30 people this question.

'Approximately how many hours do you watch TV over a typical weekend?'

Record your results in a copy of the table below.

Time (hours)	Tally	Frequency
Less than 2 hours		
2 hours or more but less than 4 hours		
4 hours or more but less than 8 hours		
More than 8 hours		

  b   Create a suitable chart for your collected data.

  c   Write a newspaper headline, based on your results.

2   For this question, change some of the sports if you wish.

  a   Ask a sample of 30 boys: 'Which of these sports do you play out of school?'

Record your results in a copy of the table below.

Sport	Tally	Frequency
Football		
Cricket		
Tennis		
Badminton		
Something else		

b Now ask a sample of 30 girls the same question.

Record their results in another copy of the table.

c Create suitable charts for each set of data.

d Make two comparisons of the results for boys and girls.

3 **a** Complete the first column of the table with the names of four of your favourite bands or singers.

b Ask a sample of 30 pupils: 'Which of these would you most like to see perform live?'

Record your results in a copy of the table below.

	Tally	Frequency

c Create a suitable chart for your collected data.

d Write a short report about your results.

MR **4** **a** Ask at least 30 people these two questions.

		Yes	No
i	'Did you go on holiday last year?'		
ii	'Are you going on holiday this year?'		

b Use your results to complete this two-way table.

	Holiday	No holiday
Last year		
This year		

c From your results, is it true to say fewer people are taking holidays this year?

Activity: Do tall people have bigger heads?

By choosing a suitable sample of 30 or more people, investigate this statement.

> Taller people have a larger head circumference.

Write a report on your findings.

Remember to:

- use a data-collection form or sheet.
- use statistical diagrams in your report.
- write a conclusion.

Ready to progress?

I can read data from pie charts where the data is given as percentages.
I can compare data using the mean and range.
I can interpret data using charts and diagrams.

I can use data to answer simple statistical inquiries.

Review questions

1   20 people were asked to name their favourite drink.

One quarter chose tea.

Seven people chose coffee.

30% of them chose cola.

The rest chose water.

Put this information onto a copy of the percentage pie chart.

Remember to give your chart a title.

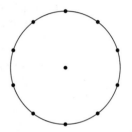

2   In a survey, a shop asked 180 customers about the quality of customer service over the last year. The pie chart shows the responses.

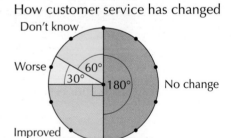

How customer service has changed

a   What fraction of those asked said that customer service had improved?

b   How many customers said there had been no change?

3   Rory and Justin play nine holes of crazy golf.

These are their scores on each hole.

| Rory | 3 | 5 | 4 | 4 | 4 | 6 | 4 | 3 | 4 |
| Justin | 4 | 5 | 4 | 5 | 4 | 5 | 5 | 4 | 6 |

a   What is the modal score for each player?

b   What is the range of scores for each player?

c   What is the median score for each player?

d   What is the mean score for each player?

e   Which player is more consistent and why?

f   Who is the better player and why?

4 Make a data-collection sheet to compare how long boys and girls usually spend on homework each week.

5 There are 30 pupils in a class.

12 of them are girls.

a What percentage of the pupils are girls?

b The pie chart is not drawn accurately.

Redraw the pie chart accurately. Label the angles.

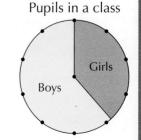

Pupils in a class

6 Reda and Jacquie run the school tuck shop.

They did a survey about chocolate.
They chose three flavours and gave out questionnaires for pupils to fill in, as shown.

Each person they asked filled in the questionnaire for each type of chocolate.

Reda and Jacquie then displayed their results on pie charts.

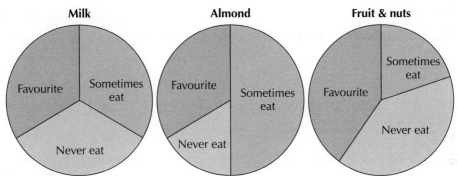

a Which flavour did most pupils choose as their favourite?

b Which flavour did most say they never eat?

c **i** Reda and Jaquie can buy the chocolate more cheaply if they buy only one flavour from the supplier.
Which flavour should they choose to buy?

ii Explain why you chose that flavour.

 7 The pie chart shows how Sandeep spent her money each week.

a She spent £30 on clothes each week.
How much did she spend on food?

b The table shows how Tom spent his money each week.

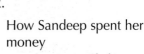

How Sandeep spent her money

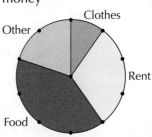

Clothes	£30
Rent	£100
Food	£80
Other	£60

Who spent the most money each week?

c Who spent a larger proportion of their money on clothes each week?

Review questions   **297**

Challenge
Dancing competition

In a dancing competition there are six couples.

Each week the couples are given scores by three judges.

Each judge gives a score out of 10. These scores are added up to give the overall scores below.

Couple	Week 1	Week 2	Week 3	Week 4	Week 5
Alexia and Gina	15.5	17.5	16.5	24.5	
Bruno and Harriet	18.5	19.0	20.0	19.5	
Carlos and Isabella	8.5	12.5	9.5	10.0	
Dmitry and Juanita	17.5	20.5	21.5	24.5	
Enrique and Kiki	10.5	10.5	11.0	11.5	
Fernando and Lucia	13.5	12.0	14.5	17.0	

In week 5 these are the judges' scores.

Couple	Judge X	Judge Y	Judge Z
Alexia and Gina	8.5	9.0	9.0
Bruno and Harriet	6.0	7.5	7.5
Carlos and Isabella	2.5	4.5	4.0
Dmitry and Juanita	5.5	6.0	5.5
Enrique and Kiki	3.0	4.0	4.0
Fernando and Lucia	7.0	7.0	7.0

Task

Write a newspaper story about the performances of the six couples.

You must include:

- the total scores for week 5
- a graph or chart to show the data for all five weeks
- statements to compare the performances over the five weeks
- comment about the judges. Is anyone harsh?
- a prediction about the winner of the competition backed up with evidence
- a headline

 Hint Copy the tables and complete the week 5 totals.
You could calculate the mean and range for each couple.
Think about the types of chart you can draw for each couple.

16

3D shapes

This chapter is going to show you:

- some 3D shapes and their names
- how to visualise 3D shapes
- how to draw 3D shapes on isometric paper
- how to draw the net of a 3D shape
- how to construct a 3D shape
- the relationship between faces, edges and vertices of 3D shapes.

You should already know:

- how to draw the net of a cube
- the meaning of the words 'face', 'edge' and 'vertex'
- how to draw a cuboid.

About this chapter

Anyone trying to enter the underground station shown here would have been disappointed! It was drawn on a street in Brussels to advertise the fast Eurostar link to London and is a 2D representation of a real 3D underground entrance. Representing 3D in 2D is an important skill – and not just for artists wanting to amaze the public. More usually, we draw plans in 2D of things that will be built in 3D – from small things such as furniture, to larger objects such as buildings and aeroplanes. Recently, computer-aided design and 3D printing have made this easier but knowing how to turn 2D dimensions into a 3D object is still a crucial skill for designers, architects and engineers.

16.1 Naming and drawing 3D shapes

Learning objectives

- To be familiar with the names of 3D shapes and their properties
- To use isometric paper to draw 3D shapes made from cubes

Key words

3D	edge
face	hexagonal prism
isometric	pentagonal prism
tetrahedron	triangular prism
vertex	

Many everyday objects are made using familiar mathematical shapes. These have three dimensions: length, width and height, so we call them three-dimensional (**3D**).

You need to be able to recognise and name these 3D shapes.

Cube

Square-based pyramid

 Cone

 Sphere

Triangular prism

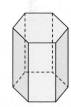
Hexagonal prism

Cuboid

 Tetrahedron

 Cylinder

Hemisphere

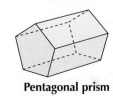
Pentagonal prism

Solid shapes have **faces**, **edges** and **vertices** (plural of vertex).

Example 1

How many faces, edges and vertices does a cuboid have?

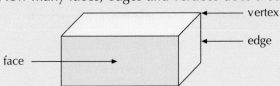

vertex

edge

face

A cuboid has 6 faces, 12 edges and 8 vertices.

You can use **isometric** paper to draw 3D shapes. This paper has dots that form a 60° grid of small triangles.

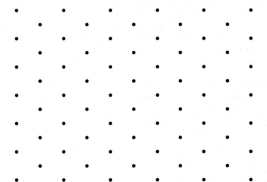

Example 2

Draw a cube and a cuboid on isometric paper.

Start by drawing a vertical line for the nearest edge and then build the diagram from there.

Draw what you would see.

All of your lines will be either vertical or at 60° to the vertical.

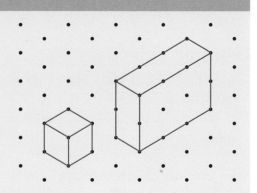

Exercise 16A

1 How many: **i** faces   **ii** vertices   **iii** edges
does each 3D shape have?

a   **b**   **c**   **d**

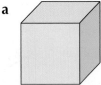

Cube   Square-based pyramid   Triangular prism   Tetrahedron

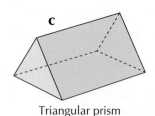

2 Copy and complete the table. Use the pictures to help you.

	Number of faces	Number of edges	Number of vertices
Cube			
Cuboid			
Square-based pyramid			
Tetrahedron			
Triangular prism			
Pentagonal prism			
Hexagonal prism			

(MR) 3 Explain why cones, cyclinders and spheres do not have just 'faces'.

(MR) 4 Decide whether each statement is *always true*, *sometimes true* or *never true*.

   a A cuboid has 8 vertices.   **b** A prism has 9 edges.   **c** A cube has 8 identical faces.

   d A cuboid is a prism.   **e** A cylinder is a prism.   **f** A hemisphere is half a sphere.

(PS) 5 This 3D shape is made by putting together a cuboid and a pyramid.

How many: **a** faces   **b** vertices   **c** edges

does the shape have?

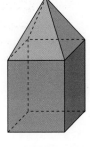

6 This cuboid is drawn on an isometric grid.
It is made from three cubes.

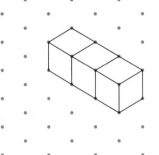

On a copy of the grid:

a add another cube to make an L-shape

b add another two cubes to make a T-shape

c add another two cubes to make a **+**-shape.

PS **7** How many cubes are required to make this 3D shape?
Use an isometric grid to draw other similar 3D shapes
of your own.

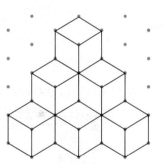

8 Draw each cuboid accurately on an isometric grid.

a

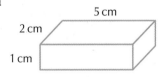

5 cm

2 cm

1 cm

b

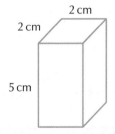

2 cm

2 cm

5 cm

c

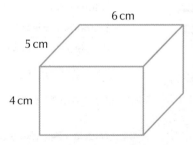

2 cm

6 cm

5 cm

4 cm

Activity: Cubes into cuboids

You will need 12 unit cubes for this activity.
Arrange all 12 cubes to form a cuboid.
How many different cuboids can you make?

16.2 Using nets to construct 3D shapes

Learning objectives

- To draw nets of 3D shapes
- To construct 3D shapes from nets

A **net** is a 2D shape that can be folded to make a 3D object.

These are nets for a cube, a tetrahedron and a square-based pyramid.

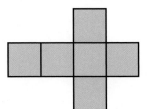 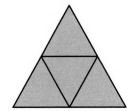 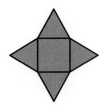

To draw nets and **construct** 3D shapes from them, you will need card, a sharp pencil, a ruler, a protractor, a pair of scissors and glue or tape.

Before folding a net you have drawn, use scissors and a ruler to score the card along the fold lines.

You can fix the edges together by using glue on the tabs or you can just use tape. If you use tabs, keep one face free of tabs and glue this face last.

Example 3

Construct a square-based pyramid.

1 Cut out the net.

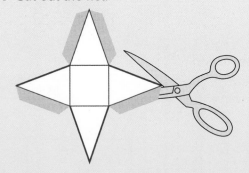

2 Score the fold lines.

3 Fold along the fold lines and glue the tabs.

4 Stick down the last face.

For questions 1 to 5, draw nets accurately on card. Cut out the nets and construct the 3D shapes.

 A cube

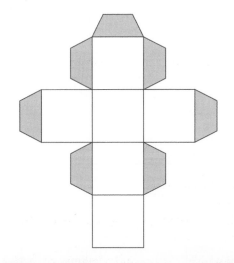

Each square has 4 cm sides.

2 A cuboid

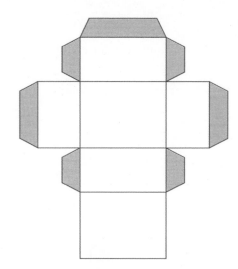

The rectangles have these measurements.

8 cm

6 cm

8 cm

4 cm

4 cm

6 cm

3 A tetrahedron

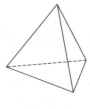

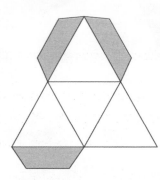

Each equilateral triangle has these measurements.

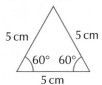

5 cm   5 cm

60°   60°

5 cm

4 A square-based pyramid

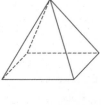

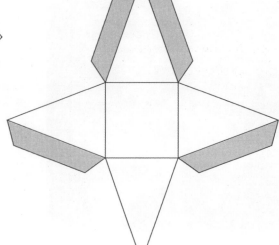

The square has these measurements.

5 cm

5 cm

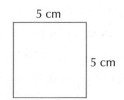

Each isosceles triangle has these measurements.

6 cm   6 cm

70°   70°

5 cm

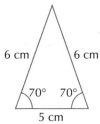

5 A triangular prism

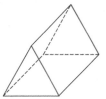

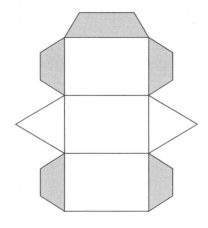

Each rectangle has these measurements.

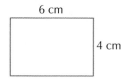

6 cm

4 cm

Each equilateral triangle has these measurements.

4 cm   4 cm
60° 60°
4 cm

PS **6** The diagram shows a net for a square-based pyramid.

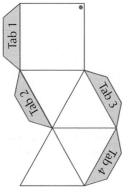

a Which edge is Tab 1 glued to? On a copy of the diagram, label this A.

b Which edge is Tab 4 glued to? On a copy of the diagram, label this B.

c The vertex marked with a red dot meets two other vertices. Label these with dots.

Activity: Nets for cubes

There are 11 different nets for a cube.

Try to draw all 11.

Use squared paper.

If you need help to find them all, look on the internet.

Cut them out and check they are all correct.

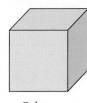

Cube

16.3 3D investigations

Learning objectives

- To work out the relationship between faces, edges and vertices for 3D shapes
- To solve problems involving 3D shapes

Leonard **Euler** was a famous eighteenth-century Swiss mathematician. He discovered the relationship between the number of faces, edges and vertices of 3D shapes.

Exercise 16C

1 **a** Copy and complete the table.

Some rows have been done for you.

	Number of faces	Number of edges	Number of vertices
Cube	6	12	8
Cuboid			
Square-based pyramid	5	8	5
Tetrahedron	4		
Triangular prism	5	9	6
Pentagonal prism			
Hexagonal prism			

b Try to work out the relationship between the number of faces, edges and vertices.

 Hint Add the number of faces to the number of vertices and compare with the number of edges.

 2 A **pentomino** is a 2D shape made from five squares that touch, side to side.

Here are two examples.

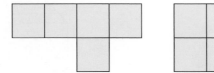

a Draw, on squared paper, as many different pentominoes as you can.

b How many of these pentominoes are nets that make an open cube?

PS **3** Four cubes

On an isometric grid, draw all the possible different solids that can be made from four cubes.

Here is an example.

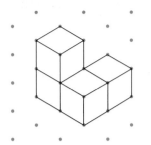

Problem solving: Isometric drawings

Here are two 3D shapes.

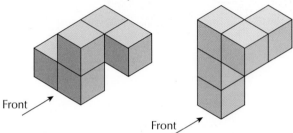

Front

Front

A Copy the diagrams onto isometric paper.

B Now draw the shapes on the isometric paper as they would look if they are turned so that they are standing on the front face.

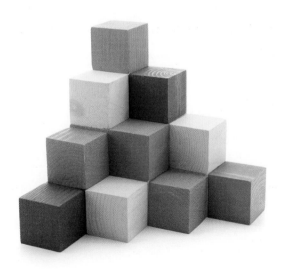

Ready to progress?

I can name 3D shapes.
I can draw nets of 3D shapes.
I can make 3D shapes from nets.
I can visualise 3D shapes.

I can describe the relationship between the number of edges, vertices and faces for a 3D shape.
I can draw 3D shapes on isometric paper.

Review questions

1 a   How many faces does this 3D shape have?

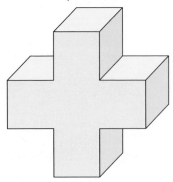

   b   How many edges does the shape have?

   c   How many vertices does the shape have?

2   Here is a net of a cube.

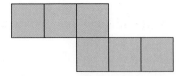

   a   How many tabs would you need, to make the cube?

   b   Draw the net with your tabs.

3   There are 10 spheres, 6 cones, 3 cubes and 1 cuboid in a bag.

    One of the shapes is picked out at random.

    What is the probability that the shape:

    a   is a sphere

    b   does not have any curved surfaces

    c   has only 1 vertex?

    Give each answer as a fraction in its simplest form.

4   The diagram shows a 3D shape made from centimetre cubes.

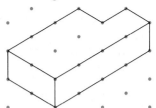

    a   What is the volume of the 3D shape?

    b   How many more centimetre cubes are needed to make a cuboid measuring 4 cm by 2 cm by 2 cm?

5   Here is a net of a cuboid.

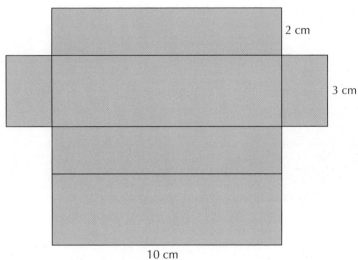

    a   Work out the volume of the cuboid.

    b   The net is cut from a piece of card measuring 20 cm by 20 cm.

    Work out the percentage of card that is wasted.

6   a   On centimetre-squared paper, draw accurately the net of this triangular prism.

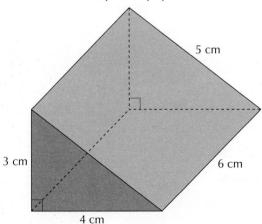

    b   The area of each triangular end is 6 cm². Work out the area of the surface of the prism.

    c   Show how you can tell that the volume of the prism is 36 cm³.

Problem solving
Packing boxes

Ivan is a delivery driver. He delivers spheres to a warehouse.

There are 2 sizes of box.

The large box is
30 cm by 20 cm by
10 cm and contains
48 spheres.

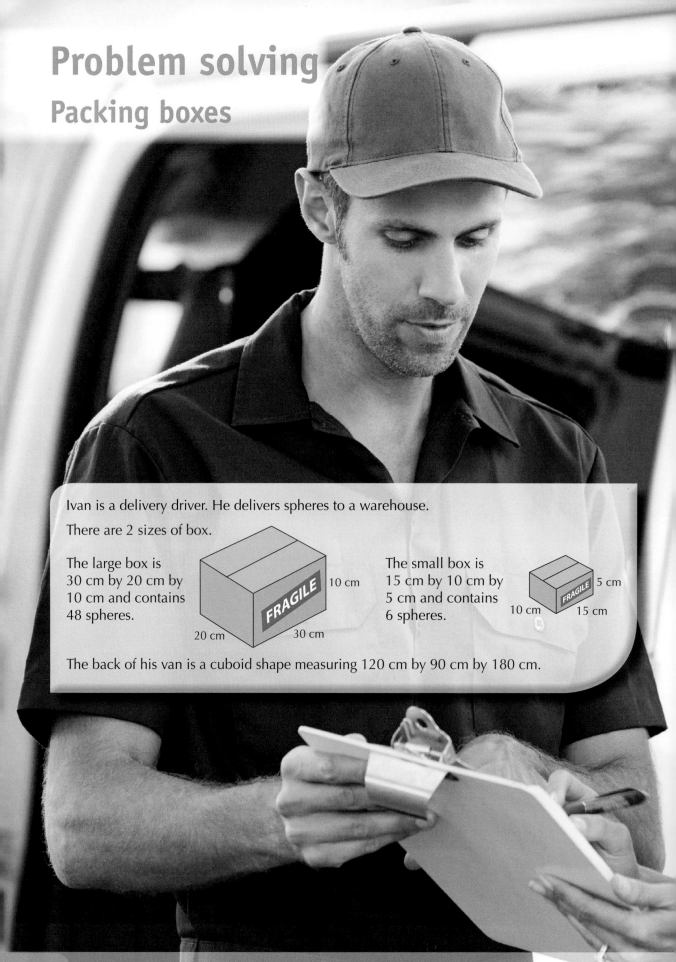

10 cm

FRAGILE

20 cm   30 cm

The small box is
15 cm by 10 cm by
5 cm and contains
6 spheres.

5 cm

FRAGILE

10 cm   15 cm

The back of his van is a cuboid shape measuring 120 cm by 90 cm by 180 cm.

Task 1

Work out:

a the number of large boxes he can fit in his van

b the number of small boxes he can fit in his van

c the number of boxes he can fit in his van, if he has the same numbers of large and small boxes

d the number of spheres he can carry on each journey.

Task 2

Ivan has to drive from the warehouse and back to the warehouse each day.

He delivers to all the five places shown on the map.

For example: Warehouse → A → B → C → E → D → Warehouse

This will be 14 + 8 + 20 + 10 + 7 + 4
= 63 miles

a Work out his shortest route.

b On one day he only visits four of the five places. He travels 38 miles.

Work out his route.

Write down the places he visited, in the correct order.

Check that the mileage is correct.

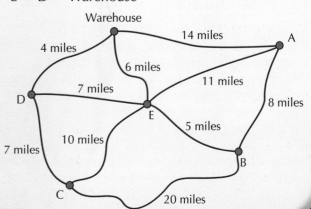

17

Ratio

This chapter is going to show you:

- how to use ratio notation
- how to use ratios to compare quantities
- how to simplify ratios
- how to use ratios to find totals or missing quantities
- the connection between ratios and fractions
- how to use ratios to solve problems in everyday life.

You should already know:

- how to simplify fractions
- how to find a fraction of a quantity
- the equivalence between simple fractions and percentages
- how to interpret bar charts and pie charts.

About this chapter

The Tour de France is one of the toughest bike races in the world. It lasts 21 days and covers all sorts of terrains, including the high and rugged Alpine mountains. Apart from being enormously fit, how do the riders cope with the steep slopes – and keep up a good speed at the same time? The answer lies in the ratios between the cogs on their bikes – one connected to the pedals and the other on the back wheel. For going uphill they would select a small gear ratio which means that the pedals are linked to a small cog driving a larger one on the wheel. This makes it easier to pedal. For going downhill they would select a large gear ratio. This helps to control the bike.

17.1 Introduction to ratios

Learning objectives

- To use ratio notation
- To use ratios to compare quantities

Key words

| quantity | ratio |

A **ratio** is a mathematical way to compare **quantities**.

To help you understand what a ratio is, look at the photo of a giraffe and an antelope.

Can you see that the giraffe is about four times as tall as the antelope?

Speaking mathematically, you could say: 'The ratio of the giraffe's height to the antelope's height is four to one.'

You could also say: 'The ratio of the antelope's height to the giraffe's height is one to four.'

When you need to write a ratio, you need to use the colon (:) symbol. You read this as 'to'.

- The ratio of the giraffe's height to the antelope's height is 4 : 1 (four to one).
- The ratio of the antelope's height to the giraffe's height is 1 : 4 (one to four).

Example 1

The mass of a lion is 150 kg.

The mass of a domestic cat is 5 kg.

What is the ratio of the mass of the lion to the mass of the cat?

Compare the masses of the two animals.

The lion is heavier than the cat.

$150 \div 5 = 30$ The lion is 30 times as heavy as the cat.

The ratio of the lion's mass to the cat's mass is 30 : 1.

Example 2

Bottled water comes in two sizes, 500 millilitres (ml) and 750 ml.

What is the ratio of the two sizes?

The larger bottle is $1\frac{1}{2}$ times bigger than the smaller one.

$1\frac{1}{2} = \frac{3}{2}$

Imagine each bottle, divided into 250 ml sections.

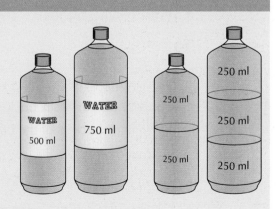

There are three sections in the larger bottle and two sections in the smaller one.

So the ratio of the capacity of the larger bottle to the capacity of the smaller one is 3 : 2 or the ratio of the capacity of the smaller to the larger is 2 : 3.

1 Ade has saved £25 and Bea has saved £100.

    a What is the missing number in this sentence?

       Bea has saved ☐ times as much as Ade.

    b Work out the ratio of Ade's savings to Bea's savings.

    c Work out the ratio of Bea's savings to Ade's savings.

2 Gary buys 500 g of rice, 250 g of pasta and 125g of coffee.

Work out the ratio of:

    a the mass of rice to the mass of pasta   **b** the mass of pasta to the mass of rice

    c the mass of rice to the mass of coffee   **d** the mass of coffee to the mass of pasta.

3 These are the ingredients to make 8 cheese scones.

Flour	200 g
Butter	25 g
Cheese	100 g
Eggs	1
Milk	2 tablespoons

Work out the ratio of:

    a the mass of flour to the mass of cheese

    b the mass of cheese to the mass of butter

    c the mass of butter to the mass of flour.

4 It is easy to make concrete. A website gives these ingredients.

    3 parts of gravel

    $2\frac{1}{2}$ parts of sand

    1 part of cement

    $\frac{1}{2}$ part of water

    a Work out these ratios.

       i gravel : cement   **ii** gravel : water

       iii sand : water   **iv** water : cement

    b Kaspar uses three buckets of cement. How many buckets of water does he need?

    c Suppose Kaspar has *N* buckets of cement.

       How many buckets of the other ingredients does he need?

5 The number of pages in a maths book is 25% of the number of pages in a science book. Work out the ratio of the numbers of pages in the two books.

6 **a** Cara's age is half of Dani's age.

       What is the ratio of their ages?

    b Elfine's age is two-thirds of Frank's age.

       What is the ratio of their ages?

7 The size of the engine in a car is given in litres.

Here are the sizes of some car engines.

Car	Engine size (litres)
Seat Ibiza	1.4
Mazda MX5	1.6
Ford Granada	2.1
Jaguar XJ8	4.2
AC Cobra	7.0

a How many times larger than the engine of the Seat Ibiza is the engine of the AC Cobra?

b Work out the ratios of these engine sizes.

   i Seat Ibiza : AC Cobra

   ii Jaguar XJ8 : Ford Granada

   iii Ford Granada : Seat Ibiza

 c The ratio of the engine size of a Lexus LFA to the engine size of a Seat Ibiza is 3 : 1.
Work out the engine size of a Lexus LFA.

 8 Here are the populations of some countries.

Country	Population (millions)
Pakistan	180
Nigeria	160
Germany	80
UK	60
Iraq	30
Sri Lanka	20

a Work out the ratios of the populations of:

   i the UK to Sri Lanka

   i the UK to Pakistan

   iii Nigeria to Germany

   iv Nigeria to Sri Lanka.

b The ratio of the population of India to the population of the UK is 20 : 1.

Work out the population of India.

c Suppose the population of the Sri Lanka is P.

Write the population of each of the other countries, in terms of P.

9 This pie chart shows an election result.

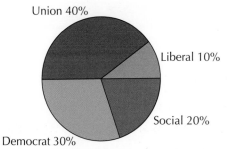

There are four parties.

Work out the ratio of:

a Union votes to Liberal votes

b Liberal votes to Democrat votes

c Democrat votes to Social votes.

10 25% of the spectators at a football match are female. The rest are male. Work out the ratio of males to females.

Investigation: Bagging coins

When customers pay cash into a bank, the coins are put into bags.

Each bag holds just one type of coin.

This is the label on a bag.

The number of coins must make up a specified value.

For example, a bag of 20p coins must be worth £10.

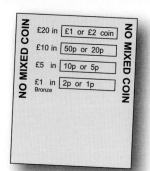

A How many coins are there in a 20p bag?

B How many coins are there in a 5p bag?

C a Work out the ratio of the number of coins in a 20p bag to the number of coins in a 5p bag.

   b Is it the same as the ratio of the values of the two bags?

D Investigate the ratios of the numbers of coins in other bags.

17.2 Simplifying ratios

Learning objective

- To write a ratio as simply as possible

Key words	
fraction	simplify

You have looked at some simple ratios such as 5 : 1 or 3 : 2.

In this section you will look at more complicated ratios. You will find out how write a ratio as simply as possible.

Example 3

The heights of two office blocks are 12 metres and 32 metres. What is the ratio of the heights of the office blocks?

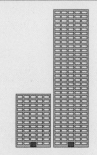

   You can write the ratio as 12 : 32.

   You can **simplify** a ratio in the same way as you do a **fraction**: divide both numbers by a common factor.

   4 is a common factor of 12 and 32.

   12 : 32 = 3 : 8

   This is the ratio in its simplest form.

You should usually write ratios using whole numbers, not fractions or decimals.

What does this mean?

$8 \div 3 = 2\frac{2}{3}$ so the larger building is more than twice the height of the smaller one.

Exercise 17B

Write your ratio answers in this exercise as simply as possible.

1 Simplify these fractions as much as possible.

    a $\dfrac{10}{15}$ **b** $\dfrac{16}{80}$ **c** $\dfrac{27}{18}$ **d** $\dfrac{150}{250}$ **e** $\dfrac{7}{210}$

2 Simplify these ratios as much as possible.

    a $5 : 20$ **b** $12 : 18$ **c** $100 : 50$ **d** $32 : 4$ **e** $40 : 60$

3 In a wood there are 40 birch trees and 100 ash trees.

    a Work out the ratio of birch trees to ash trees.

    b Work out the ratio of ash trees to birch trees.

4 Work out the ratio of yellow squares to white squares in this pattern.

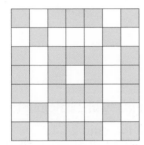

5 A drink is made from 50 ml of squash and 175 ml of water.

Work out the ratio of squash to water.

6 A council gardener plants these bulbs.

    250 daffodils

    100 crocuses

    150 snowdrops

Work out the ratio of the number of:

    a daffodil bulbs to crocus bulbs

    b crocus bulbs to snowdrop bulbs

    c snowdrop bulbs to daffodil bulbs.

(PS) **7** The label on a cardigan shows this information.

    48% viscose

    36% polyamide

    8% angora

    8% cashmere

    a Work out the ratio of viscose to cashmere.

    b Work out the ratios for some other pairs of ingredients.

8 The body of an adult female is about 60% water. For a male the figure is about 65%.

a Work out the ratio of water to other substances in the body of an adult female.

b Work out the ratio of water to other substances in the body of an adult male.

9 You can compare the masses of different elements by using their relative atomic masses.

The table shows the values for some common elements in the human body.

Element	Relative atomic mass
Hydrogen	1
Carbon	12
Nitrogen	14
Oxygen	16
Sodium	23
Phosphorus	31
Sulphur	32
Potassium	39
Calcium	40

Work out the ratio of the relative atomic masses of:

a **i** calcium to hydrogen   **ii** calcium to oxygen   **iii** calcium to sulphur.

b Find two elements with relative atomic masses in the ratio 2 : 1.

10 This bar chart shows the numbers of medals won by different countries in the 2012 Olympics.

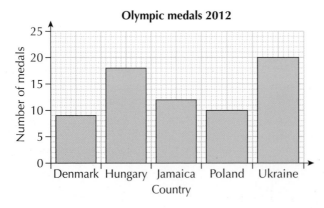

Work out the ratio of the number of medals won by:

 Hint Find the ratio of the first to the second each time.

a Hungary and Denmark   **b** Poland and Ukraine

c Jamaica and Hungary   **d** Poland and Jamaica.

11 A display has 300 coloured lights.

120 are white, 60 are blue, 45 are green and the rest are yellow.

Work out the ratio of:

a white to blue   **b** blue to green   **c** green to yellow.

Investigation: Ratios in patterns

Here are three rectangular cards, A, B and C.

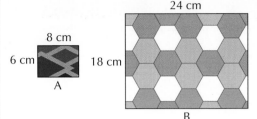

A Work out these ratios.

   a the length of A to the length of B   **b** the width of A to the width of B

   c the perimeter of A to the perimeter of B   **d** the area of A to the area of B

B Work out these ratios.

   a the length of C to the length of A   **b** the width of C to the width of A

   c the perimeter of C to the perimeter of A   **d** the area of C to the area of A

C Work out the corresponding ratios for B and C.

D Is there a pattern in the results of parts **A**, **B** and **C**?

17.3 Ratios and sharing

Learning objective

• To use ratios to find totals or missing quantities

So far, you have used ratios to compare two different quantities. You can also use ratios for sharing out a given quantity into different amounts.

Example 4

Two charities share a donation of £20 000 in the ratio 1 : 4. How much does each charity get?

The total number of shares is $1 + 4 = 5$.

Imagine that £20 000 is divided into five equal parts.

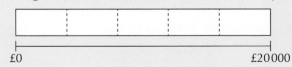

The ratio means that one charity gets 1 part or $\frac{1}{5}$ of the money and the other charity gets

4 parts or $\frac{4}{5}$.

$\frac{1}{5}$ of 20 000 = 4000 $\frac{4}{5}$ of 20 000 = 4 × 4000 = 16 000

One charity gets £4000 and the other gets £16 000.

In Example **4** you knew the total amount.

If you know one of the shares, you can use this to work out the total amount.

Example 5

Alesha makes a drink for her children by mixing juice and lemonade in the ratio 3 : 5.

She used 250 ml of lemonade.

How much of the drink will there be altogether, if Alesha adds the right amount of juice?

The number of parts is $3 + 5 = 8$.

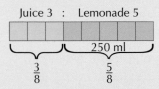

Juice is $\frac{3}{8}$ of the drink and lemonade is $\frac{5}{8}$ of the drink.

$\frac{5}{8} = 250$ ml $\rightarrow \frac{1}{8} = 250 \div 5 = 50$ ml $\rightarrow \frac{8}{8} = 50 \times 8 = 400$ ml

There are 400 ml of the drink altogether.

Exercise 17C

1 In a class of children, the ratio of swimmers to non-swimmers is 5 : 1.

  a What fraction of the class are swimmers?

  b There are 30 children in the class.

    How many are swimmers?

2 A farmer has grown oranges and lemons.

  The ratio of oranges to lemons is 4 : 1.

  a What fraction of the fruit are oranges?

  b There are 2000 oranges.

    How many lemons are there?

3 Two waitresses, Helga and Martina, shared their tips in the ratio 3 : 2.

  a What fraction did Martina receive?

  b The total of all the tips was £45.00. How much did Martina receive?

4 In a small library, the ratio of fiction to non-fiction books is 1 : 8.

  a What fraction are fiction books?

  There are 120 fiction books.

  b How many books are there all together?

 5 Harriet and Richard go shopping separately.

  They buy 66 items altogether.

  Harriet buys twice as many items as Richard.

  How many items does Harriet buy?

6 At a concert the number of men to women is in the ratio 3 : 2.

There are 150 people altogether.

How many women are at the concert?

7 100 people see a film at a cinema.

The numbers of children and adults are in the ratio 1 : 4.

How many children see the film?

8 In a fishing contest the numbers of trout and carp caught were in the ratio 1 : 2.

The total number of trout and carp caught was 72.

How many carp were caught?

9 A bakery makes 1400 white and brown loaves.

The ratio of white to brown is 4 : 3.

How many brown loaves does the bakery make?

Challenge: Mixing gold

Gold is used to make jewellery.

Gold is a soft metal and it will gradually wear away in everyday use. To make it harder it is mixed with other metals. The other metals used include copper, silver, nickel, palladium and zinc.

Gold is very expensive, so mixing it with other metals also makes the jewellery less expensive.

The purity of gold is described in carats.

Pure gold is 24 carats.

21 carat gold is 87.5% gold and the rest is other metals.

18 carat gold is 75% gold and the rest is other metals.

9 carat gold is 37.5% gold and the rest is other metals.

A A man's wedding ring has a mass of 4.0 grams.

How much pure gold does it contain, if it is made from:

  a 18 carat gold   **b** 21 carat gold   **c** 9 carat gold?

B Work out the ratio of gold to other metals in:

  a 18 carat gold   **b** 21 carat gold   **c** 9 carat gold.

C Use a ratio to compare the amount of pure gold in equal masses of 9 carat and 18 carat gold.

D Try to find out the cost of one gram of gold.

17.4 Solving problems

Learning objectives

- To understand the connections between fractions and ratios
- To understand how ratios can be useful in everyday life

Ratios are useful in practical situations.

Example 6

150 students are going on a school trip. The teacher-to-student ratio must be 1 : 8 or better.
What is the smallest possible number of teachers that can go on the trip?

If the ratio of teachers to students is 1 : 8 then the students make up $\frac{8}{9}$ of the group and the teachers make up $\frac{1}{9}$ of the total number.

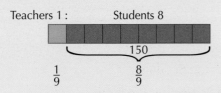

If $\frac{8}{9}$ of the total is 150, then $\frac{1}{9}$ of the total is $150 \div 8 = 18.75$.

The smallest possible number of teachers is 19. (You cannot take $\frac{3}{4}$ of a teacher!)

Exercise 17D

1 There are 350 pupils in a primary school.
The ratio of boys to girls is 3 : 2.
How many pupils are boys and how many are girls?

2 Freda has downloaded some music tracks.
75% of them are dance tracks.
What is the ratio of dance tracks to other music?

3 Two-thirds of the passengers on a bus one morning are children on the way to school.
What is the ratio of schoolchildren to other passengers?

(PS) **4** James is saving 5p and 10p coins. He has 75 coins.
The ratio of 5p to 10p coins is 7 : 8.
How much are his coins worth?

PS **5** There are 15 green and brown bottles on a wall.

The ratio of green bottles to brown bottles is 1 : 4.

One of the green bottles accidentally falls.

What is the ratio of green bottles to brown bottles now?

6 **a** Marco's age is $\frac{2}{3}$ of Pierre's age.

What is the ratio of their ages?

b The total of their ages is 60 years.

How old is Pierre?

7 This pie chart shows the populations of each country in the United Kingdom.

Population in millions

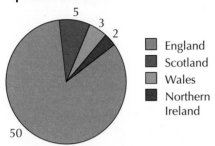

- England
- Scotland
- Wales
- Northern Ireland

a Use a ratio to compare the populations of England and Scotland.

b Use a ratio to compare the populations of Wales and Northern Ireland.

c What fraction of the population of the UK lives in England?

8 Arthur has saved £720 and Guinevere has saved £1080.

a What is the ratio of their savings?

b What fraction of their total savings does Arthur have?

They both spend £360.

c What is the ratio of their savings now?

d What fraction of their total savings does Arthur have now?

Challenge: Presents from Uncle Fred

Uncle Fred gives his nephew, Jack, and his niece, Jill, £60 between them every year at Christmas.

He splits it between them in the ratio of their ages.

A The first time he does this Jack is 1 and Jill is 3.

How much will each one get?

B How much will each one get the following Christmas?

C By the time Jack is 5, Uncle Fred has given them £300.

How much has each of them received altogether?

Ready to progress?

 I can simplify fractions.

I can use ratio notation.
I know the connection between ratios and fractions.
I know how to use ratios to compare quantities.
I know that I can simplify ratios in the same way that I simplify fractions.

 I know how to use ratios to find totals or missing quantities.

Review questions

1 This is Morag's recipe for shortcake.

   a Work out the ratio of butter to sugar.

   b What fraction of the total is semolina?

   c What percentage of the total is flour?

   (MR) d Show that if you use four times the quantity of everything, the ratio of butter to sugar will not change.

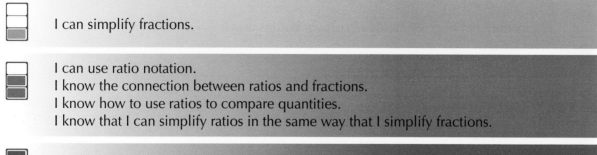

150 g of flour
150 g of butter
75 g of sugar
75 g of semolina

2 A fruit cocktail is made from mango juice and apple juice in the ratio 2 : 3.

   a What fraction of the drink is mango juice?

   b Josie wants to make 300 ml of fruit cocktail.
   How much mango juice does she need?

   c Clyde wants to make a large amount for a party. He has lots of apple juice but only has 1.5 litres of mango juice.
   What is the largest amount of fruit cocktail he can make?

3 For a cube, write down, as simply as possible, the ratio of:

   a the number of edges to the number of faces

   b the number of corners to the number of edges.

4 In 2011 in a particular town there were 146 rainy days. The rest were dry days.

   a Show that the ratio of rainy days to dry days was 2 : 3.

   b What percentage of days in the year were dry days?

(PS) 5 A football pitch is 100 metres long. The ratio of the length to the width is 5 : 2.
   Work out the perimeter of the pitch.

6 The ratio of the ages of Sam and his father is 1 : 4.

The ratio of the ages of Sam and his mother is 1 : 3.

Sam's father is 48 years old.

How old is Sam's mother?

 7 One Saturday there were football matches at Manchester City, QPR and Reading.

The attendance at Manchester City was 45 000 and at QPR was 18 000.

a Write the ratio of the Manchester City attendance to the QPR attendance as simply as possible.

b The ratio of the QPR attendance to the Reading attendance was 3 : 4.

How many were in the crowd at Reading?

PS 8 On a bicycle the large chain ring on the pedals has 45 teeth and the small sprocket on the wheel has 18 teeth.

The gear ratio is the ratio of the number of teeth on the chain ring to the number of teeth on the sprocket.

a Work out the gear ratio in this case. Write the answer as simply as possible.

b If the pedals go round once, how many times will the wheel rotate?

Simon's bike has 42 teeth on the front chain ring. On the rear he has a set of sprockets. They range from 14 teeth to 28 teeth.

c Work out the gear ratio if Simon uses:

   i the smallest sprocket   **ii** the largest sprocket.

9 These are the average distances of the planets in the Solar System from the Sun, in millions of kilometres.

Planet	Mercury	Venus	Earth	Mars
Distance (millions of km)	58	108	150	228

Planet	Jupiter	Saturn	Uranus	Neptune
Distance (millions of km)	779	1430	2880	4500

a Work out the missing number in this sentence.

The ratio of the distances of the Earth and Neptune from the Sun is 1 : ☐.

b Choose the closest whole number to complete this sentence.

The ratio of the distances of the Earth and Jupiter from the Sun is approximately 1 : ☐.

c Identify two planets for which the ratio of their distances from the Sun is approximately 1 : 2.

d Identify two planets for which the ratio of their distances from the Sun is approximately 2 : 3.

Problem solving
Smoothie bar

Recipes are for medium smoothies.

To make a small smoothie:
Use 75% of the ingredients in the medium recipe.

To make a large smoothie:
Just add 200 ml of fruit juice or milk.

Buy any two smoothies and get the cheaper one for half price!

Small	300 ml	£2.50
Medium	400 ml	£3.00
Large	600 ml	£4.00

1 Work out the recipe for a small Fruity Surprise.

2 Work out the recipe for a large Chocolate.

3 How much milk would be needed to make 50 small Breakfast Boost smoothies? Give the answer in litres.

4 Work out how many medium Breakfast Boosts can be made with 2 kg of strawberries, 1 litre of milk and 20 bananas. What extras would be needed to make 20 Breakfast Boosts?

5 How much tropical fruit would be needed to make 30 medium Tropical Fruit smoothies? Give the answer in kilograms.

Chocolate

100 g banana
50 g chocolate spread
200 ml cranberry juice

Breakfast Boost

100 g strawberries
1 banana
150 ml milk

Tropical Fruit

250 g tropical fruit
100 ml yoghurt
85 g raspberries
$\frac{1}{2}$ lime juice
1 tsp honey

Fruity Surprise

100 g mango
50 g strawberries
75 g bananas
250 ml orange juice

6 What fraction of the volume of a medium Fruity Surprise is orange juice?

7 I am buying 15 small smoothies. They are Tropical Fruit and Breakfast Boost in the ratio 2 : 3. How many of each type am I buying?

8 If I buy one smoothie of each size, how much will I save if I use the offer?

9 I have £5. Using the offer, how much change will I have if I buy a medium and a small smoothie?

10 I would like 2 small Tropical Fruits, 1 medium Tropical Fruits and 1 large Chocolate. Using the offer, how much will they cost?

Glossary

24-hour clock A method of measuring the time, based on the full twenty-four hours of the day, rather than two groups of twelve hours.

3D Having three dimensions: length, width and height.

acute angle An angle between 0° and 90°.

add Combine two numbers or quantities to form another number or quantity, known as the sum or total.

addition A basic operation of arithmetic, combining two or more numbers or values to find their total value.

algebra The use of letters to represent variables and unknown numbers and to state general rules or properties; for example: $2(x + y) = 2x + 2y$ describes a relationship that is true for any numbers x and y.

angle The amount of turn between two straight lines with a common end point or vertex.

angles at a point The angles that are formed at a point where two or more lines meet; they add up to 360°.

angles on a straight line The angles that are formed to make a straight line; they add up to 180°.

approximation A value that is close but not exactly equal to another value, and can be used to give an idea of the size of the value; for example, a journey taking 58 minutes may be described as 'taking approximately an hour'; the sign ≈ means 'is approximately equal to'.

area The amount of flat space a 2D shape occupies; usually measured in square units such as square centimetres (cm^2) or square metres (m^2).

at random Chosen by chance, without looking; every item has an equal chance of being chosen.

average A central or typical value of a set of data, that can be used to represent the whole data set; mean, median, and mode are all types of average.

axis, plural axes Fixed lines on a graph, usually perpendicular, numbered and used to identify the position of any point on the graph.

balance The amount of money in, for example, a bank account after payments in and out have been made.

bank statement A statement listing the amounts of money put into or taken out of a bank account.

bar chart or graph A diagram showing quantities as vertical bars so that the quantities can be easily compared.

biased Not random, for example, attaching a small piece of sticky gum to the edge of a coin may cause it to land more frequently on Heads than on Tails: the coin would be biased.

BIDMAS An agreed order of carrying out operations Brackets, Indices (or powers), Division and Multiplication, Addition and Subtraction.

brackets Symbols used to show expressions that must be treated as one term or number. Under the rules of BIDMAS, operations within brackets must be done first; for example: $2 \times (3 + 5) = 2 \times 8 = 16$ whereas $2 \times 3 + 5 = 6 + 5 = 11$.

calculate Work out, with or without a calculator.

capacity The volume of a liquid or gas inside a 3D shape, usually measured in litres.

cent- or centi- A prefix referring to 100; in the metric system, centi- means one hundredth; for example, a centimetre is one hundredth of a metre.

chance The likelihood, or probability, of an event occurring.

chart A diagram or table showing information.

Chinese method A method of performing multiplication by arranging the numbers in a particular layout.

class A small range of values within a large set of data, treated as one group of values.

coefficient A number written in front of a variable in an algebraic term; for example, in $8x$, 8 is the coefficient of x.

column method A method for multiplying large numbers, in which you multiply the units, tens and hundreds separately, then add the products together.

compound shape A shape made from two or more simpler shapes; for example, a floor plan could be made from a square and a rectangle joined together.

construct Draw angles, lines or shapes accurately, using compasses, a protractor and a ruler.

conversion   Expression of a unit or measurement in terms of another unit or scale of measurement.

conversion graph   A graph that can be used to convert from one unit to another, constructed by drawing a line through two or more points where the equivalence is known; sometimes, but not always, a conversion graph passes through the origin.

convert   **1** Express a unit or measurement in terms of another unit or scale of measurement; for example, you can convert inches to centimetres by multiplying by 2.54.
2 To change a number from one form to another, for example, from a fraction to a decimal.

coordinates   Pairs of numbers that show the exact position of a point on a graph, by giving the distance of the point from each axis; on an x–y coordinate graph, in the set of coordinates (3, 4), 3 is the x-coordinate, and is the horizontal distance of the point from the y-axis, and 4 is the y-coordinate, and is the vertical distance of the point from the x-axis.

cube   **1** In geometry, a 3D shape with six square faces, eight vertices and 12 edges.
2 In number and algebra, the result of multiplying a number or expression raised to the power of three: n^3 is read as 'n cubed' or 'n to the power of three': for example: 2^3 is the cube of 2 and $(2 \times 2 \times 2) = 8$.

cuboid   A 3D shape with six rectangular faces, eight vertices and 12 edges; opposite faces are identical to each other.

data   A collection of facts, such as numbers, measurements, opinions or other information.

data-collection form   A form or table used for recording data collected during a survey.

decimal   A number or number system that is based on 10; a decimal number usually means a number made up of a whole number and fractions, expressed as tenths, hundreds, thousandths, written after a decimal point.

decimal place   The position, after the decimal point, of a digit in a decimal number; for example, in 0.025, 5 is in the third decimal place. Also, the number of digits to the right of the decimal point in a decimal number; for example, 3.142 is a number given to three decimal places (3 dp).

decimal point   A symbol, usually a small dot, written between the whole-number part and the fractional part in a decimal number.

decrease   **1** Reduce or make smaller.
2 The amount by which something is made smaller.

degree   A measure of angle equal to $\frac{1}{360}$ of a complete turn.

denominator   The number below the line in a fraction, which says how many parts there are in the whole; for example, a denominator of 3 tells you that you are dealing with thirds.

deposit   Money paid as a first instalment on the purchase of something; the balance must be paid later.

diagonal   A straight line joining any two non-adjacent vertices of a polygon.

edge   The line where two faces or surfaces of a 3D shape meet.

equally likely   When the probabilities of two or more outcomes are equal; for example, when a fair six-sided die is thrown, the outcomes 6 and 2 are equally likely with probabilities of $\frac{1}{6}$.

equation   A number sentence stating that two expressions or quantities are of equal value, for example, $x + 2y = 9$; an equation always contains an equals sign (=).

equivalent   The same, equal in value.

equivalent fraction   Fractions that can be cancelled to the same value, such as $\frac{10}{20} = \frac{5}{10} = \frac{1}{2}$.

estimate   **1** State or guess a value, based on experience or what you already know.
2 A rough or approximate answer.

Euler   Leonhard Euler (1707–83), a Swiss mathematician.

Euler's formula   A formula connecting the numbers of faces (F), vertices (V) and edges (E) of a 3D shape: $F + V - E = 2$.

event   Something that happens, such as the toss of a coin, the throw of a dice or a football match.

experiment   A test or investigation made to find evidence for or against a hypothesis.

experimental probability   The probability found by trial or experiment; an estimate of the true probability.

expression   Collection of numbers, letters, symbols and operators representing a number or amount; for example, $x^2 - 3x + 4$.

face   One of the flat surfaces of a solid shape; for example, a cube has six faces.

fair   The probability of each outcome is similar to the theoretical probability.

first term   The first number in a sequence.

formula   A mathematical rule, using numbers and letters, that shows how to work out an unknown variable; for example, the conversion formula from temperatures in Fahrenheit to temperatures in Celsius is: $C = \frac{5}{9}(F - 32)$.

formulae   The plural form of formula.

fraction   A part of a whole that has been divided into equal parts, a fraction describes how many parts you are talking about.

fraction wall   A diagram that allows you to compare fractions and see which ones are equivalent.

frequency   The number of times a particular item appears in a set of data.

function machine   A diagram to illustrate functions and their inputs and outputs.

geometric sequence   A sequence in which each term is multiplied or divided by the same number, to work out the next term; for example, 2, 4, 8, 16, ... is a geometric sequence.

geometrical properties   The properties of a 2D or 3D shape that describe it completely.

graph   A diagram showing the relation between certain sets of numbers or quantities by means of a series of values or points plotted on a set of axes.

greater than, >   The symbol > shows that the amount on the left of it is greater or more than the amount on the right of it.

grid or box method   A method for multiplying numbers larger than 10, where each number is split into its parts: for example, to calculate 158×67:

   158 is 100, 50 and 8

   67 is 60 and 7.

These numbers are arranged in a rectangle and each part is multiplied by the others.

grouped data   Data that is arranged into smaller, non-overlapping sets, groups or classes, that can be treated as separate ranges or values, for example, 1–10, 11–20, 21–30, 31–40, 41–50; in this example there are equal class intervals.

grouped frequency table   A table showing data grouped into classes.

height   The vertical distance, from bottom to top, of a 2D or 3D shape.

hexagonal prism   A prism with a hexagonal cross-section and six rectangular faces; it has 8 faces, 12 vertices and 18 edges.

icon   A symbol or graphic representation on a chart or graph.

image   The result of a reflection or other transformation of an object.

improper fraction   A fraction in which the numerator is greater than the denominator. The fraction could be rewritten as a mixed number for example, $\frac{7}{2} = 3\frac{1}{2}$.

increase   **1** Enlarge or make bigger.
2 The amount by which something is made bigger.

input   The number put into a function machine.

intersect   To have a common point for example, two non-parallel lines cross or intersect at a point.

inverse   Reverse or opposite; inverse operations cancel each other out or reverse the effect of each other.

inverse operation   An operation that reverses the effect of another operation; for example, addition is the inverse of subtraction, division is the inverse of multiplication.

isometric   A grid of equilateral triangles or dots, can be used for drawing a 3D shape in 2D.

isosceles triangle   A triangle in which two sides are equal and the angles opposite the equal sides are also equal.

length   The distance from one end of a line to the other.

less than, <   The symbol < shows that the amount on the left of it is smaller or less than the amount on the right of it.

like terms   Terms in which the variables are identical, but have different coefficients; for example, $2ax$ and $5ax$ are like terms but $5xy$ and $7y$ are not. Like terms can be combined by adding their numerical coefficients so $2ax + 5ax = 7ax$.

line graph   A chart that shows how data changes, by means of points joined by straight lines.

line of symmetry   A line that divides a symmetrical shape into two identical parts, one being the mirror image of the other.

linear sequence   A sequence or pattern of numbers where the difference between consecutive terms is always the same.

litre   A metric measure of capacity; 1 litre = 1000 millilitres = 1000 cubic centimetres.

long division   A method of division showing all the workings, used when dividing large numbers.

long multiplication A method of multiplication showing all the workings, used when multiplying large numbers.

mean An average value of a set of data, found by adding all the values and dividing the sum by the number of values in the set; for example, the mean of 5, 6, 14, 15 and 45 is (5 + 6 +14 + 15 + 45) ÷ 5 = 17.

mean average *See* mean.

median The middle value of a set of data that is arranged in order; for example, write the data set 4, 2, 6, 2, 2, 3, 7 in order as 2, 2, 2, 3, 4, 6, 7, then the median is the middle value, which is 3. If there is an even number of values the median is the mean of the two middle values; for example, 2, 3, 6, 8, 8, 9 has a median of 7.

metric A system of measurement in which the basic units of mass, length and capacity are grams, metres and litres. Sub-units are obtained from main units by multiplying or dividing by 10, 100, 1000, …. For example, for mass, 1 kilogram = 1000 grams; for length, 1 kilometre = 1000 metres, 1 metre = 100 centimetres, 1 centimetre = 10 millimetres; for capacity, 1 litre = 1000 millilitres.

metric units Units of measurement used in the metric system; for example, metres and centimetres (length), grams and kilograms (mass), litres (capacity).

milli- A prefix used in the metric system of measurement to indicate a thousandth part, for example, a millimetre is one thousandth of a metre.

mirror line Another name for a line of symmetry.

mixed number A number written as a whole number and a fraction; for example, the mixed number $2\frac{1}{2}$ can be written as the improper fraction $\frac{5}{2}$.

modal The value that occurs most frequently in a given set of data.

modal class In grouped data, the class with the highest frequency.

mode The value that occurs most frequently in a given set of data.

negative number A number that is less than zero.

net A 2D shape that can be folded up to make a 3D shape.

numerator The number above the line in a fraction: it tells you how many of the equal parts of the whole you have; for example, $\frac{3}{5}$ of a whole is made up of three of the five equal parts. The number of equal parts is the denominator.

object The original or starting shape, line or point before it is transformed to give an image.

obtuse angle An angle that is greater than 90° but less than 180°.

operation An action carried out on or between one or more numbers; it could be addition, subtraction, multiplication, division or squaring.

opposite angles The angles on the opposite side of the point of intersection when two straight lines cross, forming four angles. The opposite angles are equal.

order Arrange numbers or quantities according to a rule, such as size or value.

order of operations The order in which mathematical operations should be done.

order of rotational symmetry The number of times a 2D shape looks the same as it did originally when it is rotated through 360°. If a shape has no rotational symmetry, its order of rotational symmetry is 1, because every shape looks the same at the end of a 360° rotation as it did originally.

origin The point (0, 0) on Cartesian coordinate axes.

outcome The result of an event or trial in a probability experiment, such as the score from a throw of a dice.

outlier In a data set, a value that is widely separated from the main cluster of values.

output The number produced by a function machine.

parallel Lines that are always the same distance apart, however far they are extended.

pentagonal prism A prism with a pentagonal cross-section and five rectangular faces; it has 7 faces, 10 vertices and 15 edges.

pentomino A shape made by joining five squares together side-to-side. There are 12 such shapes.

per cent (%) Parts per hundred.

percentage A number written as a fraction with 100 parts, but instead of writing it as a fraction out of 100, you write the symbol % at the end, so $\frac{50}{100}$ is written as 50%.

perimeter   The total distance around a 2D shape; the perimeter of a circle is called the circumference.

perpendicular   At right angles, meeting at 90°.

pictogram   A method of displaying data, using small pictures or icons to represent one, two or more items of data.

pie chart   A circular graph divided into sectors that are proportional to the size of the quantities represented.

place value   The value of a digit depending on where it is written in a number; for example, in the number 123.4, the place value of 4 is tenths, so it is worth 0.4 and the place value of 2 is tens, so it is worth 20.

positive number   A number that is greater than zero.

power   How many times you use a number or expression in a calculation; it is written as a small, raised number; for example, 2^2 is 2 multiplied by itself, $2^2 = 2 \times 2$ and 4^3 is $4 \times 4 \times 4$.

probability   The measure of how likely an outcome of an event is to occur. All probabilities have values in the range from 0 to 1.

probability fraction   A probability that is not 0 or 1, given as a fraction.

probability scale   A scale or number line, from 0 to 1, sometimes labelled with impossible, unlikely, even chance, etc., to show the likelihood of an outcome of an event occurring. Possible outcomes may be marked along the scale as fractions or decimals.

protractor   A transparent circular or semicircular instrument for measuring or drawing angles, graduated in degrees.

quadrant   One of the four regions into which a plane is divided by the coordinate axes in the Cartesian system.

quadrilateral   A 2D shape with four straight sides. Squares, rhombuses, rectangles, parallelograms, kites and trapezia are all special kinds of quadrilaterals.

quantity   A measurable amount of something that can be written as a number, or a number with appropriate units; for example, the capacity of a milk carton.

questionnaire   A list of questions for people to answer, so that statistical information can be collected.

random   Chosen by chance, without looking; every item has an equal chance of being chosen.

range   The difference between the greatest value and the smallest value in a set of numerical data. A measure of spread in statistics.

ratio   A way of comparing the sizes of two or more numbers or quantities; for example, if there are five boys and ten girls in a group, the ratio of boys to girls is 5 : 10 or 1 : 2, the ratio of girls to boys is 2 : 1. The two numbers are separated by a colon (:).

rectangle   A quadrilateral in which all four interior angles are 90° and two pairs of opposite sides are equal and parallel; it has two lines of symmetry and rotational symmetry of order 2. The diagonals of a rectangle bisect each other.

reduction   *See* decrease.

reflect   Draw an image of a 2D shape as if it is viewed in a mirror placed along a given (mirror) line.

reflection   The image formed when a 2D shape is reflected in a mirror line or line of symmetry; the process of reflecting an object.

reflective symmetry   A type of symmetry in which a 2D shape is divided into two equal parts by a mirror line.

reflex angle   An angle that is greater than 180° but less than 360°.

relationship   An association between two or more items.

remainder   The amount left over after dividing a number.

repeated subtraction   A type of division involving the process of repeatedly subtracting the same number or amount; for example, $35 - 5 - 5 - 5 - 5 - 5 - 5 - 5 = 0$ so $35 \div 5 = 7$, remainder 0.

right angle   One quarter of a complete turn. An angle of 90°.

rotational symmetry   A type of symmetry in which a 2D shape may be turned through 360° so that it looks the same as it did originally in two or more positions.

round   In the context of a number, to express to a required degree of accuracy; for example, 653 rounded to the nearest 10 is 650.

round down   To change a number to a lower and more convenient value; for example, 451 rounded down to the nearest ten is 450.

round up   To change a number to a higher and more convenient value; for example, 459 rounded up to the nearest ten is 460.

rounding   Expressing to a required degree of accuracy; for example, 743 rounded to the nearest 10 is 740.

rule   The way a mathematical function is carried out. In patterns and sequences a rule, expressed in words or algebraically, shows how the pattern or sequence grows or develops.

sample   A selection taken from a larger data set, which can be researched to provide information about the whole data set.

sector   A region of a circle, like a slice of a pie, bounded by an arc and two radii.

sequence   A pattern of numbers that are related by a rule.

short division   The division of one number by another, usually an integer, that can be worked out mentally rather than on paper.

simplest form   **1** A fraction that has been cancelled as much as possible.
2 An algebraic expression in which like terms have been collected, so that it cannot be simplified any further.

simplify   To make an equation or expression easier to work with or understand by combining like terms or cancelling; for example, $4a - 2a + 5b + 2b = 2a + 7b$, $\frac{12}{18} = \frac{2}{3}$, $5 : 10 = 1 : 2$.

solve   To find the value or values of a variable (x) that satisfy the given equation.

square   A quadrilateral in which all four interior angles are 90° and all four sides are equal; opposite sides are parallel, the diagonals bisect each at right angles; it has four lines of symmetry and rotational symmetry of order 4.

square number   A number that results from multiplying an integer by itself; for example, $36 = 6 \times 6$ and so 36 is a square number. A square number can be represented as a square array of dots.

square root   For a given number, a, the square root is the number b, where $a = b^2$; for example, a square root of 25 is 5 since $5^2 = 25$. The square root of 25 is recorded as $\sqrt{25} = 5$. Note that a positive number has a negative square root, as well as a positive square root; for example, $(-5)^2 = 25$ so it is also true that $\sqrt{25} = -5$.

squaring   Multiplying a number or expression by itself; raising a number or expression to the second power; for example, $3^2 = 9$.

statistical survey   The collection of statistical information.

straight-line graph   A graph of a linear function or equation, such as $y = 2x + 3$, for which all the points lie in a straight line.

substitute   Replace a variable in an expression with a number and evaluate it; For example, if we substitute 4 for t in $3t + 5$ the answer is 17 because $3 \times 4 + 5 = 17$.

subtraction   Taking one number or quantity away from another, to find the difference.

tally   A mark made to record a data value; every fifth tally is drawn through the previous four.

tally chart   A chart with marks made to record each object or event in a certain category or class. The marks are usually grouped in fives to make counting the total easier.

term   **1** A part of an expression, equation or formula. Terms are separated by + and − signs.
2 A number in a sequence or pattern.

term-to-term rule   The rule that shows what to do to one term in a sequence, to work out the next term.

tessellation   A pattern made of one or more repeating shapes that fit together without leaving any gaps between them.

tetrahedron   A 3D shape with four triangular faces; in a regular tetrahedron, the faces are equilateral triangles. A tetrahedron has 4 faces, 4 verticals and 6 edges.

timetable   A table showing when events take place.

trial   An experiment to discover an approximation for the probability of an outcome of an event; it will consist of many trials where the event takes place and the outcome is recorded.

triangle   A 2D shape with three straight sides; the interior angles add up to 180°. Triangles may be classified as:

- scalene – no sides are equal, no angles are equal
- isosceles – two of the sides are equal, two of the angles are equal
- equilateral – all the sides are equal, all the angles are equal
- right-angled – one interior angle is equal to 90°.

triangular number A number in the sequence 1, 1 + 2, 1 + 2 + 3, 1 + 2 + 3 + 4, …. 55 is a triangular number since 55 = 1 + 2 + 3 + 4 + 5 + 6 + 7 + 8 + 9 + 10. A triangular number can be represented by a triangular array of dots, in which the number of dots increases by 1 in each row.

triangular prism A prism with a triangular cross-section and three rectangular faces; it has 5 faces, 6 vertices and 9 edges.

units digit The digit that appears furthest right in a whole number, or before the decimal point in a decimal number; for example, in 315, the units digit is 5 and in 123.4 the units digit is 3.

unknown number A number that is represented by a letter; it can be treated as a number, following the rules of arithmetic (BIDMAS).

variable A quantity that may take many values.

vertex The point at which two lines meet, in a 2D or 3D shape.

vertically opposite angles *See* opposite angles.

vertices The plural of vertex.

volume The amount of space occupied by a 2D shape.

width The distance from one side of a 2D shape to the other, usually taken to be shorter than the length.

x-axis The horizontal axis of a two-dimensional x–y Cartesian coordinate graph, along which the x-coordinates are measured.

x-coordinate The horizontal distance of the point from the y-axis; the position of a point along the x-axis.

y-axis The vertical axis of a two-dimensional x–y Cartesian coordinate graph, along which the y-coordinates are measured.

y-coordinate The vertical distance of the point from the x-axis; the position of a point up the y-axis.

Index

William Collins's dream of knowledge for all began with the publication of his first book in 1819. A self-educated mill worker, he not only enriched millions of lives, but also founded a flourishing publishing house. Today, staying true to this spirit, Collins books are packed with inspiration, innovation and practical expertise. They place you at the centre of a world of possibility and give you exactly what you need to explore it.

Collins. Freedom to teach.

Published by Collins
An imprint of HarperCollins*Publishers*
77–85 Fulham Palace Road
Hammersmith
London
W6 8JB

Browse the complete Collins catalogue at
www.harpercollins.co.uk

© HarperCollins*Publishers* Limited 2013

10 9 8 7 6 5 4 3 2 1

ISBN-13 978-0-00-753772-3

The authors Kevin Evans, Keith Gordon, Trevor Senior, Brian Speed and Chris Pearce assert their moral rights to be identified as the authors of this work.

British Library Cataloguing in Publication Data
A catalogue record for this publication is available from the British Library.

Commissioned by Katie Sergeant
Project managed by Elektra Media Ltd
Development edited by Lindsey Charles
Copy-edited and proofread by Joan Miller
Illustrations by Ann Paganuzzi, Nigel Jordan and Tony Wilkins
Typeset by Jouve India Private Limited
Cover design by Angela English

Printed and bound by L.E.G.O. S.p.A. Italy

Acknowledgements

The publishers wish to thank the following for permission to reproduce photographs. Every effort has been made to trace copyright holders and to obtain their permission for the use of copyright materials. The publishers will gladly receive any information enabling them to rectify any error or omission at the first opportunity.

Cover Nikonaft/Shutterstock, p 6 eska2005/Shutterstock, p 16t Claudio Del Luongo/Shutterstock, p 16b RIA Novosti/Alamy, pp 24–25 hxdyl/Shutterstock, p 26 Bletchley Park Trust/Contributor/Getty Images, pp 42–43 Alexander Tihonov/Shutterstock, p 44 Aerial Archives/Alamy, p 62 kstudija/Shutterstock, pp 62–63 Vladimir Badaev/Shutterstock, p 64 Alexey Rezaykin/Shutterstock, pp 80–81 oliveromg/Shutterstock, p 82 Anton Gvozdikov/Shutterstock, pp 102–103 CDH_Design/iStock, p 104 bbbrrn/iStockphoto, pp 126–127 Mark Herreid/Shutterstock, p 128 Hadrian/Shutterstock, pp 146–147 Samot/Shutterstock, p 148 Diego Barbieri/Shutterstock, pp 166–167 Svetlana Lukienko/Shutterstock, p 168 nikkytok/Shuttrstock, p 192 StockLite/Shutterstock, pp 192–193 Kekyalyaynen/Shutterstock, p 194 sfam_photo/Shutterstock, pp 214–215 Andrey Yurlov/Shutterstock, p 216 Makushin Alexey/Shutterstock, p 228 spirit of america/Shutterstock, p 229 neelsky/Shutterstock, p 231 Sergey Chirkov/Shutterstock, pp 232–233 Rtimages/Shutterstock, p 234 Lightroom Photos/Alamy, pp 248–249 Sarah2/Shutterstock, p 250 Melissa Brandes/Shutterstock, p 262l FloridaStock/Shutterstock, p 262cl Sylvana Rega/Shutterstock, p 262cr holbox/Shutterstock, p 262r sgame/Shutterstock, p 264t Ratikova/Shutterstock, p 264b Alastair Wallace/Shutterstock, p 265t vadim kozlovsky/Shutterstock, p 265c WDG Photo/Shutterstock, p 265b f9photos/Shutterstock, pp 264–265 RuthChoi/Shutterstock, p 266 Jane Sweeney/Getty Images, p 267 ollyy/Shutterstock, pp 284–285 zhu difeng/Shutterstock, p 286 ineskoleva/iStockphoto, pp 298–299 Dmitry Morgan/Shutterstock, p 300 Barcroft Media/Contributor/Getty Images, p 305 Ann Paganuzzi, p 306 Alexey V Smirnov/Shutterstock, pp 312–313 Monkey Business Images/Shutterstock, p 314 Radu Razvan/Shutterstock, p 315 TanArt/Shutterstock, pp 328–329 Africa Studio/Shutterstock.